THE CENTENARY OF THE FIRST WORLD WAR

FIRST WORLD WAR
CENTENARY
2014–2018
DCMS
Centenary
Publications

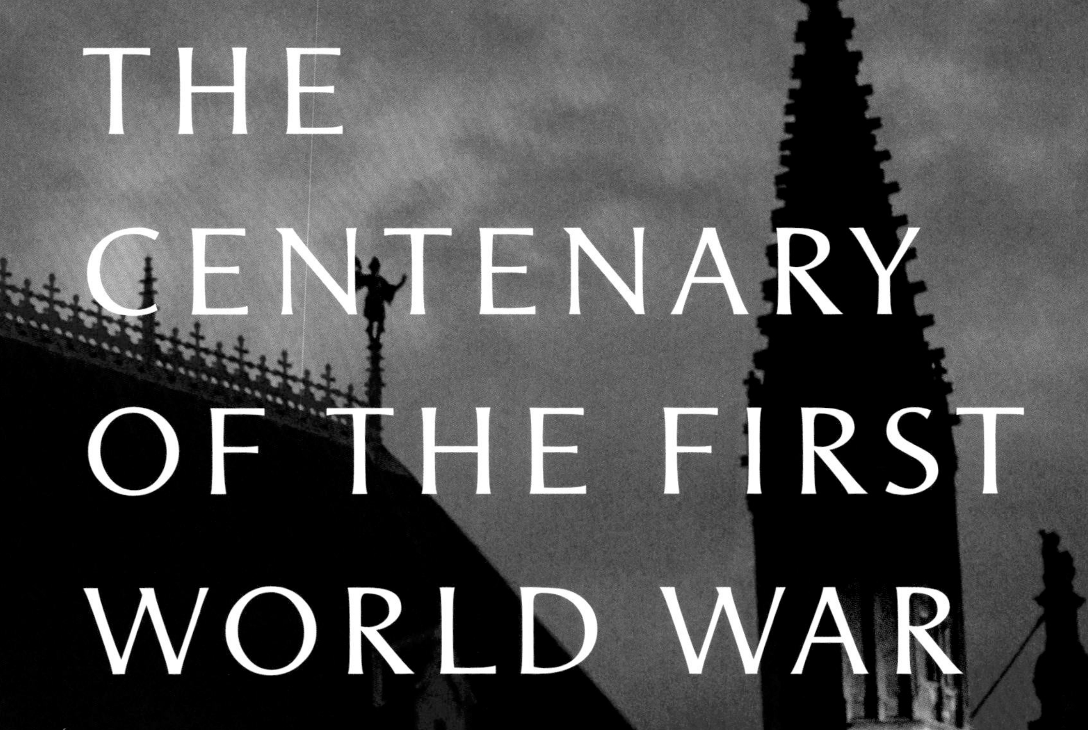

THE CENTENARY OF THE FIRST WORLD WAR

How the Nation Remembered

Contents

2016 COMMEMORATIONS

2017 COMMEMORATIONS

2018 COMMEMORATIONS

2014–18 PROGRAMMES

The Right Honourable Theresa May MP
The Prime Minister of the United Kingdom of Great Britain
and Northern Ireland

10 DOWNING STREET
LONDON SW1A 2AA

A century after the guns fell silent on the Western Front, only a handful of people have any memory of the First World War. But the passage of time has given us all a greater perspective of the causes of the conflict, a greater appreciation of the sacrifice of those who played their part, and the ways in which the conflict shaped – and continues to shape – our society and our country.

The importance of the First World War – not just to our history but also to our present and future – was the reason why, in 2012, the government announced plans to mark the centenary of the conflict with a wide-ranging programme of national events and local projects.

Focused on the key themes of youth, remembrance and education, the commemorations have brought traditional services of remembrance together with music, poetry and the visual and performing arts to create a rich tapestry of events that will long linger in the memories of all who witnessed them.

From August 2014, when families across the UK shut out their lights and placed a single candle in the window, to November 2018, when the faces of those who died were etched into beaches and washed away by the tide, the opportunity to learn, reflect and remember has been embraced by millions of people.

Just as the war touched every community in the United Kingdom, so the centenary programme has reached people in every corner of our nation.

Lottery grants have been awarded to more than 2,000 projects exploring the war and its legacy. The conservation and repair of some 560 war memorials has been funded. More than 4,000 organisations have joined the Imperial War Museums' Centenary Partnership. More than 6,500 pupils and teachers from more than 2,000 secondary schools have visited First World War battlefields on tours organised for the centenary commemorations, and the community projects they have completed on return have reached more than 1.9 million of their school friends, families and local communities.

No words can ever adequately pay tribute to those who sacrificed so much in the First World War. But the events of the past four years – events chronicled by this book – have ensured that another generation will take forward the baton of remembrance. That their names will indeed live for ever more. And that, at the going down of the sun, and in the morning, we will remember them.

Introduction and Overview

DR ANDREW MURRISON MP

Dr Andrew Murrison MP, Prime Minister's Special Representative for the Centenary of the First World War.

Planning for the centenary with partners at home and abroad began in 2011 as the country prepared for two major events the following year – the London Olympics and the Queen's Diamond Jubilee. When Prime Minister David Cameron appointed me to come up with a plan with the incomparable Department for Culture, Media and Sport (DCMS), there was no roadmap and no measure of the public's appetite or how it would be sustained over more than four years. We need not have worried. Above all, this is a story of how our wonderful public rose to the occasion and how the nation united in remembrance.

It is impossible to capture the full extent of activity since the start of the centenary in August 2014. However, we have attempted in this book to cover the journey's main waypoints, its essence and its spirit.

I hope it accurately portrays a country at its best from top to tail and at every level, from major state ceremonial watched by millions to battlefield tours and school debates, to far more intimate things experienced by just a few. So much has been played out in communities, groups and schools up and down the country, where a tapestry of commemoration has been worked that emphasises the personal and parochial, intensely human, experience of the war. This was '*how the nation remembered*'.

The first thing was to set the tone. That required an understanding of where public sentiment lay. I found a quiet pride in predecessors, a sense of awe at the sheer scale of the sacrifice and no appetite for jingoism. There was a desire to learn more and a particular interest in the lived experience of the war.

It was not difficult to come up with the centenary's three principal themes: remembrance, youth and education. We were clear from the outset that it was not the place of government to impose a narrative or a four-year history lesson, but rather to facilitate exploration and interpretation of the material. We now know that understanding of the conflict has improved as people have reflected on the great geopolitical events of the time alloyed with the daily experiences of their predecessors. Government has been keen to facilitate exposure to lesser known material and to offer the chance of gaining fresh perspectives. The role of women and ethnic minorities has played into this, as has the involvement of theatres beyond the Western Front.

Drawing on the acclaimed London Olympics cultural wraparound, it was proposed that exploration of the centenary should be further advanced through an artistic and cultural dimension aimed at improving reach. This has given us some of the most powerful elements of the programme, many of the iconic moments featured here being delivered through a bespoke lottery funded organisation, 14–18 NOW. We have seen artists responding to themes of war in music, art and performance. These elements have touched audiences as only art can, prompting us to reconsider a period that has generated so much of the national cannon of iconic art and poetry. Such has been its success, evident in the pages of this book, that it is inconceivable that any future national commemorative endeavour would not have a substantial artistic dimension.

The centenary, drawing people and communities closer at home and bringing countries together in the commemoration of shared history, has honoured the fallen in the best way imaginable. From South Africa to Germany to Ireland, a mature, reflective approach to a past that is so often complex and nuanced has eased tensions and strengthened bonds. That is a legacy to be proud of.

Readers flicking through the pages of this book will quickly realise that the centenary was above all a joint effort. Government departments could not have carried it off alone. Fortunately a platoon of non-governmental and arms-length bodies, from the Imperial War Museum to the Commonwealth War Graves Commission and The Royal British Legion, have done much of the heavy lifting and, themselves, evolved in the process.

Our big events have often been logistically challenging because much of the activity has taken place in other countries. That has meant working with foreign government at all levels using our outstanding embassies for support in navigating unfamiliar systems. The effort has been repaid by the warmth and generosity of local people living in close proximity with the cemeteries and memorials of the Great War. For them, remembrance is a daily experience.

The scope of the centenary has been broadened and deepened by a staggering array of local initiatives, tributes and events, often associated under the IWM-led light touch Centenary Partnership. They have set much of its character and been a fount of discovery and learning. Very often they have been worked up by small groups that have reinvigorated the capacity of communities to organise and be creative. It seems likely those skills and that habit will endure long after the centenary.

Dr Andrew Murrison MP visiting Tyne Cot Cemetery with students from Clarendon School in Wiltshire on a government-funded centenary battlefield tour.

We hardwired youth into the commemorations because young people were principally in the frame a century ago and today's youngsters will be carrying forward the torch of remembrance. Throughout, young people have a been a constant, from the schools battlefields tours programme, at events of all shapes and sizes, in the Great War debates series, to CWGC's centenary internship scheme and the international Never Such Innocence poetry and art competition.

In the end, commemoration is all about people – those caught up in the extraordinary events of a hundred years ago, the custodians of remembrance in the decades since and those whose privilege it is to build and mark the centenary. It is also about the future and how people will remember and reflect in the century ahead.

I hope we have made a good start.

Andrew Murrison

2014 COMMEMORATIONS

2014 INTRODUCTION

1 Volunteers at the Tower of London installing the 888,246 ceramic poppies that created *Blood Swept Lands and Seas of Red* by artist Paul Cummins and designer Tom Piper.

Marking the centenary of the outbreak of the First World War was, by its nature, a momentous undertaking. It was also going to break new ground. Previous events commemorating significant wartime milestones in the 20th and 21st centuries had focused on veterans' participation. These would be the first of such commemorations without any living veterans. Commemorating the outbreak of the war, rather than the end, also presented a new challenge.

It was hard to gauge what the public reaction would be to the planned events or to the overall tone. There was speculation in the press that the programme could

2 'Now the Last Poppy has Fallen' was a project that focused on the lives of individuals, families and communities in Essex during the First World War.

3 The Imperial War Museum was founded in 1917, to record the civilian and military war effort during the First World War. Their collection includes this poster, part of a recruiting campaign organised by *Punch* magazine in 1914.

be ill-judged, or perhaps an opportunity for inappropriate jingoism. It was clear that the launch of the programme in 2014 – on both a national and a local level – had to capture the mood of the centenary appropriately, focusing on the themes of youth, remembrance and education. With no living veterans, the personal connections were in danger of becoming lost as the war became more and more distant. The involvement of the families of those whose ancestors had served or had been on the home front helped to reignite that personal connection, and to inspire others to explore their own family history.

The commemorative events and activities were supported by the contributions of a number of historians, military associations, educational charities and other partners, including the inspiring collections of the Imperial War Museums (IWM).

The year 2014 saw a combination of major national events, numerous local initiatives and the first 14–18 NOW artistic moment, *Lights Out* (see pages 38–39). This range of activity meant that a great number of people was able to reflect on the conflict and be involved. While many projects had been planned well before 2014, for all of them the start of the year led to a new urgency. Increasingly the nation focused on August 2014, as the centenary of the start of the 'war to end all wars' loomed ever closer.

IWM London: First World War Galleries

4 View of the new First World War Galleries. An array of trench signs reflects the dangers of life on the front line.

On 19 July 2014, the new First World War Galleries opened to the public at IWM London. Four years earlier, a small team of IWM historians and curators had been brought together to see the project through from concept to realisation. The first task was to map out a storyline – to give the most devastating conflict in Britain's history a fresh perspective with historical integrity, while being relevant and engaging.

Audience research showed that there were four key questions to answer – why did the war begin, why did it continue, how did the Allies win, and what was the impact of the war? In accordance with IWM's remit, the team set out to answer these questions from the perspective of British and Empire experiences. The fruits of their deliberations were translated into 14 main 'Story' areas, each of which had a number of 'Substories'.

Once the framework had been agreed, a trawl of the collections was undertaken and objects large and small plotted into the spaces. IWM's First World War collections are unrivalled in their breadth and depth,

and the selection process was a challenge. The final selection showcases 1,300 pieces, large and small. They range from uniforms and equipment to intensely personal items such as letters home and lucky charms. Some objects are familiar, many are not, but they all have powerful stories to tell, not only of destruction and loss, but also of endurance, innovation, courage, duty and devotion.

IWM's First World War Galleries were the first at the museum to be created about events outside of living memory. This cultural shift was to inform every decision. Academic advisors and curators provided context and meaning, while a Youth Panel contributed to texts and captions, helping the youngest visitors understand and learn from the objects around them.

The galleries have proved to be a tremendous draw to the public, and are helping to fulfil the words of King George V who, when he opened the Imperial War Museum in 1920, hoped that it would be 'an inspiration for future generations'.

5 A section of the galleries, exploring the Battle of the Somme, during installation. Objects include a captured rifle, a heavy artillery piece and an officer's bloodied jacket.

6 First-hand, contemporary accounts of the war form part of the fabric of the galleries. Here an officer describes the lethal firepower of modern weapons.

HLF: The People's Centenary

As a distributor of funds raised by National Lottery players, the Heritage Lottery Fund (HLF) was keen to ensure that people and communities right across the UK could get involved in marking the centenary of the First World War.

First World War Then and Now – a community grants programme – was launched in May 2013 (and continued until 2019) to give thousands of groups the chance to explore the fascinating local and personal stories of the war. Alongside this, HLF continued to offer support through its larger grant programmes, which welcomed applications for more substantial projects. Many of these have had a profound impact on the way we view the First World War and its legacy.

The achievements were impressive. By the end of 2018 HLF had awarded £97 million to 2200 projects that span the length and breadth of the UK and touch nearly every community, with awards in 95% of local authority areas. Alongside multi-million-pound

7 Children learning about the story of the poppy as part of 'The Moving Poppy' project, which toured schools and hard-to-reach communities across Scotland.

8 Artwork by schoolchildren in response to the *First World War In the Air* exhibition, which opened in December 2014 at the Royal Air Force Museum, Hendon.

9 Project volunteer and former nurse Eileen Brereton, dressed in First World War nursing uniform, talking to a visitor at the Heritage Day Exhibition in Northallerton, March 2016.

10 A participant in the project 'Great War to Race Riots' looking at archival documents that highlight the plight of black servicemen, workers and seafarers in Liverpool.

awards for projects such as restoring HMS *Caroline* (last survivor of the Battle of Jutland, now docked in Belfast), redeveloping the First World War Galleries at IWM London, and the inspiring programme of artistic commissions created by 14–18 NOW, there was a groundswell of community activity – with almost 1,700 projects demonstrating how powerfully the centenary captured the public imagination.

Communities were able to explore, reflect on and share the heritage of a conflict that affected not only their locality and their ancestors' lives, but also re-shaped the world. Thousands of personal stories were researched, such as those behind the names on war memorials (or those omitted), and what became of the members of a sports club and other such groups who volunteered to serve. Projects looked at life on the home front, letters from home to the trenches, conscientious objectors and dissent, and how medical care – including artificial limbs and treatment of so-called 'shell shock' – developed as a direct result of the conflict.

The changing role of women, many of whom worked in munitions factories or replaced men in agriculture or other jobs, was a prominent theme. The centenary also provided new opportunities for diverse cultural and faith communities, including the African, Caribbean, Chinese, Muslim, Sikh and Jewish communities, to research and share stories of their ancestors' contribution to the conflict. A small number of projects looked at the German experience, both in Germany and in the UK, as well as that of refugees.

All HLF-funded projects were generous in sharing their experiences and their heritage. More than 10 million people took part in activities supported by HLF funding. Young people under 19 and older people over 60 were particularly well represented. Volunteers across the nations were inspired to get involved too, with some 26,500 people giving 240,000 days of volunteering.

HLF's aim with its centenary funding was to create a greater understanding of the First World War and its impact on communities in the UK. This is perhaps best encapsulated by a participant in 'Unheard Voices: the Civilian Experience of the First World War in Yorkshire':

> I had no idea of the richness of this collection [University of Leeds, Liddle Collection] and the picture that these ordinary everyday lives paint of civilian life during the First World War; from hearing the Zeppelin land at Scarborough, being evacuated from the Quaker school in York to watching soldiers have their hair cut in the market square. I felt humbled to be allowed to dip into these people's lives and have made a promise that I will be back for more.

CWGC: Centenary Planning

It is perhaps difficult for those of us who have grown up with remembrance of the war dead to fully appreciate what a revolutionary concept it was in 1914. The First World War changed the world in which we live, and it also changed the way we remember our war dead. A vital component of that was the creation of the Imperial (now Commonwealth) War Graves Commission (CWGC) in 1917.

For a century, the CWGC has cared for the graves of, and memorials to, those who died – the physical form on which our remembrance of the war dead is focused. Pilgrims have always come to CWGC sites, but the centenary of the First World War presented a unique opportunity to show the relevance of the commission's work and the importance of ongoing remembrance, as well as to encourage and inform existing and new visitors. With those aims in mind, planning began early.

As a first step it made sense to establish a baseline from which to work. A public survey showed there was a strong desire to mark the centenary, but respondents felt that they needed help to better understand the conflict, the history behind the sites, and the stories of those commemorated. It was a clear message that the centenary was more than just marking anniversaries. It was a chance to use those commemorations to tell the human stories behind the names engraved on more than one million headstones and memorials.

The centenary also marked a shift in how the CWGC saw itself and its task. From a modest and self-effacing organisation, that felt it was merely the custodian of the cemeteries, it became more central to the commemorative activities. The CWGC even found time to celebrate its own centenary in 2017, one of the highlights of which was an award-winning garden at the RHS Chelsea Flower Show.

With a newly established emphasis on the visitor experience, the CWGC recruited historians to tell its story, and professional archivists to conserve and promote its internationally important records to a wider audience. They installed interpretation at many sites and, for the first time, newly recruited interns gave the organisation a human presence at key locations.

11 A new monument. The first Cross of Sacrifice in the Republic of Ireland was unveiled at Glasnevin Cemetery, Dublin, on 31 July 2014. Irish President Michael D. Higgins and CWGC President HRH The Duke of Kent spoke of the sacrifices made by the Irish in the First World War.

12 Lyness Royal Naval Cemetery, Orkney, is one of the largest CWGC sites in the UK. It was begun in 1915 when Scapa Flow was the base of the British Grand Fleet. It has 445 First World War Commonwealth burials, and the graves of 14 sailors of the German Navy (the High Seas Fleet was interned at Scapa Flow after the Armistice).

Their findings revealed that many visitors did not stray beyond a well-trodden path. Some cemeteries attract hundreds of thousands of pilgrims, while others, just a short distance away, receive just a handful. That did not feel right, and people were encouraged to broaden their remembrance horizons with the use of new themed war-grave trails.

To increase awareness of the work of the CWGC in the UK – where the graves and memorials to more than 300,000 Commonwealth war dead are cared for, at a staggering 13,000 locations – Living Memory was launched. This was a UK-wide initiative in partnership with Big Ideas Company, timed to coincide with the anniversary of the Battle of the Somme.

Living Memory challenged the public to visit their local war graves, take a personal interest in those buried there, organise a commemoration of their own, and champion the sites in the future. The aim was to have 141 groups and to hold 141 events, to mark the anniversary of the Battle of the Somme. In fact, more than 250 groups, from members of the Women's Institute to football supporters, took part.

In partnership with 14–18 NOW, the CWGC brought the iconic Poppies: *Wave* sculpture to the naval memorial at Plymouth. Hosting the poppies in Plymouth, at a CWGC memorial bearing the names of those who died at sea, helped reach a wider audience, and was a fitting tribute to the sometimes overlooked sacrifice of those who served and died at sea.

Throughout the centenary CWGC played a key part in the work of honouring and remembering those who died in the First World War. But it also acted to ensure that those who lost their lives will be remembered in the future, and that the CWGC has a strong foundation for the next 100 years.

13 Schoolchildren from Kingston School, Bristol, learning about the First World War as part of the CWGC's Living Memory project. On its launch, Colin Kerr, Director of External Relations at CWGC, said: 'The Living Memory Project aims to reconnect the British public to the commemorative heritage on their doorstep'.

The Service for the Commonwealth

On the morning of 4 August 2014 a special service was held at Glasgow Cathedral to mark the centenary of the day that the British Empire entered the First World War, and to commemorate the Commonwealth contribution to the ensuing conflict. Reflecting the Commonwealth theme, the 12th-century cathedral was decorated with flowers from all the Commonwealth countries that fought in the war.

The service took place the day after the closing ceremony of the 2014 Commonwealth Games, hosted by Glasgow. While echoing the spirit of unity and shared history with Commonwealth partners at the Commonwealth Games, the commemoration obviously had a very different tone. The service focused on the extraordinary courage, commitment and sacrifice of all those who served from the Commonwealth nations.

The event referred to our 'Commonwealth brothers and sisters'. For example, over a million Indians served overseas, with 54,000 losing their lives. Some 60,000 from the African continent fought for the Allies, with 7,000 fatalities, while 59,000 of the 416,000 who enlisted from Australia lost their lives.

Guests included HRH The Duke of Rothesay (as the Prince of Wales is known in Scotland), UK Prime Minister David Cameron and Scottish First Minister Alex Salmond, as well as other UK and Irish politicians. Many Commonwealth heads of government were also present. A poignant selection of readings was introduced by broadcaster Sir Trevor McDonald and journalist Kate Adie. At the end of the ceremony, candles were passed to young people, to inspire the next generation to continue the journey of remembrance and learning.

Following the service, the Duke of Rothesay laid the first of many wreaths at Glasgow's Cenotaph in George Square. The Pipes and Drums of the Scots Guards, the band of the Parachute Regiment, and representatives of the Army, Royal Navy and Royal Air Force, all stood in silent tribute. As a lone bugler

14 HRH The Duke of Rothesay and the Lord Provost of Glasgow, Sadie Docherty, processing down the nave at Glasgow Cathedral.

played the Last Post, two women in a corner of the square lifted a small home-made banner embroidered with the words 'Lest we Forget'. A march-past in the square then took place, in the presence of the Prime Minister and the First Minister of Scotland. Later that day HM The Queen attended a special service at Crathie Kirk near Balmoral.

In Edinburgh, on 10 August 2014, the start of the five-year Scottish Commemorations Programme was marked with a service and military parade.

15 A Drumhead Service on the Esplanade of Edinburgh Castle, 10 August 2014, marked the start of the five-year Scottish Commemorations Programme.

16 Military bands and Tri-Service Guards, watched by thousands, processing down the Royal Mile in Edinburgh accompanied by 100 marching veterans and 100 cadets on 10 August.

Commemoration at the CWGC St Symphorien Military Cemetery

17 British and German servicemen and women walking through the graves at St Symphorien Military Cemetery in Mons. They carry lanterns, ready for the evening ceremony to commemorate the outbreak of the First World War.

On 4 August 1914, the British Empire declared war on Germany for violating the neutrality of Belgium. One hundred years on, while commemorative activities were taking place all over the UK, so too were events happening further afield. The UK government delivered an event close to where the opening shots of the war on the Western Front were fired, and where the first casualties fell.

The St Symphorien Military Cemetery at Mons in Belgium was established by the German Army in 1916, following a decision to exhume those who had died at Mons and to re-inter them in a single location. Significantly, British and German soldiers were buried side-by-side. After the war, responsibility for the cemetery was taken on by the Imperial War Graves Commission (later to become the Commonwealth War Graves Commission, CWGC).

By holding the event at the cemetery, the intention was to reflect on how the world moved from peace to war in 1914. Supported by the City of Mons and the CWGC, the themes were those of light and darkness, the shift from peace to war, and the accompanying feelings of anticipation and apprehension. The event reflected on the thoughts of those affected by the start of the war, both at home and in the field in the armies of the British Empire and Germany.

The commemoration was attended by TRH The Duke and Duchess of Cambridge, HRH Prince Harry, UK Prime Minister David Cameron, Irish President Michael D. Higgins and President Joachim Gauck of the Federal Republic of Germany. The King and Queen

18 HRH The Duchess of Cambridge, HRH Prince Harry, and the Most Revd and Rt Hon. Justin Welby placing lanterns at the Cross of Sacrifice during the ceremony at the St Symphorien Military Cemetery.

19 HRH The Duke of Cambridge, King Philippe of Belgium and Prime Minister David Cameron among those laying wreaths at the foot of the Cross of Sacrifice in the evening ceremony.

ST SYMPHORIEN MILITARY CEMETERY

The cemetery at St Symphorien was established by the German Army during the First World War as a final resting place for British and German soldiers killed at the Battle of Mons. Among those buried here is Private John Parr of the Middlesex Regiment, who was fatally wounded during an encounter with a German patrol two days before the battle, thus becoming the first British soldier to be killed in action on the Western Front.

The cemetery also contains the graves of Commonwealth and German soldiers who died in the final days of the conflict, including George Ellison of the Royal Irish Lancers and George Price of the Canadian Infantry. Ellison and Price were killed on 11 November 1918, and are believed to be, respectively, the last British and Commonwealth combat casualties of the war on the Western Front. See page 164 for the 2018 commemoration that took place here.

There are 229 Commonwealth and 284 German servicemen buried or commemorated at St Symphorien, of whom 105 remain unidentified.

20 View of British and German graves at the St Symphorien Military Cemetery.

21 A lone soldier standing at the Cross of Sacrifice during the ceremony.

of the Belgians, along with Prime Minister Elio Di Rupo, represented Belgium at the event. Descendants of some of the soldiers buried in the cemetery also attended. German readers and musicians participated alongside British performers, reinforcing the theme of reconciliation.

The theme of light permeated many of the events on 4 August, inspired by the now famous comment in 1914 from the British Foreign Secretary, Sir Edward Grey, on the eve of Britain's entry into the war: 'The lamps are going out all over Europe, we shall not see them lit again in our life-time.'

This poignant observation was reflected in the St Symphorien ceremony. As darkness fell, lamps were laid at the cemetery's Cross of Sacrifice.

A Solemn Commemoration of the Outbreak of the First World War

While lamps were being lit at Mons in Belgium, an evening service was taking place in Westminster Abbey. Starting at 10pm, an hour before war was officially declared a hundred years earlier, the event was televised live in its entirety on BBC2.

In solemn recognition of Sir Edward Grey's remark in August 1914 – that the lamps were going out all over Europe – the theme of light that featured in Mons continued in Westminster Abbey. Candles were extinguished in stages throughout the service, with a symbolic candle being extinguished along with participants' candles in consecutive areas of the abbey. Every light had been extinguished by the end of the service except for a Paschal candle in the Lady Chapel.

The event reflected on family connections and international relations. It was attended by HRH The Duchess of Cornwall along with senior ministers. The Duchess of Cornwall lost three great-uncles at the Battle of the Somme in 1916, all of whom were killed within six weeks of each other.

22 The candlelit vigil and prayer service at Westminster Abbey on 4 August 2014 to commemorate the centenary of the outbreak of the First World War.

23 Chelsea Pensioners lighting candles. The lighting and extinguishing of candles was a key element of the service.

A poignant focal point of the ceremony was the Grave of the Unknown Warrior. As Big Ben struck 11pm, the Duchess of Cornwall extinguished an oil lamp at the grave in memory of the 17 million lives lost in the war.

Commemorating the centenary of the outbreak of war, it was appropriate that the Westminster Abbey service focused on the last moments of peace before the British Empire declared war on Germany. The horrors of war were still to come, and the readings and music aimed to capture the contemporaneous attitudes of those preparing for war. Among the anticipation and apprehension, there were some who relished the prospect, but many others dreaded it.

24 HRH The Duchess of Cornwall extinguishing the single oil lamp at the Grave of the Unknown Warrior..

THE GRAVE OF THE UNKNOWN WARRIOR

Located at the west end of Westminster Abbey's nave, the Grave of the Unknown Warrior has long been a site of commemoration and reflection. Four unknown British servicemen, exhumed from the battle areas of the Aisne, the Somme, Arras and Ypres, were covered by Union flags and one chosen at random to be brought back for a state funeral at Westminster Abbey on 11 November 1920.

25 The grave contains soil from France and is covered by a slab of black Belgian marble. The inscription was written by Herbert Ryle, Dean of Westminster from 1911 to 1925.

In 2009 the grave took on a new significance, following the death of the last of the men from the British Isles who had fought in the war. HM The Queen laid a wreath at the grave to mark the passing of Harry Patch, the last of the First World War generation.

Step Short's Commemorative March and the Unveiling of the Memorial Arch

Folkestone was a crucial communications hub throughout the First World War. Millions of fighting men marched down 'The Slope' to the harbour, to embark on ships to France and the front line. At the top of the road the troops would hear the order 'step short' – to shorten their stride and negotiate the slope safely. The charity Step Short was set up in 2008 to improve the setting of this historic road (now the Road of Remembrance).

Step Short's commemorative events on 4 August 2014 began with a march to the newly erected Memorial Arch at the top of the Road of Remembrance. The classic steel design is a testament to Folkestone's status as a gateway to the Western Front. The arch's commemorative plaque was unveiled by HRH Prince Harry, who then took the salute as servicemen and women, supported by the Band of the Brigade of Gurkhas, marched through the arch and down the hill to the harbour. The Prince also laid a wreath at the nearby war memorial on behalf of the nation.

Like many other centenary initiatives, Step Short has maintained an ongoing educational programme, along with other activities, throughout each year of the commemorations.

The public support and enthusiasm shown at Folkestone's events were reflected in many other local community events, which were to have a similar reception.

26 The Road of Remembrance street sign during Step Short's commemorative events in Folkestone, Kent, on 4 August 2014.

27 Folkestone's striking steel Memorial Arch was designed by specialist architectural company Foster Gearing for the 2014 commemorations.

Victoria Cross Memorial Plaques

28 For each country represented by the Victoria Cross recipients, a bronze plaque was displayed, along with a banner highlighting a particular recipient. The plaque shown here honours the five US VC recipients, and the banner relates the story of Bellenden Hutcheson, a doctor whose heroism on the front line saved countless lives.

Britain's highest military honour, the Victoria Cross, was won by 175 men from overseas during the First World War – comprising nearly one in three of the total number awarded during the conflict. To commemorate the recipients' extraordinary courage and sacrifice, 11 bronze memorial plaques (one for each country represented) were unveiled at a launch event at London's Lancaster House in June 2014.

HRH The Duke of Kent and Baroness Warsi, Senior Minister of State in the Foreign Office and Minister for Faith and Communities, hosted the event. Two of the nine Victoria Cross holders alive in the world today – British Lance Sgt Johnson Beharry VC and Australian Cpl Mark Donaldson VC – attended; other guests included descendants of those being honoured and representatives of the 11 countries.

The plaques were then gifted to the recipients' home countries – Canada, Australia, New Zealand, South Africa, India, USA, Pakistan, Nepal, Denmark, Belgium and Ukraine – to be displayed at a prominent public location as a symbol of the gratitude felt towards them by the people of the UK.

29 HRH The Duke of Kent, Baroness Warsi, Cpl Mark Donaldson VC and Lance Sgt Johnson Beharry VC at the event.

14–18 NOW: Introduction

30 French street theatre company Royal de Luxe brought giant puppets to the streets of Liverpool for Memories of August 2014, an event jointly staged by Liverpool City Council and 14–18 NOW.

14–18 NOW led the UK's arts programme for the First World War centenary, with the aim to engage as many people as possible with the First World War through the contemporary arts. Throughout the centenary, 14–18 NOW commissioned new artworks and projects by leading artists from around the world in many art forms – including the visual arts, film, theatre, literature, mass-participation events, music, fashion, digital projects, poetry, dance and opera. Artists were invited to create new works inspired by the period 1914–18, exploring how the war impacted on the world we live in now.

14–18 NOW was founded on a firm belief in the transformative power of the arts to bring the stories of the First World War to life. Many of the projects were highly innovative, involving the public through mass participation and digital engagement. With no living veterans left to tell their experiences of the First World War, the arts proved to be potent in engaging

31 Thousands of volunteers dressed as First World War soldiers silently filled public spaces across the UK to mark the Somme centenary in 2016. The event, entitled *we're here because we're here*, was conceived and created by artist Jeremy Deller in collaboration with the National Theatre and others.

contemporary audiences, especially those who felt little connection to the conflict.

Looking at momentous events of the past through the artistic output of the time is often revealing. The vital role that poets, painters, filmmakers and others played in shaping public perceptions of the First World War, as the conflict happened, was a key inspiration for 14–18 NOW's programme. One hundred years later, the artists of the 21st century have opened up new perspectives on the present as well as the past.

All the projects were co-commissioned in partnership with arts and heritage organisations across England, Scotland, Northern Ireland, Wales and beyond. 14–18 NOW also organised the UK tour of the iconic poppy sculptures by artist Paul Cummins and designer Tom Piper.

Engaging people through the arts is a powerful way to bring the past to life. In total, 14–18 NOW commissioned over 125 artworks that were seen by over 35 million people throughout the UK. The programme was supported by the Department for Digital, Culture, Media and Sport (DCMS), the National Lottery through the Heritage Lottery Fund (HLF), and Arts Council England, with additional support from leading trusts and foundations, including The Backstage Trust and Bloomberg Philanthropies, corporations and philanthropists.

32 Close-up of ceramic poppies at the Yorkshire Sculpture Park, the first stop of the 14–18 NOW Poppies Tour in 2015.

14–18 NOW: 2014 Season

The first season of 14–18 NOW's programme focused on the centenary of the outbreak of war. New artworks, created in many different media, were launched across the UK, including commissions that engaged local communities and involved large numbers of participants. In total the season was experienced by over 19 million people.

The poignant *Letter to an Unknown Soldier* project was inspired by Charles Jagger's famous statue in Paddington Station of a soldier reading a letter. Neil Bartlett and Kate Pullinger invited everyone in the UK to write a letter to the soldier, expressing their thoughts and feelings about the First World War. This was a new kind of war memorial, made only of words and created by thousands of people. Over the six weeks of the project, 21,500 people wrote letters. These are now archived in the British Library, and a selection was published by William Collins. All those written in Gaelic were published in a collection by BBC Alba.

33 The *Letter to an Unknown Soldier* project was inspired by the statue in Paddington Station of a First World War soldier reading a letter. Everyone was invited to write a letter to the soldier, creating an extraordinary memorial in words.

A 6,000-strong audience experienced an extraordinarily moving day of remembrance on 3 August 2014 in Cornwall, at a dawn-till-dusk theatrical event entitled *100: The Day Our World Changed*. A collaboration between Wildworks Theatre and The Lost Gardens of Heligan, the event recreated the wartime lives of families from the Cornish parishes of Mevagissey, Gorran and St Ewe.

National Theatre Wales's large-scale, site-specific theatre production *Mametz* by Owen Sheers – performed in ancient woodland in Monmouthshire – gave audiences a vivid glimpse of life and death in

34 Community performers, musicians, stewards and gardeners were among those joining Wildworks Theatre and The Lost Gardens of Heligan to create *100: The Day Our World Changed*. The day-long event re-created the wartime lives of families from three Cornish parishes.

35 *Mametz*, inspired by Owen Sheers's poem 'Mametz Wood', was staged in Monmouthshire woodland by the National Theatre of Wales. In July 1916, 4,000 members of the 38th (Welsh) Division were killed or wounded at Mametz Wood.

the trenches and on the battlefields of the Somme. BalletBoyz's *Young Men* was a staged dancework exploring the bonds that form between men that train and fight together, and how these bonds can fracture under pressure. The work was later adapted for a full-length dance film commissioned with the BBC. In *Does it Matter?*, a series of short films commissioned with Channel 4, five artists with disabilities presented unorthodox, irreverent and unexpected takes on the legacies of war and disability in Britain today.

Visual art projects ranged from the Dazzle Ships series (see pages 36–37) to Anya Gallaccio's installation for the Aldeburgh Festival that was inspired by the landscape on which the British military conducted its early experiments in flight. Photographer Chloe Dewe Mathews created *Shot at Dawn*, a series of images showing the locations at which soldiers of different nations were executed for cowardice and desertion during the war.

In literature, Lavinia Greenlaw, one of Britain's most eminent poets, invited ten writers from countries involved in the war to respond to the title of Robert Graves's famous book, *Goodbye to All That*. Essays by Jeanette Winterson, Ali Smith, Kamila Shamsie and others considered the impact of war on artists.

Music events included a collaboration with WOMAD festival, performances by musician Richard Thompson, and – on 4 August 2014, as the nation remembered Britain's entry into the war 100 years before – a special Late Night Prom featuring the work of composer John Tavener. Activist and musician Billy Bragg curated a set at Glastonbury Festival featuring six musicians performing new songs inspired by the First World War.

36 Work by Zimbabwean music collective Siyaya featured at WOMAD. The Shona name 'Siyaya' means 'we are on the move'. Their work with schools and communities shows how a healthy musical culture can transcend tumultuous social change such as war.

14–18 NOW: Dazzle Ships

Introduced during the First World War, dazzle was a style of ship camouflage characterised by brilliant, glaring geometric patterns. Unlike other forms of camouflage, the intention was not to conceal but to mislead – the enemy would not be able to assess a ship's course properly. The British Navy and merchant navy used dazzle extensively, and in 1918 the artist Norman Wilkinson took the technique across the Atlantic to the US Navy.

37 Venezuelan artist Carlos Cruz-Diez's *Dazzle Ship*, Liverpool. The ship is the *Edmund Gardner*, owned and conserved by Merseyside Maritime Museum.

To commemorate this striking and ingenious tactic, five modern dazzle ships were co-commissioned by 14–18 NOW and Liverpool Biennial as a 14–18 NOW project that spanned all five years of the centenary. Each of the ships was designed by a different artist, with two being shown in Liverpool and the other three showcased in London, Edinburgh and New York.

The Dazzle Ships project was launched in 2014 with the unveiling of Venezuelan artist Carlos Cruz-Diez's *Dazzle Ship* in Liverpool. Cruz-Diez used a historic pilot ship, the *Edmund Gardner*, which was owned and conserved by Merseyside Maritime Museum. The ship is situated in a dry dock adjacent to Liverpool's busy Albert Dock, and has become a much-loved new public monument.

In London, HMS *President 1918* was 'dazzled' by the German artist Tobias Rehberger. One of only three surviving Royal Navy warships from the First World War, the ship had actually served as a dazzle ship during the war when it was named the HMS *Saxifrage*.

The third of the Dazzle Ship commissions was by renowned British pop artist Sir Peter Blake, who created a new design for one of the Mersey ferries in Liverpool. Blake covered the *Snowdrop* with a pattern that he titled *Everybody Razzle Dazzle*. The 'dazzled' ship continued its regular commuter service, making this the first of the Dazzle Ship commissions to be a working vessel.

The project then moved to Scotland with a fourth commission, entitled *Every Woman*, by Ciara Phillips. Phillips 'dazzled' the MV *Fingal*, berthed at the Prince of Wales Dock in the historic port of Leith in Edinburgh. The launch of this dazzle ship was timed to mark the centenary of the Battle of Jutland in May 2016, and the ship formed a central element of that year's Edinburgh Art Festival.

38 In 2014 HMS *President 1918* was converted to a dazzle ship – for the second time in its history – by German artist Tobias Rehberger and moored in London. During the war it had served in dazzle camouflage as HMS *Saxifrage*.

39 *Everybody Razzle Dazzle*, Sir Peter Blake, 2015. The famous British Pop artist used a working Mersey ferry, the *Snowdrop*, to create his dazzle ship.

40 14–18 NOW and Edinburgh Art Festival unveiled *Every Woman* by Ciara Phillips in May 2016, to mark the centenary of the Battle of Jutland. The ship is the MV *Fingal*, berthed at Leith in Edinburgh.

41 *Flow Separation*, Tauba Auerbach, 2018. The artist repainted a historic New York fireboat, the *John J. Harvey*, with a design based on First World War dazzle ships and fluid dynamics.

Finally, the project moved to the United States, with a commission by American artist Tauba Auerbach in New York City. The artist transformed a decommissioned fireboat, the historic *John J. Harvey*, into a floating artwork, commemorating the centenary of the Armistice and the dazzle camouflage programme of the US Navy.

By responding to this little-known episode of design history, the ships' eye-catching liveries have been seen by millions of people, and continue to draw attention to the important role played by the Royal Navy and the merchant navy in the Allies' wartime survival.

14–18 NOW: *Lights Out*

On 4 August 1914, Britain's ultimatum to Germany expired at 11pm, resulting in Britain's declaration of war. This moment in history was marked by 14–18 NOW's free UK-wide event, *Lights Out*. Echoing Sir Edward Grey's famous reference in 1914 to the lamps going out across Europe, between 10pm and 11pm on 4 August 2014 over 16 million people in the UK turned off their lights, allowing just a single light to shine or a single candle to burn in the darkness.

Lights were not only extinguished in homes across the country, but also in over 1,000 local authorities, along with iconic buildings and national organisations, including the BBC and the Royal British Legion.

As a further response to the idea of a single light shining through the darkness, four artworks were commissioned by 14–18 NOW. The artists were Nalini Malani, Bedwyr Williams, Bob and Roberta Smith, and Ryoji Ikeda.

At dusk on 4 August a pillar of intense white light appeared in the London sky. For the next seven nights, from sunset until dawn, it beamed upwards from a series of static high-powered searchlights positioned near the Palace of Westminster. Created by Ryoji Ikeda, the work was visible across London. Visitors to the site of the installation itself could walk within the grid of spotlights and experience a soundscape of pure sine waves that accompanied this monumental column of light. The work was entitled *spectra*.

42 *spectra*, Ryoji Ikeda, 2014. Created with static high-powered searchlights, the pillar of intense white light was visible in the night sky from all over London.

43 *In Search of Vanished Blood*, Nalini Malani, 2014. Malani, a video and installation artist based in Mumbai, combined imagery from Eastern and Western cultures to create visual and aural projections using the façade of the Scottish National Gallery in Edinburgh.

In Bangor, Bedwyr Williams's *Traw* took the form of a large-scale video and sound installation presented at the site of the North Wales Memorial Arch, while Nalini Malani used large-scale projections and shadow play in Edinburgh to cover the façades of the Scottish National Gallery for the work *In Search of Vanished Blood*. Bob and Roberta Smith took over the City Hall grounds in Belfast to create an installation constructed with local artists and community groups. It used candles to illuminate the statement: *What unites human beings, ears, eyes, loves, hopes and toes is huge and wonderful. What divides human beings is small and mean.*

In addition, artist Jeremy Deller designed an app featuring four short films that were released daily before 'vanishing' at the stroke of 11pm each night, for four nights. The culmination of the artwork, at 10pm on 4 August, was when the final *Lights Out* film was available for just one hour.

44 In the grounds of Belfast's City Hall, candles are lit on the artwork *What unites human beings, ears, eyes, loves, hopes and toes is huge and wonderful. What divides human beings is small and mean*, by Bob and Roberta Smith.

First World War Memorials Programme

The aftermath of the First World War saw the biggest ever single wave of public commemoration. As a result, war memorials can be found in almost every town and village throughout the country. They stand as eloquent witnesses of the tragic impact of the war on local communities and the sacrifices they made. While many memorials continue to form the focus of remembrance ceremonies and are cherished by the communities they serve, at the beginning of the centenary it was clear that some needed extra support to allow them to continue to act as fitting tributes to the fallen.

In response, the Department for Digital, Culture, Media and Sport (DCMS) funded Historic England in partnership with Civic Voice, Imperial War Museums and War Memorials Trust, to form the First World War Memorials Programme. This partnership worked closely with the public throughout the centenary period to ensure that war memorials across Britain are protected and the people they commemorate are remembered.

War memorials are tragic reminders not only of those who died but of the many ways in which the war affected lives on the home front and across the Commonwealth. They can vary in size from grand

45 During the First World War, 49,076 members of the Royal Regiment of Artillery lost their lives. In 2014 the Royal Artillery Memorial at Hyde Park Corner, London, was upgraded from Grade II* to Grade I in recognition of its artistic and historical significance.

national monuments to small village memorials, and in form from traditional stone monuments to more practical ones such as drinking fountains, street lamps and church organs.

Throughout the centenary Historic England and its partners worked with the public to ensure that all memorials – regardless of size, shape or who they commemorated – were cared for and protected, and that online information about their history, condition and protected status was as easily accessible as possible. War Memorials Trust worked with communities and memorial custodians, administering

46 Detail of the Royal Artillery Memorial, Hyde Park Corner, London. This impressive memorial was cleaned by specialists at the beginning of the centenary, as part of the First World War Memorials Programme.

47 The Wagoners' Memorial at Sledmere, Yorkshire, has carved scenes of the Wagoners' Reserve, including German soldiers committing atrocities. During the centenary, this extremely unusual memorial was upgraded to Grade I to recognise its significance.

48 Memorial in Carlton Colville, Suffolk, commemorating a scoutmaster and sea scouts who died in a sailing accident in 1914.. Two years later, Stanley Wood, the sole survivor of the accident, was killed at the Battle of the Somme aged 19. His name was added to the memorial.

over £2 million in grant funding to repair and conserve memorials. To support this, conservation specialists from Historic England prepared advice and training for heritage professionals to ensure they had the skills needed to care for the nation's war memorials.

Historic England also sought to recognise the importance of memorials to our shared heritage, and to protect memorials by adding and upgrading 2,500 war memorials on the National Heritage List for England. For the first time in a project of this scale volunteers were invited to play a part in the process. The national civic charity, Civic Voice, went out into communities to help people research, care for and protect their local memorials. Equally important to the long-term survival of war memorials is ensuring that the next generation understand their significance and how to care for them. Historic England and War Memorials Trust have worked with schools to help children learn more about their local memorials and how they can help with their care and protection.

Blood Swept Lands and Seas of Red

Created at the Tower of London in 2014, *Blood Swept Lands and Seas of Red* by artist Paul Cummins and designer Tom Piper quickly became an icon of the First World War centenary commemorations. The scale of the artwork was intended to reflect the magnitude of the centenary, and to create a powerful visual commemoration. It was seen by an estimated five million people from across the world.

The artwork comprised 888,246 handmade ceramic red poppies, each representing a British and Colonial life lost at the Western Front in the First World War. The impression of a surging sea of red was given further impact by the inclusion of poppies appearing to flow out of a window in Legge's Mount in the West Moat (the 'Weeping Window'), cascading down the wall on the wharf side of the moat ('Over the Top'), and curling over the main causeway into the Tower on a free-standing twisted metal sculpture (the 'Wave').

To create so many poppies, 497,000 kg of Etruria Marl-based Etruscan red earthenware were needed. Individually handmade at Paul Cummins's ceramics works in Derbyshire and at Johnson Tiles in Tunstall, Stoke-on-Trent, the poppies were progressively 'planted' by a team of about 17,500 volunteers between 17 July and 11 November 2014. The artwork was unveiled on 5 August, with a visit by TRH The Duke and Duchess of Cambridge and HRH Prince Harry.

At around sunset each day between 1 September and 10 November, the names of 180 First World War service personnel – nominated by members of the public to appear on a Roll of Honour – were read aloud by a Yeoman Warder or guest reader, followed by the bugle call of the Last Post.

Members of the public were able to pre-order a ceramic poppy for £25 each, and in the months following the dismantling of the artwork the poppies travelled to destinations far and wide around the globe. A share of the proceeds (estimated at more than £15 million) went to six service charities: COBSEO, Combat Stress, Coming Home, Help for Heroes, the Royal British Lergion and SSAFA.

Two elements of the original artwork, entitled Poppies: *Wave* and Poppies: *Weeping Window*, went on a tour of the UK organised by 14–18 NOW. The Poppies Tour concluded at the Imperial War Museums in 2018 as part of the Armistice commemorations.

49 The moat gradually filled with poppies as the artwork evolved. In the early days of the First World War, the moat was used as a training ground for the Stockbrokers' Battalion, made up of City of London workers who had enlisted.

50 View of the *Wave* sculpture, on the main causeway of the Tower.

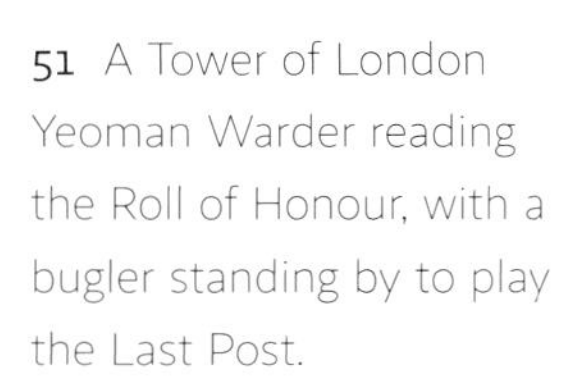

51 A Tower of London Yeoman Warder reading the Roll of Honour, with a bugler standing by to play the Last Post.

London Transport Museum

To commemorate the First World War centenary, London Transport Museum restored into operational condition a 1914-built London bus – B2737. Over 1,000 of these B-type buses were requisitioned for war service, serving as troop transports, ambulances and even mobile pigeon lofts. The restoration of B2737 (known as 'Battle Bus') was completed in 2014, and was part of a five-year community learning programme exploring the war's impact on Londoners. The project was funded by the Heritage Lottery Fund, London Transport Museum Friends and public donations.

In 2014 Battle Bus participated in various London events in its original red-and-cream London General Omnibus Company (LGOC) livery. It took part in a cavalcade of 48 buses displayed on Regent Street, and a recreation of its original route as the No. 9 bus from Barnes to Liverpool Street. In September, the bus was converted into a military troop carrier. Undertaken in the museum, in public view and captured on time-lapse cameras, the conversion included fitting the windows with protective boarding and painting the body in military khaki.

The bus then departed for a commemorative tour of the Western Front. For ten days, the bus and a mobile exhibition toured Belgium and France, visiting locations where London buses are known to have served. The tour included the bus participating in the Last Post Ceremony at the Menin Gate in Ypres, Belgium, and a visit to Bus House Cemetery, named after the wreck of a London bus that was hit by a shell and remained where it was hit throughout the war.

52 Battle Bus in its red-and-cream livery at London's Piccadilly Circus, August 2014.

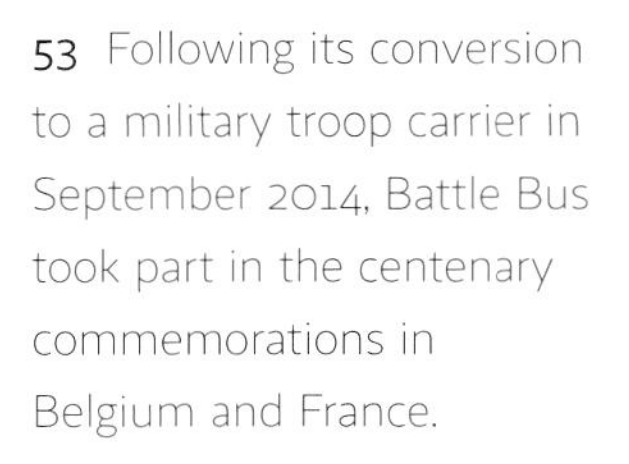

53 Following its conversion to a military troop carrier in September 2014, Battle Bus took part in the centenary commemorations in Belgium and France.

People's History Museum

People's History Museum (PHM) is the national museum of democracy, telling the story of its development in Britain: past, present, and future. Exhibitions and activities inspire people of all ages to explore issues such as equality, social justice and a fair world for all.

A Land Fit for Heroes: War and the Working Class 1914–1918 opened in May 2014, looking at how the First World War radically altered British society. By Christmas 1914 the trade union movement had contributed 250,000 men to the war effort. This mass support is often overlooked. John Ward, MP for Stoke-on-Trent and leader of the navvies and labourers union, raised three pioneer battalions and fought in France, Italy and Russia. Labour Party leader Arthur Henderson joined the War Cabinet. Service in the armed forces defined the future of countless politicians. At the same time, the roles of women changed dramatically. Photographs and letters showed exhibition-goers how the needs of women working in factories were represented by suffragette societies, who had suspended their fight for the vote to support the war effort.

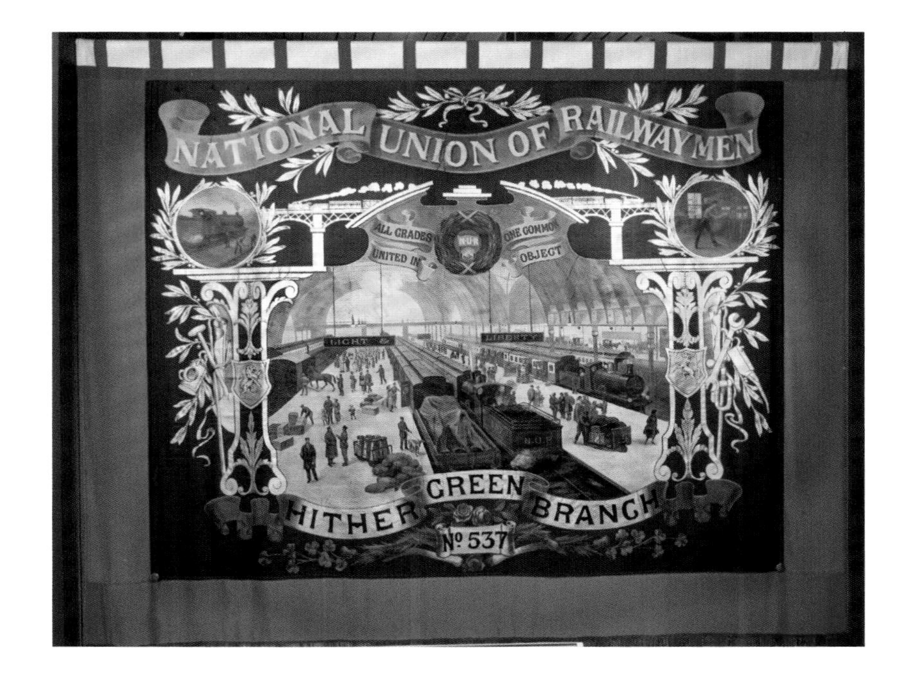

54 The National Union of Railwaymen's magnificent Hither Green branch banner shows how railway workers supported the war effort.

55 View of the exhibition, showing how the war prompted changing attitudes to women.

RAF Museum

The First World War in the Air opened at the RAF Musuem in December 2014, exploring the unique role of air power during the First World War. The wider programme included activities for formal education, lifelong learning, volunteering, apprenticeships and public events. The exhibition and events were made possible with grants from the Heritage Lottery Fund plus funds from ongoing partnerships with BAE Systems and the Esmée Fairbairn Collections Fund.

Exhibits included iconic aircraft such as the Sopwith Camel, the Fokker D VII and the Avro 504, built in the factory set up by Claude Grahame-White at the outset of the war. In 1911 he had bought a plot of land in Hendon, and set up a flying school with aviation pioneer Louis Blériot. The thrilling story of the evolution of flight, from early experimentation to fighting machines, was underpinned by stories of people 'on the ground'. Theatrical media installations, such as an animated dogfight, plus hundreds of smaller, personal items from the museum's collections, brought the story to life. The exhibition also explored how the Royal Flying Corps and Royal Naval Air Service, comprising 1,800 men in 1914, became a Royal Air Force of 290,000 men and women at the end of the war. The museum also launched RAF Museum Storyvault (www.rafmuseumstoryvault.org.uk), featuring digitised archive documents such as casualty cards, the 1918 Muster Roll and the 1918 Air Force List.

56 View of *The First World War in the Air* exhibition.

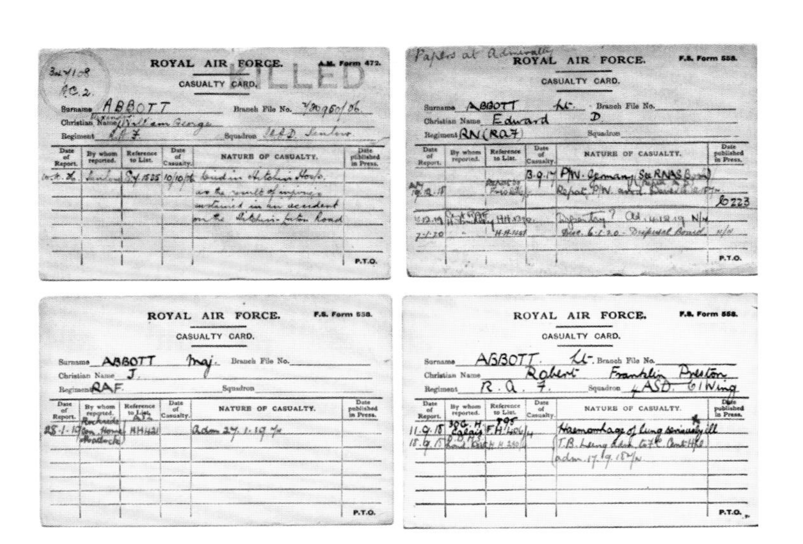

ROYAL AIR FORCE. A.M. Form 472.
CASUALTY CARD.
KILLED
Surname ABBOTT Branch File No.
Christian Name William George
Regiment R.A.F.

Date of Report.	By whom reported.	Reference to List.	Date of Casualty.	NATURE OF CASUALTY.	Date published in Press.
			10/10/18		

P.T.O.

ROYAL AIR FORCE. F.S. Form 558.
CASUALTY CARD.
Papers at Admiralty
Surname ABBOTT Lt. Branch File No.
Christian Name Edward D
Regiment RN (RAF) Squadron

Date of Report.	By whom reported.	Reference to List.	Date of Casualty.	NATURE OF CASUALTY.	Date published in Press.
			3.9.17	P/W. Germany	
					6223
7.1.20					

P.T.O.

ROYAL AIR FORCE. F.S. Form 558.
CASUALTY CARD.
Surname ABBOTT Maj. Branch File No.
Christian Name J.
Regiment RAF Squadron

Date of Report.	By whom reported.	Reference to List.	Date of Casualty.	NATURE OF CASUALTY.	Date published in Press.
25.1.19		HH421		Adm 27.1.19	

P.T.O.

ROYAL AIR FORCE. F.S. Form 558.
CASUALTY CARD.
Surname ABBOTT Lt. Branch File No.
Christian Name Robert Franklin Preston
Regiment R.A.F. Squadron 4 ASD. 61 Wing

Date of Report.	By whom reported.	Reference to List.	Date of Casualty.	NATURE OF CASUALTY.	Date published in Press.
11.9.18	30 G. H. Calais			Haemorrhage of lung seriously ill	
18.9.18				T.B. Lung	
				adm. 17.9.18	

P.T.O.

57 Casualty cards have been digitised for RAF Museum Storyvault.

National Memorial Arboretum

The National Memorial Arboretum is the UK's year-round centre of remembrance and a maturing 150-acre arboretum. Since planting began in 1997, it has been a special place for honouring those who served and continue to serve.

The Arboretum's diverse First World War centenary programme was launched in the spring of 2014 with the introduction of three special self-led trails, enabling visitors of all ages to discover the trees and memorials that are linked to the First World War by the stories of people's wartime experiences.

On the evening of 4 August 2014, marking 100 years since Britain entered the First World War, the Arboretum held a candlelit vigil at the top of the Armed Forces Memorial to commemorate all who served. Open to all, the poignant service included prayers, readings, music and poetry, and the event gave visitors a rare opportunity to explore the Arboretum's grounds in the evening.

58 The candlelit vigil was a public event to mark the start of the First World War and to reflect on all those whose lives were changed forever by the conflict.

Commemorative Football Matches

The Christmas Truce was a series of unofficial ceasefires along the Western Front in 1914. Men from both sides ventured into no-man's-land on Christmas Eve and Christmas Day, and exchanged food and souvenirs and in some cases sang carols and even played football. British and German soldiers playing football together on the front line became one of the most enduring images of the First World War. The Christmas Truce is often portrayed as the last human element of the war before the intensification of trench warfare.

In 2014, the theme of commemorative football matches was played out on a global scale. In the UK, the Premier League, the Football Association and the Football League organised matches in partnership with the British Council as part of the Football Remembers campaign. More than 30,000 schools received a British Council education pack with resources to help children learn about the truce – including eye-witness accounts, photos, drawings and letters from soldiers.

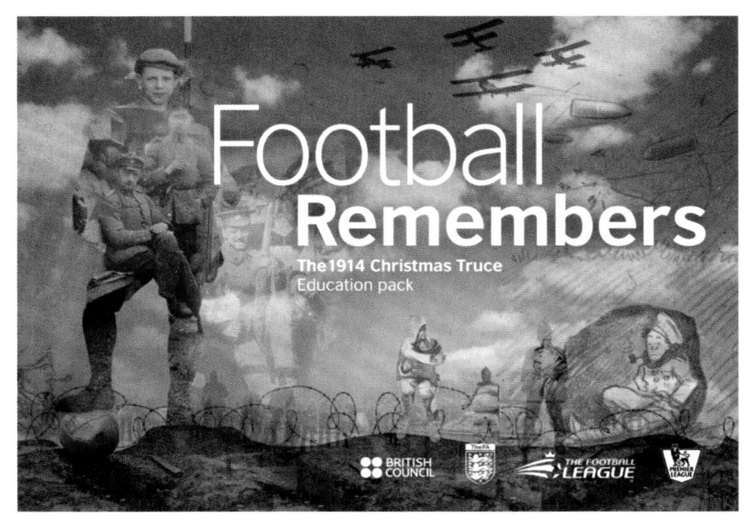

59 Front cover of the Football Remembers education pack, issued to schools across the UK by the British Council.

The Football Remembers memorial was unveiled at the National Memorial Arboretum in Staffordshire, on 12 December 2014, by HRH The Duke of Cambridge and the England national football team manager, Roy Hodgson. The handshake inside a football design was by ten-year-old schoolboy, Spencer Turner, winning a UK-wide competition. It was turned into a striking bronze memorial by British sculptor Georgie Welch.

Staff at British embassies, high commissions and consulates around the world marked the Christmas Truce by hosting a series of football matches. A key part of the events was ensuring that young people

60 The Football Remembers memorial at the National Memorial Arboretum in Alrewas, Staffordshire.

around the world learnt more about the First World War and the powerful message that the truce conveys about peace and reconciliation.

Examples of commemorative football matches include the British Embassy in Bolivia playing against Oruro Royal Football Club. Football was introduced in Bolivia by British railway engineers; Oruro Royal was the first football club in Bolivia. In Brazil, the British and German consulates in Rio played alongside people from the local community and the police – demonstrating how football can be a tool for promoting social inclusion, fair play and respect.

The British Embassy in Tel Aviv organised a football tournament involving 200 young players from Arab and Jewish communities, while in Sri Lanka the High Commission hosted football matches with around 50 youngsters, as well as a multilingual carol service, in conjunction with the Sri Lanka Unites programme to promote reconciliation. In Ghana a game was played between teams made up of youngsters from broken homes, as part of a wider charity programme aimed at giving them hope and direction.

61 A team from the British Embassy in Bolivia (white shirts) and the Oruro Royal Football Club (striped shirts) took part in a friendly game in La Paz, on 9 December 2014, to remember the 1914 Christmas Truce football matches.

62 On Christmas Eve 2014, British and German soldiers commemorated the Christmas Truce in this football game on the heliport of the ISAF headquarters in Kabul, Afghanistan.

2015
COMMEMORATIONS

2015 INTRODUCTION

Following the positive public response to the commemorations in 2014, events in 2015 sought to build on this momentum and continue to engage and inspire. During the early part of the year the focus was on the Gallipoli campaign and the war outside Europe. Other significant battles were also marked, such as those of Neuve Chapelle and Loos, which provided opportunities to recognise the important role of forces from the Commonwealth and beyond. In addition, a wide range of commemorative activities in the UK was held locally by various communities, with people of all ages taking part. This was an opportunity for less well-known stories to come through, as well as to develop further the educational projects that had been established in 2014.

63 At the London Gallipoli commemoration in April 2015, military personnel and descendants of those who fought in the campaign marched down Whitehall to the Cenotaph.

64 War Memorials Trust and Historic England worked with pupils from Ashby Willesley Primary School, Leicestershire, to undertake a condition survey of the Ashby de la Zouch war memorial. It was originally unveiled in 1922.

65 The Muslim Burial Ground, near Woking, Surrey, commemorates Muslim soldiers who lost their lives far from home. It was begun in 1915. During the centenary, data held about memorials was linked in one central source on the IWM War Memorials Register.

IWM North: Centenary of Neuve Chapelle

The Battle of Neuve Chapelle in March 1915 was the first large-scale planned British offensive on the Western Front. Despite heavy losses, the offensive in the Artois region successfully broke through at the village of Neuve Chapelle. It was here that the Indian Corps fought its first major action of the war and played a key role in the battle.

Commemorating the centenary of the battle, events took place in both India and the UK to honour the significant contribution of the Indian troops. One such event, in tribute to the diverse make-up of those who fought at the battle, was the multi-faith commemorative evening held at IWM North in Manchester exactly 100 years later – on 10 March 2015. Religious leaders from the Muslim, Hindu and Sikh communities were joined by Culture Secretary Sajid Javid, along with serving personnel and schoolchildren from the north-west, for an evening of traditional Indian dance, readings and poems.

The evening was an important opportunity for communities to explore and learn more about their connections to the war, as they heard how men from modern-day India, Pakistan, Bangladesh and Nepal had taken up arms alongside soldiers from across the UK.

THE JULLUNDUR BRIGADE AT NEUVE CHAPELLE

One of the first units from the Indian Army to go into action on the Western Front was the Jullundur Brigade. Just three weeks into the war, the Jullundur Brigade were part of a 21-ship transportation to Marseilles, France. Their arrival was an enormous morale boost to the Allies, and the Indian troops were cheered as they marched towards the Western Front.

On 10 March 1915 the attack on Neuve Chapelle began, with the Jullundur Brigade fighting as part of the Lahore Division. At that time the brigade comprised the 1st Manchesters (who were serving in India when the First World War broke out), the 47th Sikhs, the 15th Ludhiana Sikhs, the 59th Scinde Rifles and the 4th Battalion, Suffolk Regiment (Territorial Force), who had joined the brigade in November 1914. For four long days men from across the British Empire fought side-by-side, advancing ever closer to Neuve Chapelle.

66 Photograph of Indian troops in France marching to the front, taken in 1915.

IWM North: From Street to Trench, a World War that Shaped a Region

At the same time as the Neuve Chapelle event took place at IWM North, there was a major exhibition in the galleries looking at the impact of the early days of the war on the home front. The largest exhibition ever created to explore the lives and experiences of people from the north-west of England during the First World War, it showcased more than 200 personal objects, films, sound recordings, photographs, artworks and letters. Walking down a northern terraced street, visitors could follow the journey of those who went to the trenches of the Western Front and beyond. Items from IWM's unrivalled collections, complemented by objects on loan, revealed how lives were shaped by the conflict. From poet Wilfred Owen and future Prime Minister Clement Attlee, to Victoria Cross recipients and first-hand accounts by civilians on the home front, the exhibition revealed the remarkable experiences of individuals through previously unpublished and personal items.

67 View of *From Street to Trench* at IWM North. Visitors could play hopscotch on the replica of a wartime northern terraced street, while finding out about the impact of war and the changes that happened on the home front.

68 Large-scale paintings from the period vividly brought to life the atmosphere of wartime industry – such as Anna Airy's *The 'L' Press. Forging the Jacket of an 18-inch Gun: Armstrong-Whitworth Works, Openshaw*, 1918, seen in this view of the exhibition. The Manchester workers are making the barrel of an 18-inch gun, one of the largest artillery guns used by British forces.

Commonwealth and Ireland Service to Commemorate the Centenary of the Gallipoli Campaign

69 The lighthouse on the Gallipoli peninsula, with HMS *Bulwark* moored in the Dardanelles Strait behind for the centenary commemorations of the Gallipoli campaign.

Between April 1915 and January 1916, the Gallipoli peninsula was the scene of an attempt by Allied forces to capture the Ottoman capital of Constantinople (now Istanbul). An initial naval attack was repelled and, after eight months of fighting, the ensuing land campaign was abandoned. There were heavy casualties on both sides. In 2015, commemorations took place in both the UK and on the site of the former battlefields.

On 24 April 2015, themes of conflict and reconciliation featured in events in Turkey to commemorate the Gallipoli campaign. Events took place at key locations throughout the day. At 11.30am, HRH The Prince of Wales and HRH Prince Harry went aboard HMS *Bulwark*, the Royal Navy's then flagship, anchored for the occasion in the Dardanelles Strait. Here they met 15 descendants of British and Irish men who had fought at Gallipoli. The inclusion of HMS *Bulwark* reflected the role of the Royal Navy at Gallipoli, both at sea and on land, and the significant losses sustained.

Today, men from both the Ottoman and Allied forces lie close together in separate cemeteries on the Gallipoli peninsula. Honouring the theme of reconciliation between former enemies, the 2015 events took place at both of them. At an international service at the Çanakkale Martyrs' Memorial, on the southern end of the peninsula, HRH The Prince of Wales laid a wreath. The memorial commemorates the services of approximately 253,000 Turkish soldiers who participated in the Gallipoli campaign. During the war, the town of Çanakkale was the chief supply port for reinforcements to the peninsula, and was heavily defended.

70 HRH Prince Harry, HRH The Prince of Wales and Captain Nick Cooke-Priest on HMS *Bulwark*, at a reception held with relatives of veterans of the Gallipoli campaign on 24 April 2015.

This was followed by the Commonwealth and Ireland Service at Cape Helles. The Helles Memorial is a Commonwealth War Graves Commission memorial on the tip of the peninsula, with a stone obelisk standing at over 30 metres high. It serves the dual function of being a Commonwealth battle memorial for the whole Gallipoli campaign, and a place of commemoration for Commonwealth servicemen who died there and have no known grave, including those lost in Gallipoli waters. Over 20,000 names are commemorated on the memorial.

The service focused on the heroism shown by both sides, the courage shown in the face of huge adversity and horrendous conditions, and the reconciliation and friendship which has blossomed since the end of the war. HRH The Prince of Wales read an extract from John Masefield's book *Gallipoli*, and wreaths were laid by representatives including the President of Ireland, Michael D. Higgins, Australian Prime Minister Tony Abbott, New Zealand Prime Minister John Key and the President of Turkey, Recep Tayyip Erdoğan.

71 The Helles Memorial on the Gallipoli peninsula, Turkey.

72 HRH Prince Harry speaking at the Commonwealth and Ireland Service at the Helles Memorial on 24 April 2015. Wreaths were laid and a memorial stone was unveiled.

73 A piper playing at the Commonwealth and Ireland Service at the Helles Memorial.

National Commemoration of the Centenary of the Gallipoli Campaign and Anzac Day

74 Military representatives from the combatant nations that took part in the campaign arriving at the Cenotaph.

In a combined event, a wreath-laying ceremony and parade was held at the Cenotaph in London. It began with two minutes' silence following the striking of Big Ben at 11am. HM The Queen laid the first wreath, followed by Prime Minister David Cameron, UK government representatives, and representatives from Australia, New Zealand and Turkey. Senior representatives from all the other nations who fought at Gallipoli also laid wreaths. Bangladesh, Canada, France, India, Ireland, Nepal, Pakistan, Russia and Sri Lanka represented Britain's allies in the campaign. Germany was also represented at the ceremony, as was Belgium, in recognition of the number of Anzacs who lost their lives in Flanders.

Gallipoli was the first campaign in the First World War where the Australian and New Zealand Army Corps (Anzac) suffered major casualties. Anzac Day was originally devised to honour those who gave their lives during the campaign, but has since become a national day of remembrance in those countries. It gave rise to a new sense of national identity, and as such has a special place in the hearts of many Australians and New Zealanders today. While Gallipoli has become almost synonymous with the role of the Anzacs, of the 550,000 Allied soldiers involved, over 400,000 came from Britain alone. The centenary of the campaign was an opportunity to highlight the significant role of the British as well as to commemorate Anzac Day.

Other nations which commemorate Anzac Day – Tonga, Malta, South Africa and Papua New Guinea – also laid wreaths at the Cenotaph.

The royal family was represented by HM The Queen, HRH The Duke of Edinburgh and HRH The Duke of Cambridge. They were accompanied by representatives of military charities, senior serving military and senior politicians, and representatives from various commemorative partners. Watching the event in a special VIP area were 2,000 descendants of those who were involved in the Gallipoli campaign, while thousands of others joined a procession to

march past the Cenotaph in honour of their ancestors. The event was also watched by members of the public, lining the streets to pay their respects.

Unusually, the service included an art installation erected near the Cenotaph. *Gallipoli* 1915, a small-scale reproduction of part of the Gallipoli 1915 memorial at the National Memorial Arboretum in Staffordshire, was designed by Turkish-born artist Nadir Imamoglu.

75 HRH The Queen and the Rt Hon. David Carter MP, Speaker of the New Zealand House of Representatives, laying wreaths at the Cenotaph.

76 Nadir Imamoglu's *Gallipoli 1915* at the Cenotaph, and the march-past getting underway behind.

The sculpture was constructed from young oak trees, aged between 16 and 23 years old, to represent the average age of those fighting at Gallipoli. Branches evoked the raised hands of injured soldiers, reaching out for help during the evacuation of the peninsula.

Young people from the UK, Australia, New Zealand and Turkey gave readings during the service, including Atatürk's message to bereaved pilgrims read by 14 year-old Ecenur Bilgiç from Turkey. The music, led by the Band of HM Royal Marines, the Turkish Air Force Band and the choir of Chelmsford Cathedral, included a specially commissioned piece 'Remembering Gallipoli' created by Michael McDermott, which incorporated

77 Viewing the event from a specially allocated area next to the Cenotaph were 2,000 descendants of those who were involved in the Gallipoli campaign.

78 Reflecting both sides of the Gallipoli campaign, music was performed by the Turkish Air Force Band and the Band of the Grenadier Guards.

a reading of an extract from Leon Maxwell Gellert's poem, 'The Attack at Dawn'.

The march past the Cenotaph following the service was led by contingents from the Royal Navy, the Fleet Air Arm, the Submarine Service, representatives of the Maritime Reserves and other military associations and regiments, and included representatives from the armed forces of other countries who fought at Gallipoli. They were followed by descendants of those whose ancestors were involved in the Gallipoli campaign and those who march past the Cenotaph every year to commemorate Anzac Day.

79 Representatives of military associations marching past the Cenotaph.

80 Principal Director of Music, Lt Col. Nick Grace, Royal Marines, conducting the massed bands.

Conservation of HMS *M.33*

The only surviving naval vessel from the ill-fated Gallipoli campaign of 1915, HMS *M.33* occupies pride of place alongside HMS *Victory* and the *Mary Rose* in Portsmouth Historic Dockyard. She is one of just three Royal Navy warships to remain that fought during the First World War (the others being HMS *Caroline* and HMS *President*).

Her first active operation was the support of the British landings at Suvla during the Gallipoli campaign in August 1915. She remained stationed at Gallipoli until the evacuation in January 1916. HMS *M.33* was known as a lucky ship. Although the Gallipoli campaign claimed 100,000 lives, no casualties were recorded among the 75 men who served on her.

81 At Portsmouth Historic Dockyard, HMS *Victory*, veteran of the Battle of Trafalgar in 1805, can be seen from the compass platform of HMS *M.33*, veteran of the Gallipoli campaign of 1915.

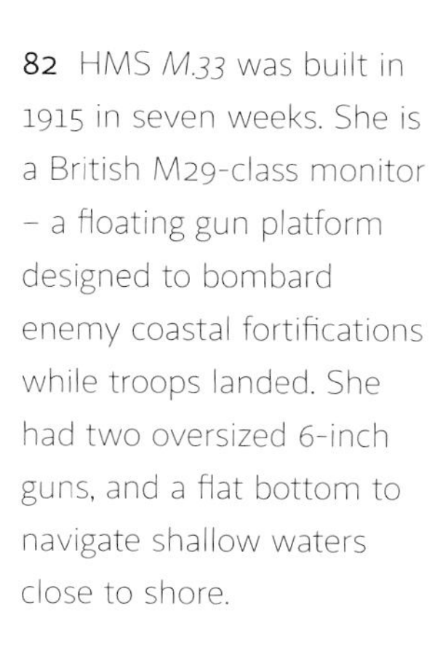

82 HMS *M.33* was built in 1915 in seven weeks. She is a British M29-class monitor – a floating gun platform designed to bombard enemy coastal fortifications while troops landed. She had two oversized 6-inch guns, and a flat bottom to navigate shallow waters close to shore.

Thanks to a grant of £1.8 million from the Heritage Lottery Fund (HLF), the small ship with a big history has welcomed many thousands of visitors since opening to the public exactly a hundred years after she first saw action. The National Museum of the Royal Navy and Hampshire County Council worked together on HMS *M.33* as part of the museum's Great War at Sea 1914–1918 programme, marking the Royal Navy's role in the First World War. A special exhibition, *Gallipoli: Myth and Memory*, opened in March 2015.

The plan was not to restore the ship, but to conserve it. Specialists worked to consolidate and conserve the original steelwork in order to expose her original features. Later layers of paint were painstakingly stripped back by hand, exposing the authentic and cracked paint surface below. This mammoth task absorbed over 3,600 hours of work on the project, and more than 275 litres of protective wax. The treatment was tailored to each area of the ship in order to retain as much of the historic surface as possible, while also carefully removing ineffectual, modern surface treatments.

83 Open to the public in No.1 Dock at Portsmouth Historic Dockyard, HMS *M.33* is painted in the 'dazzle' camouflage she wore at the end of 1918.

84 Throughout the ship's conservation, as much of the original surface area was kept as possible.

Centenary of the Quintinshill (Gretna) Rail Disaster and the Battle of Loos

A Memorial Service, in the presence of HRH The Princess Royal, was held on Friday 22 May 2015 at Gretna Green for the victims of Britain's worst rail disaster when three trains crashed at Quintinshill in Dumfries and Galloway on 22 May 1915. Most of the soldiers who died were buried in a communal grave in Rosebank Cemetery, Leith, where a further service in the presence of HRH The Princess Royal and Vice Admiral Sir Tim Laurence was held on Saturday 23 May 2018.

85 The Royal Scots marching to Rosebank Cemetery for the Quintinshill (Gretna) Centenary Service of Remembrance.

86 Vice Admiral Sir Tim Laurence, Vice Chair of the Commonwealth War Graves Commission, and the Rt Hon. Nicola Sturgeon, First Minister of Scotland, paying their respects at the Memorial in Rosebank Cemetery, Leiths.

The British attack at Loos was launched on 25 September 1915 as part of a French-led plan to defeat German forces across northern France from Artois to Champagne. The battle lasted for approximately two weeks. An estimated 30,000 Scots fought at Loos. Heavy casualties in the battle affected communities throughout Scotland. Dundee, for example, lost 230 men killed or wounded out of 420 of the 1/4th Battalion Black Watch, while the losses of the 9th Black Watch were felt by families in Angus, parts of Fife, Perthshire, Aberdeenshire, Stirlingshire, Lanarkshire and Ayrshire.

Scotland commemorated the 100th anniversary of the start of the Battle of Loos with a weekend of events in Dundee, beginning on Friday 25 September 2015 with the annual lighting of a beacon at dawn at Dundee War Memorial, on top of Dundee Law. The next day, around 250 service personnel and 300 veterans marched through the streets to join over 1,000 people in City Square, which had been transformed into an open-air 'cathedral' for the national Centenary Commemorative Service. In attendance were First Minister Nicola Sturgeon and TRH The Duke and Duchess of Rothesay.

87 Three hundred veterans joined over 1,000 people in Dundee's City Square to commemorate the 100th anniversary of the start of the Battle of Loos.

88 TRH The Duke and Duchess of Rothesay unveiling a plaque in Dundee's Marryat Hall, commemorating those who fought in the Battle of Loos.

14–18 NOW: 2015 Season

89 Rehearsal photo for *Young Men*, performed by ground-breaking dance company BalletBoyz at Sadler's Wells, London.

90 *Dazzle Island* at Childwall Sports and Science Academy. Working with Studio Hato, the pupils used bespoke digital tools to help create the final design.

The first season of 14–18 NOW's evocative arts programme had a deep impact on audiences, with many people expressing a deeper connection to the First World War. The 2015 season was set to be equally resonant, and across the UK the innovative arts programme engaged people with stories and activities that took them back to the tumultuous events of 100 years ago.

The season began with the immensely powerful stage show *Young Men* by BalletBoyz at Sadler's Wells, London. With choreography by Iván Pérez and music by Keaton Henson, the show explored the bonds that form between men that train and fight together.

In Liverpool, pupils from Childwall Sports and Science Academy, Greenbank Primary and Childwall Valley Primary were inspired by Sir Peter Blake's dazzle-ship artwork *Everybody Razzle Dazzle* to create *Dazzle Island*. This new permanent artwork, for the playground of Childwall Sports and Science Academy, was created in collaboration with designers Studio Hato. At Tate Britain in London, Turner Prize winner Susan Philipsz installed *War Damaged Musical Instruments*. Developed over a number of years, this was a haunting sound installation created with musical instruments that had been disfigured in conflict. Played by musicians from Britain and Germany, the damaged instruments conveyed the physical suffering of war in an extraordinary way.

On tour in 2015 was *The Notebook*, a play from theatre company Forced Entertainment that was first staged the year before. Two performers are trapped in a single voice and shared perspective, weaving in dark and subversive humour as they recount wartime hardships.

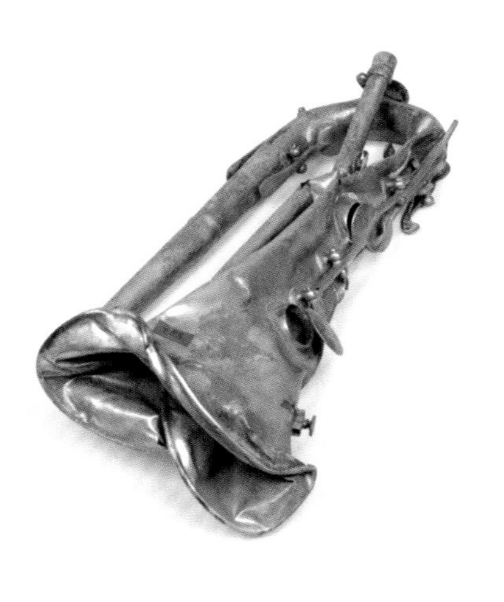

91 For *War Damaged Musical Instruments* at Tate Britain, Susan Philipsz recorded musicians playing instruments such as this crushed klappenhorn (keyed bugle), salvaged from Berlin in 1945.

92 *The Notebook*, a stage play by Forced Entertainment, tells the story of twin brothers evacuated to the countryside.

Centenary of Edith Cavell's Death

In 1907 British nurse Edith Cavell became director of the first professional school of nursing in Belgium. With the outbreak of the First World War, she continued to work in what became occupied Belgium, nursing soldiers from both sides of the conflict as well as helping more than 200 Allied soldiers escape the country. On 12 October 1915, she was shot at dawn by a German firing squad in Brussels. Her execution received worldwide condemnation and extensive press coverage. In 1919 her remains were brought back to Britain, and after a state funeral at Westminster Abbey her body was buried at Norwich Cathedral.

93 The centenary memorial service on 10 October 2015, taking place at the grave of Norfolk-born Edith Cavell at Norwich Cathedral.

Events were held simultaneously in the UK and Belgium to mark the centenary of her death. On 10 October 2015 a ceremony was held at her graveside at Norwich Cathedral, led by the Bishop of Norwich, the Right Revd Graham James. Attending the service was Guy Trouveroy, Belgian ambassador to the UK; Colonel Frank Hartwig, who represents German forces in the UK; Brenda Arthur, Lord Mayor of Norwich; and members of the armed forces and nursing organisations. Wreaths were laid in her memory.

On the exact centenary of Cavell's execution, a ceremony was hosted by the Cavell Nurses' Trust at the Edith Cavell memorial statue in St Martin's Place,

94 A year after the 2015 event, Edith Cavell's grave was rededicated with a new headstone and improved access, thanks to a £50,000 grant from the Department for Digital, Culture, Media and Sport (DCMS).

95 Nurses from the Royal London Hospital, in historical uniforms, laid a wreath at the statue of Edith Cavell, St Martin's Place, London, at the ceremony hosted by the Cavell Nurses' Trust on 12 October 2015.

London. Representatives from nursing, the UK and Belgian governments, the armed forces and veterans organisations attended. The British government was represented by Heritage Minister Tracey Crouch, and the Belgium government by Jan Bayart, Deputy Head of Mission at the Belgian Embassy in London. As part of the centenary commemorations, the Heritage Lottery Fund awarded £91,000 to the Cavell Nurses' Trust to explore stories about her life and death, including the ceremonial repatriation of her body.

On 15 October 2015, there was a ceremony in the Belgian Senate, the location of Edith Cavell's trial by a German court martial in 1915. After the ceremony, HRH The Princess Royal joined Princess Astrid of Belgium for the unveiling of a commemorative bust designed by Belgian sculptor, Natalie Lambert.

96 Edith Cavell's words, inscribed at the base of her statue in St Martin's Place, formed a poignant focal point to the ceremony exactly 100 years later.

CWGC: Behind the Scenes

The trenches, battlefields and fortifications of the First World War may have all but disappeared, or returned to their pre-war use, but the CWGC's cemeteries and memorials remain as a physical reminder of the battles fought and their human cost. It was natural, therefore, that many of the commemorative events to remember those who served and those who died took place at CWGC cemeteries and memorials. Preparing them to host events both large and small, with a huge increase in visitors, was a challenging prospect.

Long before the centenary programme got underway, the CWGC recognised that this period would see a level of intense activity. To ensure that the sites were ready and accessible, many major structural and horticultural restoration programmes were brought forward (or condensed) so that they would be complete before 2014. Inevitably, this put pressure on teams and resources as routine work continued – for example, the equivalent of almost 1,000 football pitches is mowed every week.

Over their vast commemorative estate, the work was completed. Name panels were replaced at the Menin Gate and Arras memorials, an entire cemetery in Belgium was 'raised' by 1.2 metres to prevent flooding, a new memorial was built in Africa (raising awareness of the contribution and sacrifice of African troops during the war) and, elsewhere, turf reinforcement at the more visited locations ensured that lawns were ready for the thousands of pairs of feet that would walk on them.

Of course, many of the larger, set-piece commemorations required additional work and support. The infrastructure to host large-scale events at cemeteries, and the impact it can have on a site, all had to be factored in. But the CWGC staff rose to the challenge, proud to help mark these momentous anniversaries. The sites were ready and, perhaps more importantly, the people came and continue to come to remember those who died.

97 In 2015, restoration work at the Helles Memorial in Turkey included the removal of damaged panels.

98 Harefield St Mary churchyard in Middlesex has 120 First World War graves, mostly of Australians who died at No. 1 Australian Auxiliary Hospital at Harefield Park. Renovations included new turf laid in March 2015, in anticipation of increased visitor numbers.

99 In 2015 the CWGC began to restore the Colne Valley Cemetery, north of Ieper (Ypres) in Belgium. Adjacent land had been raised due to industrial activity, causing regular flooding. The rear wall had collapsed, and access was often restricted.

100 At Colne Valley Cemetery everything was measured, numbered and dismantled. The ground level was raised by approximately 1.2 metres, and the cemetery was then reconstructed. The city of Ieper supplied a pumping installation to prevent future flooding.

101 TRH The Duke and Duchess of Cambridge thanking gardeners at St Symphorien Military Cemetery, Mons, 4 August 2014.

First World War Memorials Programme

102 Spalding War Memorial in Lincolnshire is one of 44 memorials in England designed by Sir Edwin Lutyens, one of the principal architects for the Commonwealth (then Imperial) War Graves Commission. The memorial was upgraded to Grade I in 2015 in recognition of its special significance.

At the beginning of the centenary there were more telephone boxes on the National Heritage List for England (NHLE) than war memorials. (The NHLE is the official register of nationally protected historic buildings and sites, comprising listed buildings, scheduled monuments, protected wrecks, registered parks and gardens, and battlefields.) Historic England sought to rectify the situation by listing and upgrading 2,500 war memorials by November 2018.

In 2015 all 44 of the First World War memorials in England by Sir Edwin Lutyens, the architect of the Whitehall Cenotaph, had their listing revised. The lack of a famous artist or architect, however, does not make a memorial any less precious to the community it serves. Many smaller, local memorials were listed too, in recognition of their importance as part of our cultural heritage and their role as witnesses to the tragic impact of the First World War.

War memorials are testaments to the multiple experiences of the war – not only the loss of life and the impact on the home front, but also the displacement of those living in conflict zones and the imprisonment of soldiers. Many of the memorials listed or upgraded during the centenary, such as the Belgium Monument to the British Nation in London or the German Prisoner of War Memorial in Dorset, commemorate these experiences.

In addition to protecting memorials through listing, grants were also awarded to repair and conserve war memorials across the UK. Throughout the centenary,

103 Crich Stand Memorial, Derbyshire, required extensive repairs to its dome and tower.

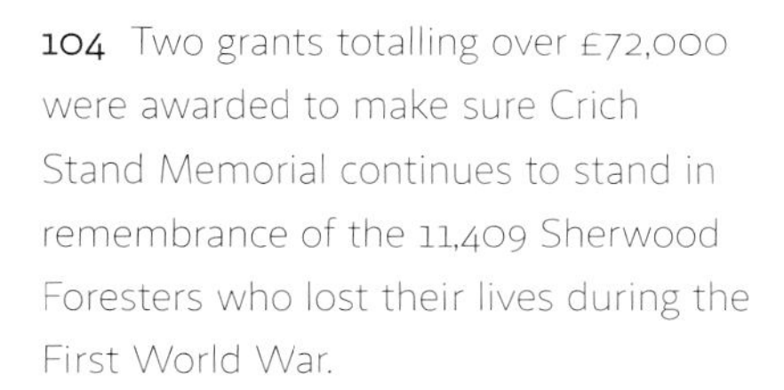

104 Two grants totalling over £72,000 were awarded to make sure Crich Stand Memorial continues to stand in remembrance of the 11,409 Sherwood Foresters who lost their lives during the First World War.

War Memorials Trust distributed grants to over 600 war memorials of all scales. In 2015, War Memorials Trust and Historic England worked with the custodians of Crich Stand, a colossal memorial to the Sherwood Foresters Regiment. At almost 20 metres tall, this memorial tower stands proud over the Derbyshire landscape. This unusual memorial needed specialist conservation and repair work to ensure that it remains standing for the next 100 years.

Equally important as the current repair of war memorials is their future preservation. This can only be achieved by ensuring that younger generations understand the significance of war memorials to our shared history and the need to protect them. Throughout the centenary Historic England and War Memorials Trust have been helping schoolchildren not only to research the names listed on their local war memorials but to understand how to care for and protect them in the future.

105 Cleaning the Belgium Monument to the British Nation in Westminster. It was built as a tribute to Britain, from the people of Belgium, in recognition of the welcome extended to refugees from the German invasion of Belgium in August 1914. During the centenary it was upgraded from Grade II to Grade II*.

14–18 NOW: Poppies Tour 2015

In 2014 *Blood Swept Lands and Seas of Red* by artist Paul Cummins and designer Tom Piper was presented at the Tower of London. Created in conjunction with Historic Royal Palaces, it was only intended to last for four months. The phenomenal response to the piece, however, lead to two key sculptures from the original installation – newly titled Poppies: *Wave* and Poppies: *Weeping Window* – being saved for the nation and taken on a UK-wide tour by 14–18 NOW.

106 and 107 The first stop on the tour was the Yorkshire Sculpture Park, where Poppies: *Wave* rose up from the park's Lower Lake, reached over the historic Cascade Bridge, and was reflected in the water below.

108 Poppies: *Weeping Window* at Liverpool's St George's Hall. During the First World War, this Grade I-listed building became the rallying point for the famous Liverpool Pals, when speakers including Lord Derby and Lord Kitchener appealed for 100,000 men to form a new army.

109 Poppies: *Weeping Window* made its first tour appearance at Woodhorn Museum in Northumberland, cascading 55 feet down from the winding wheel of the No. 1 Heapstead, a well-known symbol of the industrial heritage of the region.

The Tank Museum

110 Nicknamed Little Willie, the world's first tank was the result of a project initiated by the UK's Landship Committee in 1915.

On 9 September 2015, The Tank Museum celebrated the 100th birthday of the world's first tank, known as Little Willie. Agricultural firm William Foster & Co. of Lincoln were contracted in 1915 to build a prototype machine to tackle the problems of trench warfare. Designers William Tritton and Walter Wilson came up with a set of workable tracks, fitted to a 'landship'. By the time Little Willie was built, however, they had already had the idea of a machine with tracks running all the way around the vehicle, which would become the classic British tank design of the First World War. Little Willie never saw active service.

The 2015 event marked the start of 100 years of tank design, the results of which can be seen on today's battlefields. Little Willie was covered in a tarpaulin, similar to the one used to conceal the new invention during testing in 1915, and unveiled in a ceremony by descendants of Walter Wilson.

National Memorial Arboretum

The UK's first national memorial in honour of the 130,000 Sikh men who fought in the First World War was unveiled on 1 November 2015 in the grounds of the National Memorial Arboretum. Despite comprising only 1% of the Indian population at the time of the war, Sikhs made up 20% of the British Indian Army, and were represented in over a third of the regiments.

Designed by sculptor Mark Bibby, the memorial was funded through a Kickstarter campaign by the WW1 Sikh Memorial Fund. People from across different faiths and backgrounds contributed to the campaign. The unveiling event included speeches from dignitaries, a British Army band and a re-enactment troop. The memorial was sanctified with a traditional Sikh prayer, and a minute's silence held to remember all those who fought.

111 Depicting a uniformed soldier wearing medals, the WW1 Sikh Memorial was unveiled in 2015.

Tyne & Wear Archives & Museums

Exploring life, loss and love on Tyneside during the First World War, *Tributaries* was a collaborative project with Tyne & Wear Archives & Museums, US artist Halsey Burgand and local volunteers.

Taking the form of a location-sensitive mobile app, *Tributaries* is an immersive audio stream. Readings by local volunteers are heard against a soundscape of music by Halsey Burgund, who explained: 'Users of the app are immersed in music and a stream of voices that flows like the water of the Tyne.' Readings include the diaries of Ruth Dodds, an author, playwright and political activist caught between her job of making munitions and her pacifist ideals; the diary of Frederick Tait, conscientious objector; and letters between long-distance lovers. These are juxtaposed with readings of newspaper articles, classified ads, sports results and recipes, illustrating a continuing sense of normality. The app also allowed users to make their own recordings, adding to the work's evolving map of collective memory.

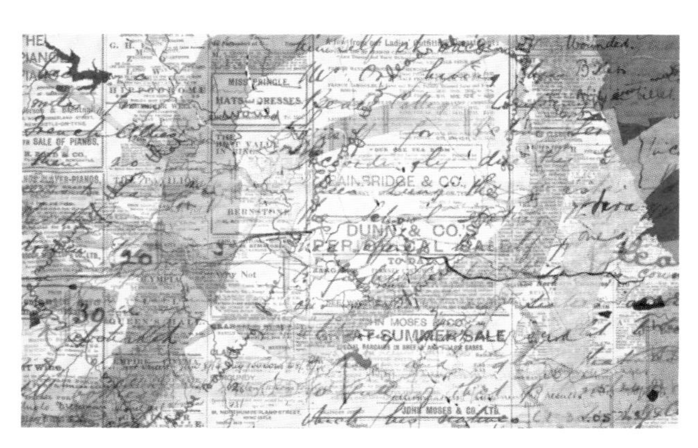

112 Composite graphic by Halsey Burgund, representing *Tributaries*.

Stage Production of *Birdsong*

This critically acclaimed stage adaptation of Sebastian Faulks's bestselling novel was seen by over 75,000 people on its debut tour in 2013. To mark the centenary of the First World War, the play was re-mounted by The Original Theatre Company and Birdsong Productions Ltd., and toured the UK and Ireland during 2014 and 2015.

A mesmerising story of love, courage and sacrifice, *Birdsong* follows the journey of young Englishman Stephen Wraysford – from pre-war France, where he embarks on a passionate and dangerous affair with the beautiful Isabelle Azaire, to the horrors of trench warfare where he must lead his men through the carnage with only the memory of Isabelle for comfort as his world explodes around him.

113 A scene from *Birdsong*, with George Banks as Stephen Wraysford.

Museum of Science & Industry

In 1915, David Lloyd George was appointed to the newly created position of Minister of Munitions in response to desperate shortages on the Western Front. In a subsequent visit to Manchester, Lloyd George appealed to the city's scientific and engineering minds for help. Marking 100 years since the establishment of the new Ministry, the Museum of Science & Industry opened its first ever war exhibition, *The Innovation Race: Manchester's Makers Join the First World War*, in March 2015.

114 Box of hand tools belonging to Mr Lomas, an engineer at Ferranti Ltd. Used to maintain machinery at the factory, some of them are marked 1915.

Through a fascinating collection of artefacts, photographs and documents, largely drawn from the museum's extensive archives, the exhibition illustrated how the region was affected by the munitions appeal. It included the story of how Oldham factory owner and electrical engineer Sebastian Ziani de Ferranti converted his factory output from domestic goods to shells and fuzes. Others were busy contributing to the war effort too, with Mather & Platt's sprinkler systems, Thornton Pickard's aerial reconnaissance cameras, and Beyer Peacock's switch from locomotive manufacturing to anti-aircraft gun carriages and bomb-throwers for ships. The role of the Munitions Inventions Department was also explored. Visitors were invited to design and create their own solutions to wartime problems.

115 The Lancashire Anti-Submarine Committee worked on the River Mersey to develop ways of countering the devastating U-Boat threat.

116 Visitors at the exhibition looking at designs for inventions.

Royal Pavilion, Brighton & Hove

By the end of 1914 the Indian Army to the Middle East made up almost a third of the British Expeditionary Force. As medical facilities in France were not considered adequate, several sites in Brighton were chosen. The Royal Pavilion was converted into a state-of-the-art Indian hospital, with new plumbing and toilet facilities and 600 beds. X-ray equipment was installed, and the Great Kitchen became one of two operating theatres. The first patients arrived in early December 1914. The hospital closed in January 1916, after the British had redeployed the Indian Army to the Middle East in late 1915. In April, it reopened as a hospital for British amputees. Between 1916 and 1920 it treated and rehabilitated over 6,000 soldiers who had lost arms or legs during the war.

To commemorate the centenary, an audio tour was launched in 2015 in collaboration with members of the Chattri Memorial Group in Brighton, exploring the Royal Pavilion's use as a First World War hospital.

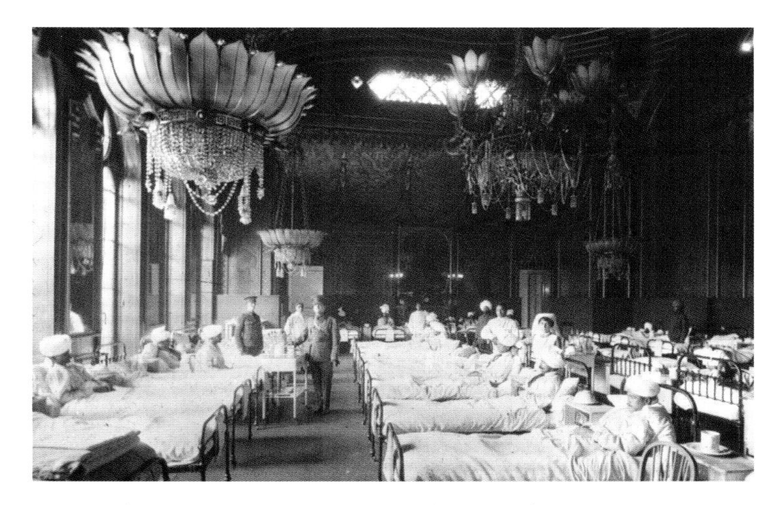

117 Ward 1, The Banqueting Room, Brighton Pavilion, c.1915.

London Transport Museum

To ease the labour shortage created by war, women were recruited for a variety of roles in the transport industry for the first time from 1915. One of the most visible and controversial of these was the role of bus conductor. The Battle Bus learning project (see page 44) commemorated the role of women in the war effort with a programme that engaged female bus drivers. They explored the experiences of wartime conductresses and other women working in transport during the war, and reflected on their own experiences 100 years later. Their experiences were featured in a pop-up exhibition that launched at the London Transport Museum and went on to tour bus garages and libraries. The participants were also offered the chance to experience driving Battle Bus.

118 In 2015, female bus drivers drove Battle Bus in memory of the women who served as wartime conductresses and mechanics 100 years earlier.

2016 COMMEMORATIONS

2016 INTRODUCTION

For 2016 the main focus was on two key milestones – the Battle of Jutland and the Battle of the Somme. In many people's minds, these are the most emblematic battles of the war at sea and the war on land during the First World War. The centenary of the Battle of Jutland provided an opportunity to focus on the war at sea and the role of the Royal Navy and the Mercantile Marine. Both battles resulted in huge loss, but there are also tales of bravery, heroism and sacrifice.

Stories of individuals and families were commemorated at both local and national level, with a wide range of activities and events. In addition, the government-delivered events saw close cooperation with international partners. Jutland centenary commemorations were organised with the help and support of the German federal government; the events to mark the centenary of the Somme with France.

As with previous years, the events sought to convey the experiences of those who were there, using contemporaneous accounts to place descendants at the heart of the event. A range of other activities took place to tell less well-known stories at the two battles, alongside many other stories of the war around the world.

119 Jack Cornwell, aged 16, was fatally wounded on 31 May 1916 on board HMS *Chester* at the Battle of Jutland after refusing to leave his post. He was posthumously awarded the Victoria Cross. The Royal Navy held a centenary ceremony in Coronation Gardens, Leyton, London.

120 The powerful 'Mud Dance' was part of the Heaton Park concert on 1 July 2016 in Manchester. Over 19,240 free tickets were made available for the concert, representing the number of lives lost on the first day of the battle of the Somme.

121 Actor Hugh Dennis, CWGC Living Memory Project Ambassador, in the war graves plot of St Pancras Cemetery, London, April 2016. The project worked with many communities to remember the stories behind the UK's 300,000 commemorative memorials.

Centenary of the Battle of Jutland

122 St Magnus Cathedral, Orkney, with the sculpture Poppies: *Weeping Window* at the west end.

From 31 May to 1 June 1916, the Battle of Jutland took place in the North Sea, near the coast of Denmark's Jutland peninsula. Britain's Royal Navy Grand Fleet, under Admiral Jellicoe, fought against the Imperial German Navy's High Seas Fleet, under Vice Admiral Reinhard Scheer. The British lost more ships and twice as many sailors, but succeeded in containing the German fleet.

Orkney played a vital role in hosting and supporting the Grand Fleet throughout the war. The presence of thousands of sailors in the sheltered anchorage of Scapa Flow, a natural harbour in the heart of Orkney, had a major impact on the lives of ordinary Orcadians. It was therefore fitting that, as part of the commemorative events, guests were taken across Scapa Flow from mainland Orkney to the island of Hoy.

On the morning of Tuesday 31 May 2016, a service was held at St Magnus Cathedral in Kirkwall, Orkney, accompanied by a combined Royal Marine and Federal German Navy brass ensemble. Those invited to attend reflected the main theme of this event – nations meeting in peace and friendship – including First Minister Nicola Sturgeon, HRH The Princess Royal and the First Sea Lord, Admiral Sir Philip Jones, together with German President Joachim Gauck and Chief of the German Navy, Vice Admiral Andreas Krause. Representatives of countries most closely connected with the battle (Australia, Canada, Ireland, Japan, Malta, New Zealand and South Africa) also attended. As with all the national events, descendants of those who fought in the battle were at the heart of the commemorations.

123 The service at St Magnus Cathedral was conducted in both English and German, in front of a large international congregation.

124 HRH The Princess Royal, German President Joachim Gauck and Lord-Lieutenant of Orkney Bill Spence viewing the sculpture Poppies: *Weeping Window* at St Magnus Cathedral.

125 Moored in Scapa Flow for the centenary events, SMS *Schleswig-Holstein* (left) and HMS *Kent* (right) provided an evocative backdrop to the commemorative service at Lyness Royal Naval Cemetery.

To complement this poignant event, the *Weeping Window* ceramic poppy sculpture, part of 14–18 NOW's cultural programme, was installed at the cathedral for the commemoration. This was its first venue in Scotland (see page 116).

In the afternoon of 31 May 2016, many of those who attended the service at St Magnus Cathedral were transferred across Scapa Flow to a commemorative service at the Lyness Royal Naval Cemetery on the island of Hoy. This is the final resting place for more than 450 service personnel who died in the First World War, including sailors killed at Jutland.

Modern British warship HMS *Kent* was anchored in Scapa Flow, alongside the German Navy's SMS *Schleswig-Holstein*. The ships highlighted the role, contribution, loss and sacrifice of those on both sides. HMS *Kent* gave a 21-gun salute as Royal Navy P2000 Fast Inshore Patrol Craft carrying HRH The Princess Royal and President Joachim Gauck went past.

Wreaths were laid at the Cross of Sacrifice, after which, in keeping with the event's theme of education and youth, schoolchildren from Hoy joined descendants in laying commemorative crosses at the graves. Victoria Wallace, Director General of the CWGC, Andreas Wagner, Mayor of Wilhelmshaven, and Monsignor Rainer Schadt, Leitender Militärdekan of the Federal German Navy, accompanied the children as they laid crosses on all the German graves.

On the same day, sailors of the Royal Navy and the Federal German Navy came together some 300 nautical miles to the south-east of Scapa Flow. Over the wrecks of HMS *Invincible*, HMS *Queen Mary*, SMS *Lützow* and SMS *Pommern*, their modern-day counterparts (HMS *Duncan* and FGS *Brandenberg*) honoured all those lost at the battle. A service of reconciliation and commemoration was held, and sailors from both nations scattered symbols of remembrance – British poppy petals and German forget-me-nots.

126 German President Joachim Gauck, Vice Admiral Sir Timothy Laurence, HRH The Princess Royal and Admiral Sir Philip Jones laying wreaths at the cemetery's Cross of Sacrifice.

Battle of Jutland Events in Scandinavia

Despite their neutrality, Denmark, Sweden and Norway experienced first-hand the horrific impact of the First Word War when wreckage and bodies were washed ashore after the Battle of Jutland. As a result, numerous British, Commonwealth and German graveyards date from this period in those locations. In May and June 2016, hundreds of people joined events when the embassies in each country marked the centenary of the battle.

In Denmark, the British Embassy, supported by the CWGC, re-dedicated the grave of a previously unknown British sailor, Harry Gasson, at Esbjerg. The British Embassy, along with representatives from the German Embassy in Copenhagen, helped inaugurate a new Memorial Park in Thyborøn to 18 sailors, 11 of whom are unknown. Nick Jellicoe and Rheinhart Scheer-Hennings, direct descendants of the British and German admirals at the Battle of Jutland, attended.

In Norway, the British Embassy commemorated the centenary at Fredrikstad, where seven known and 11 unknown sailors are buried, while in Sweden, the British Embassy and the German Embassy held a joint memorial service at Kviberg Cemetery, Gothenburg. In the afternoon, the two embassies organised a public seminar on the Battle of Jutland at the Gothenburg City Museum.

The events were well attended by local people and those from further afield, ensuring that both the local history and the fallen servicemen were remembered.

127 Research by the CWGC and volunteers in Denmark established the identity of a previously unknown British sailor, buried at Esbjerg. Harry Gasson's grave was re-dedicated in 2016, with three of his descendants attending the ceremony.

128 Reinhard Scheer-Hennings, great grandson of Admiral Scheer, and Nicholas Jellicoe, grandson of Admiral Jellicoe, during an event in Trafalgar Square, London, to commemorate the Battle of Jutland. A few weeks later they both attended the opening of the Thyborøn Memorial Park in Denmark.

Battle of Jutland UK Naval Memorial Events

The Royal Navy held remembrance events on 31 May 2016 in Portsmouth, Plymouth and Chatham, to commemorate those lost at the Battle of Jutland whose only grave is the sea.

Sailors from HMS *Sultan* and HMS *Collingwood*, led by the Royal Marines Band Collingwood, were joined by veterans to march to Southsea Common for a 2pm service at Portsmouth Naval Memorial. Many of those who lost their lives at Jutland had been attached to Portsmouth. The event included wreath-laying, readings, and the traditional drumhead ceremony with drums piled to form an altar.

Plymouth was greatly affected by the loss of the city's warships at Jutland. At the Royal Naval Memorial, descendants laid wreaths, and poignant pre-recorded readings from the past were played. A 21-gun salute fired from HMS *Monmouth* in Plymouth Sound was followed by a two-minute silence and the sounding of the Last Post.

Naval chaplain Ernie Grimshaw led the ceremony at Chatham, which was attended by Ros Kelly (commissioner of the Commonwealth War Graves Commission), Viscount De L'Isle MBE, Lord Lieutenant of Kent, Rear Admiral Richard Stokes and Admiral Sir Trevor Soar OBE, along with descendants of those who had fought at Jutland. The war memorial had recently been given Grade 1 listed status.

129 Commodore Jeremy Rigby, Portsmouth Naval Base Commander, laying a wreath at the Portsmouth Naval Memorial during the Battle of Jutland centenary ceremony.

130 Battle of Jutland memorial service at the Royal Naval Memorial, Plymouth, 31 May 2016.

Battle of Jutland Centenary Events at Rosyth and South Queensferry

131 HRH The Princess Royal laid a wreath during the service at Rosyth Parish Church, marking the centenary of the Battle of Jutland.

132 HRH The Princess Royal and Vice Admiral Sir Timothy Laurence at the Commonwealth War Grave Cemetery in South Queensferry.

Scotland's national memorial event commemorating the centenary of the Battle of Jutland was held at Rosyth and South Queensferry on 28 May 2016. Hundreds of people lined the streets to commemorate

100 years since ships based in the Firth of Forth joined the remainder of Britain's Royal Navy Grand Fleet to intercept the Imperial German Navy's High Seas Fleet. Three days later, the two fleets met at the Battle of Jutland.

The port of Rosyth was the departure point of the 52 ships of the British Battle Cruiser Fleet – a Royal Navy formation of fast battle cruisers led by Admiral Beatty. These were the first ships to see action in the Battle of Jutland. Construction of the Rosyth Naval Dockyard had begun in 1909, when the Royal Navy was strengthening its presence along the eastern seaboard of the UK as part of the naval arms race with Germany.

Rosyth marked the start of the commemorations, in the presence of HRH The Princess Royal and Vice

Admiral Sir Timothy Laurence, with a service of remembrance in Rosyth Parish Church. Wreaths were laid, followed by a minute's silence and the ringing of a bell made from the hull of battle cruiser HMS *Tiger*. Despite suffering many hits by German shells, the ship suffered only light damage during the Jutland campaign.

The dignitaries then crossed the Forth for a commemoration ceremony at the CWGC Cemetery in South Queensferry, where 40 casualties from the Battle of Jutland are commemorated or buried. HRH The Princess Royal and Vice Admiral Sir Timothy Laurence attended the service, and afterwards met with descendants of those who served at the battle.

The day concluded at Hawes Pier in South Queensferry, where a large crowd enjoyed a Beating Retreat by the Band of HM Royal Marines (Scotland). A gun was fired by HMS *Kent* in the Forth, and HRH The Princess Royal unveiled a commemorative plaque.

133 Ships leaving the Firth of Forth, in a symbolic gesture remembering the Battle Cruiser Fleet's departure 100 years ago. On the left is dazzle ship MV *Fingal*, painted by artist Ciara Phillips to mark the centenary of the battle.

134 The Band of HM Royal Marines (Scotland) performing by the Forth Rail Bridge in South Queensferry, as part of the centenary commemoration of the Battle of Jutland.

Battle of Jutland and Irish Sailor Commemoration

135 HMS *Caroline* in Belfast, photographed the day before the Battle of Jutland commemoration.

136 HRH Prince Michael of Kent, GCVO, performed the official opening of HMS *Caroline* following the ship's extensive restoration.

HMS *Caroline*, as the sole survivor of the Battle of Jutland and the only ship of her type surviving anywhere in the world, provided a significant element of the commemorative programme. On 31 May 2016 she was officially opened as a refurbished museum ship at Alexandra Dock, Belfast. At the same time, an act of commemoration took place alongside her – marking the service and sacrifice of the Irish Sailor, both Naval and Mercantile, in the First World War.

Throughout the war over 20,000 sailors from all parts of the island of Ireland served in the Royal Navy and the merchant navy, as well as being part of fishing fleet crews and maritime rescue services. Over 350 of those lost at the Battle of Jutland were from Ireland. As well as sending thousands of sailors to sea, Belfast made a significant contribution to the war effort through the shipyards of Harland & Wolff and Workman, Clark & Co.

137 The band of the Royal Marines Scotland playing at the centenary ceremony at Alexandra Dock in Belfast.

138 Wreaths were dropped into the sea from the deck of the restored HMS *Caroline* as part of the centenary ceremony.

At the Battle of Jutland, HMS *Caroline* took part in the Destroyer action between the main fleets, firing her 6-inch main armament and torpedoes before withdrawing under heavy fire. After Jutland she continued her service, and in 1918 she was modified to allow light aircraft to launch from an on-board platform – another example of her innovative past. She finally berthed in Belfast in 1923.

Thanks to £11.5 million Heritage Lottery Funding, HMS *Caroline* was restored to reflect her warship history, and to act as a living memorial to the lives of the seamen from Ireland and beyond who died both at Jutland and throughout the First World War.

The National Museum of the Royal Navy organised the commemoration ceremony to the Irish Sailor and the official opening of HMS *Caroline* on 31 May 2016. HRH Prince Michael of Kent, GCVO, performed the official opening. It was attended by the Secretary of State for Northern Ireland, Rt Hon. Theresa Villiers MP, and Paul Kehoe TD, Minister of State at the Department of Defence, along with descendants of sailors from both the Royal Navy and Mercantile Marine.

Service and Vigil for the Centenary of the Battle of the Somme

139 View of the congregation and choir in Westminster Abbey during the service on 30 June 2016 to mark the eve of the centenary of the Battle of the Somme.

On 1 July 1916, the British and French armies launched an offensive near the River Somme in Picardie, France. Early in the morning, soldiers moved into forward trenches and advanced into no-man's-land, preparing for 'zero-hour' at 7.30am. As the bombardment lifted, the first wave of Allied troops attacked along a 40km front. On the south part of the front, the French made good progress and British units took Mametz and Montauban. But in the north – at Gommecourt, Serre, Beaumont-Hamel, Thiepval, Ovillers and La Boisselle – the British Army suffered terrible losses for very little gain. On that first day 19,240 British soldiers were killed. The French had 1,590 casualties and the German 2nd Army lost between 10,000 and 12,000 men.

Lasting nearly five months, the Somme series of battles would become one of the bloodiest and most famous campaigns of the First World War. Marking 100 years since the battle began was a key part of the commemorative programme in 2016. A sense of anticipation, and of silence and reflection, characterised these events.

On the evening of 30 June, a service took place at Westminster Abbey. Prayers were said for the dead of the First World War, and hymns sung by a congregation that included descendants of those who fought at the Somme. HM The Queen laid a wreath of roses on the Grave of the Unknown Warrior, before a bugler sounded the Last Post from the Lantern Tower.

140 HM The Queen preparing to lay a wreath at the Grave of the Unknown Warrior, as part of the evening service on 30 June 2016.

141 The Last Post was sounded from Westminster Abbey's Lantern Tower on a bugle that was played at the Battle of the Somme.

The Grave of the Unknown Warrior became the focal point of an all-night vigil which followed the service. The vigil remembered those lost in the battle – both on 1 July, notorious as one of the bloodiest days in the history of the British Army, and on the 141 days that the battle would last. Those who served on all sides were represented by groups of service personnel and others who kept vigil in 15-minute watches throughout the night. The final watch took up its position at 7.15am on the morning of 1 July.

Vigils were also held across the UK, including at the Scottish National War Memorial in Edinburgh Castle, the National War Memorial in Cardiff, and at Somme Museum Clandeboye, County Down. This was mirrored at the Thiepval Memorial (see pages 96-99), where 72,337 British and South African soldiers with no known grave are commemorated.

At 7.25am the Left Half Battery of the King's Troop, Royal Horse Artillery, fired from Parliament Square for 100 seconds. This was followed by a reading of 'An Account of the Battle' by Corporal George Ashurst (1895–1988), 1st Battalion, Lancashire Fusiliers. At 7.30am – exactly 100 years since the Battle of the Somme began – Second Lieutenant Matthew Narey, 2nd Battalion, Yorkshire Regiment, blew a trench whistle that had been issued in 1915. The final watch then departed from the Grave of the Unknown Warrior through the Great West Door, in silence, as a piper from the Irish Guards played 'Flowers of the Forest'. This ancient Scottish folk tune commemorated the defeat of the Scottish army of James IV at the Battle of Flodden in 1513, and has come to be played only at funerals or memorial services.

Afterwards a Requiem service was held by the Dean of Westminster, the Very Reverend Dr John Hall, at the Abbey's Lantern Altar. Prayers were offered to the fallen at the Somme.

142 Service personnel and civilians kept a vigil of 15-minute watches throughout the night at the Grave of the Unknown Warrior, finishing at 7.30am to mark the moment the Battle of the Somme began.

143 Those who had undertaken the final watch of the vigil processed in silence through the Great West Door, while a piper from the Irish Guards played 'Flowers of the Forest'.

Somme Vigil and Centenary Commemoration

While the overnight vigil was taking place at Westminster Abbey, Thiepval was the chosen location of events taking place in the heart of the Somme battlefields. When the battle got underway on the morning of 1 July 1916, Thiepval was well fortified by the Germans and they fought with great determination. The British coordination of infantry and artillery deteriorated after the first day, due to confusion caused by fighting in a maze of trenches, dugouts and shellcraters.

The commemorative events at Thiepval began on 30 June with a short, intimate service of remembrance as the sun set over the farmland of Picardie. Before attending the service, TRH The Duke and Duchess of Cambridge and HRH Prince Harry climbed to the top of the Thiepval Memorial, newly renovated for the centenary commemorations, to view the battlefield. Guests at the service included 200 descendants of those named on the Thiepval Memorial.

144 HRH Prince Harry and TRH The Duke and Duchess of Cambridge attended the events marking the eve of the 100th anniversary of the Battle of the Somme.

CWGC THIEPVAL MEMORIAL TO THE MISSING OF THE SOMME

Designed by Sir Edwin Lutyens, the Thiepval Memorial is the largest CWGC memorial to the missing in the world. It commemorates more than 72,000 men of British and South African forces who died in the Somme sector before 20 March 1918 and have no known grave. The majority died during the Somme offensive of 1916.

Construction began in 1928. While the foundations were being dug, to a depth of 30 feet, wartime tunnels and unexploded ordnance were discovered. The memorial comprises intersecting arches which increase in height and proportionate width. It was unveiled on 1 August 1932 by HRH Prince Edward, Prince of Wales, in the presence of many veterans and families.

145 Located on high ground overlooking the River Somme, the Thiepval Memorial dominates the surrounding landscape.

At 10pm local time the overnight candlelit vigil began, held by service personnel from the British Army, French Army, Australian Army and New Zealand Defence Force. This was an opportunity to reflect on the mindset of the troops of a hundred years ago, as they made final preparations and thought about the upcoming battle. The vigil ended at 7.30am the following morning, marking the beginning of the Battle of the Somme on 1 July 1916.

A large-scale commemorative service was held at the Thiepval Memorial. The event began at noon with the King's Troop, Royal Horse Artillery, bringing First World War guns into position. The presence of the British guns was mirrored by two French guns

146 A poignant overnight vigil took place at the Thiepval Memorial. Standard bearers were provided by the British Legion.

147 Viewed from the Thiepval Memorial, members of the royal family and representatives from the UK, France, Germany and Ireland watching the King's Troop, Royal Horse Artillery, as they move into position at the beginning of the event.

from the period, the famous '75s'. By noon a century earlier, nearly 20,000 British men lay dead or dying in the surrounding fields.

Some 10,000 guests were invited, many of whom were descendants of those involved with, or directly affected by, the battle. They were joined by HRH The Prince of Wales, HRH The Duchess of Cornwall, TRH The Duke and Duchess of Cambridge, HRH Prince Harry and TRH The Duke and Duchess of Gloucester. Also in attendance were representatives of all those nations involved in the battle, along with senior military personnel, politicians, figures from various military charities and faith leaders.

Readings from contemporaneous letters and accounts let the soldiers and their families tell their own, first-hand stories of the battle.

Following this poignant tribute, footage of the cemetery behind the memorial was screened to the guests. The cemetery faces the fields that the British attacked that day. Six hundred bodies are buried here, half beneath Commonwealth headstones, half under French stone crosses. Six hundred schoolchildren – half from Britain, half from France – laid a wreath at every grave.

Dignitaries laid wreaths at the Cross of Sacrifice, and then made way for the 10,000 members of the public to make the pilgrimage around the memorial and leave their own mark of respect. Many of them, too, laid wreaths.

The Royal British Legion (RBL) held a small event at the Theipval Memorial every day from 2 July through to 17 November, before hosting a significant final act of commemoration on 18 November – the last of the 141 days of the Battle of the Somme. At home the RBL launched a toolkit to support communities in arranging their own Somme commemorations. Throughout the four-year period, the RBL generously provided standard bearers in support of the national commemorative events.

148 Events included a big-screen viewing of the edited version of the Imperial War Museums' film *Battle of the Somme* (1916).

149 During a two-minute silence, 10,000 poppies and cornflowers (the French flower of remembrance) fluttered down from the top of the Thiepval Memorial.

THIEPVAL, FRANCE

150 The Irish Guards standing at ease before the event.

151 The French guard was provided by cadets from the École spéciale militaire de Saint-Cyr.

152 HRH The Prince of Wales and HRH The Duchess of Cornwall chatting to some of the English and French schoolchildren who stood in attendance behind the cemetery's 600 graves after the service.

153 The wreath laying at the Cross of Sacrifice.

CWGC: Thiepval Memorial Renovation

The restoration of the Thiepval Memorial – ahead of the 100th anniversary commemorations of the Battle of the Somme in July 2016 – was one of the most important projects ever undertaken by the CWGC.

Like all historic monuments, over the years the memorial had been exposed to the elements, resulting in damage to its structure. Although regularly maintained, there comes a point when more extensive work is required. The work at Thiepval addressed a number of issues with the memorial, particularly that of water ingress and drainage.

The restoration was divided into two phases. Phase One tackled the memorial's roofs and pointing, with the aim of keeping the structure watertight. Wherever possible existing materials – including the memorial's distinct red bricks – were reused or restored. Phase Two saw a complete overhaul of the memorial's internal rainwater drainage system.

154 A CWGC engraver ensuring that the names on the Thiepval Memorial are legible.

155 Extensive work was carried out to repair the roof and drainage of the Thiepval Memorial.

The new drainage system was designed to contain, remove and discharge water away from the memorial.

The whole project was supported by the UK Government's Department for Digital, Culture, Media and Sport (DCMS). £1.6 million was provided towards the restoration and enhancement of the memorial as part of the First World War commemorations.

As Phase One of the restoration neared completion, the memorial's flagpoles – each weighing an astonishing 480 kilos and measuring 12 metres in height – were restored to the memorial's highest point by one of the largest cranes in Europe. The flagpoles are topped with British and French crowns, symbolising the memorial's dual function as a memorial to the missing and a memorial to the joint nature of the Allied effort on the Somme. The original French crown was destroyed during a lightning strike in the 1960s, and the British crown moved into storage for safe keeping. Both were made anew by master craftsmen in Belgium.

The final touch to the memorial's restoration was the installation of the lighting system, which illuminated the memorial for the first time on the eve of the Somme commemorations (30 June). As the sun set, and the lighting took hold, the newly restored memorial looked stunning. The stage was set for the following day's tribute to those who died during the Somme offensive of 1916.

156 The memorial sees some 250,000 visitors a year. Here a member of the team is cutting the grass in preparation for the centenary events.

157 Repointing and repairing some of the stone features of the memorial, ready for the commemorative events of 2016.

Centenary of the Battle of the Somme Commemorative Service

The 36th (Ulster) Division earned the honour of being the only Allied division at the Somme to reach its objective on 1 July 1916. Their role was to take the German Schwaben Redoubt and the villages of Saint Pierre Divion and Grandcourt. Their attack began at 7.30am on 1 July from Thiepval Wood, and at first things went well. The situation changed, however, when other divisions were unable to capture the villages of Thiepval and Beaumont-Hamel, and German guns were turned on the attacking Ulster Division. In just two days of fighting the division lost 5,500 men – killed, wounded or missing. The 36th (Ulster) Division gained many awards for bravery, including four Victoria Crosses.

Dedicated in 1921, the Ulster Memorial Tower stands on what was the German front line during the Battle of the Somme, opposite Thiepval Wood. It is a replica of the Ulster landmark, Helen's Tower, on the Dufferin and Ava estate at Clandeboye, County Down. On the outbreak of the First World War, the

158 The 1st and 2nd Battalions of the Royal Irish Regiment with members of the Somme Association at the Ulster Memorial Tower in Thiepval.

159 Colour parties from the 1st and 2nd Battalions of the Royal Irish Regiment during the Somme centenary service at Ulster Memorial Tower.

160 HRH The Prince of Wales with Colour Sergeant Ross from the 2nd Battalion, Royal Irish Regiment, at the Somme centenary service.

161 Wreaths were placed at the base of the Ulster Memorial Tower.

estate was used as a training camp; the newly formed Ulster Division trained in the shadow of Helen's Tower before leaving for France.

The Somme Association, in conjunction with the UK government, was responsible for organising the commemorations in France. The main event for which the association is responsible takes place every year on 1 July at the Ulster Memorial Tower. For 2016, of course, this was especially poignant.

Guests came from Northern Ireland, Ireland, England, Scotland, Wales, France, Belgium, Canada, Australia and USA, and included TRH The Prince of Wales and Duchess of Cornwall, TRH The Duke and Duchess of Gloucester, the Secretary of State for Northern Ireland, the Rt Hon. Theresa Villiers MP, First Minister of Northern Ireland, the Rt Hon. Arlene Foster MLA, and Heather Humphreys TD, Minister for Arts, Heritage, Regional, Rural and Gaeltacht Affairs. Representatives from all the main churches in Ireland attended, along with the Archbishop of Canterbury. The 1st and 2nd Battalions of the Royal Irish Regiment provided two Colour Parties, a Cenotaph party and wreath bearers.

14–18 NOW: *we're here because we're here*

162 Uniformed volunteers singing in Glasgow Central station.

163 Participants gathered at Belfast Central station, before dispersing on foot to shopping centres, streets and markets.

Devised by artist Jeremy Deller in collaboration with Rufus Norris, director of the National Theatre, *we're here because we're here* was a large-scale event that took place across the UK on 1 July 2016 – the 100th anniversary of the first day of the battle of the Somme. Commissioned by 14–18 NOW, it was produced by Birmingham Repertory Theatre and the National Theatre, with Lyric Theatre Belfast, Manchester Royal Exchange, National Theatre of Scotland, National Theatre Wales, Northern Stage, Playhouse Derry-Londonderry, Salisbury Playhouse, Sheffield Theatres and Theatre Royal Plymouth.

This contemporary memorial involved thousands of volunteers dressed in First World War uniforms, who emerged unannounced in public spaces across the UK. If approached they remained silent, and simply handed out a card that bore the name and age of a soldier who had died in the war on that day, 100 years earlier. The details were accompanied by the hashtag #wearehere.

The line 'we're here because we're here' was sung at intervals by the groups of uniformed men as a haunting echo of the same refrain that was often heard in the trenches of the First World War. It was sung repeatedly to the tune of 'Auld Lang Syne' as a reaction to the tedium of life in the trenches.

The event had a profound effect on the public, and gained social media and press coverage around the world. It remains one of the most impactful projects from the 14–18 NOW programme, and is an example of innovation in the arts as well as how national moments are marked.

After the event, 14–18 NOW and the National Theatre presented a touring exhibition at the theatres and venues across the UK who had helped organise the project in secret. The exhibition told the story of the one-day memorial through images of the volunteers. A BBC documentary that charted the making of the project was also produced, and a year later, on the battle's 101st anniversary, Jeremy Deller and 14–18 NOW published a book containing 100 photographs of the event.

164 Soldiers standing in silence at the top of Llanberis Path, Mount Snowdon.

165 A group of volunteers sitting at Eldon Square, Newcastle.

Somme Commemoration

As the centenary events at Thiepval drew to a close, attention moved back to the UK. The city of Manchester was chosen to lead the national commemorations, honouring the large numbers of Pals Battalions that came from cities in the north of England.

Early in the war, these battalions were formed through local recruiting drives, with the promise of serving alongside friends, neighbours and colleagues. Larger towns and cities were able to form several battalions each – Manchester, for example, raised four battalions in August 1914, and four more three months later. The Pals Battalions were hard hit in the Battle of the Somme, especially on the northern sections of the front.

On 1 July 2016, the Manchester events focused on links to communities and the impact of the war on those waiting at home. Events started at 1pm with a two minute silence at the Cenotaph in St Peter's Square followed by a wreath-laying ceremony. There was then a parade from Albert Square to Manchester Cathedral where at 3pm a National Service of Remembrance took place, attended by HRH the Duke of York.

Later in the day, Heaton Park became the focal point of the commemorations (it had been a military training ground for many recruits who enlisted together in the Pals Battalions). Afternoon activities included the HLF-funded Experience Field, which hosted talks, displays and films to give visitors a taste of the First World War battlefields, and of life on the home front.

The final pieces were laid in 'The Path of the Remembered', a project that invited the public to design tributes to individuals and to entire communities of men and women involved in the war effort. From an

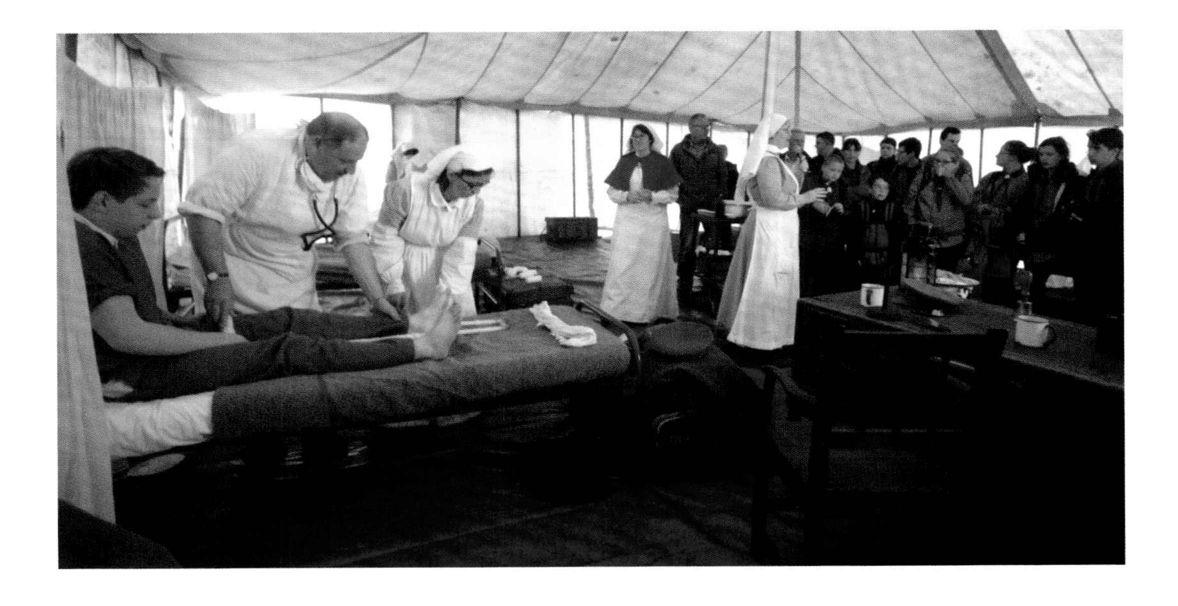

166 The Band of the Royal Air Force standing to attention during wreath laying at the Cenotaph in St Peter's Square.

167 The Experience Field at Heaton Park re-created scenes from the battlefields of the Somme.

168 'The Path of the Remembered', with its tile 'memory squares' designed by members of the public.

169 Professional dancers were joined by some 300 local volunteers for the *Somme 100 Pals* performance, Heaton Park.

online gallery, 5,000 designs were chosen to be printed on to ceramic tiles, as 'memory squares', for a pathway honouring the sacrifices made in the war.

At 7.30pm a free concert took place in the grounds of Heaton Hall, attended by thousands of people and featuring a national children's choir, film, dance and Manchester's acclaimed Hallé Orchestra. This was a day of remembrance and reflection, but also a day to learn more about the experiences of those involved.

170 A bugler of the Grenadier Guards plays the Last Post in Heaton Park.

Battle of the Somme (1916)

To commemorate the centenary of the battle, IWM made their digitally restored film *Battle of the Somme* available for members of IWM's First World War Centenary Partnership to screen for free. The restoration had taken four years and was undertaken by Dragon Digital Intermediate. IWM had also commissioned a new score from composer Laura Rossi, which had premiered on 22 October 2006 at the Queen Elizabeth Hall, London, alongside the newly restored film.

Battle of the Somme is a truly unique piece of cinema, and a star object in IWM's collection. In the first three months of its release the film was seen by around 20 million people in Britain and Ireland, informing and challenging the public with its images of warfare, and changing the way cinema was perceived.

The film shows British forces, mainly the 7th and 29th Divisions, on 1 July 1916 – the first day of the Somme offensive. Tens of thousands of soldiers went 'over the top' at 7.30am that morning; nearly 20,000 British soldiers died. Present that day were cameramen Geoffrey Malins and John McDowell. Malins had been dispatched to the Western Front in November 1915, tasked with shooting footage for short newsreels. In late June 1916, he was joined by McDowell. Together they filmed the British Army gearing up for, and then launching, the largest battle it had ever fought. When their reels arrived in London, the decision was made to present the silent footage as a feature film.

One hundred years later, over 350 members of the Partnership screened the film in an incredibly wide variety of settings – from small community groups and church halls to national and international commemorations at Thiepval, Manchester and Belfast. Tours of the film were arranged across the UK. The Poetry School and the Lake District Summer Music Festival held performances of creative responses to the film. Festivals in York, Belfast and Edinburgh screened the film, and live streams were arranged with schools in Scotland, through Poppyscotland.

SCALA THEATRE,
CHARLOTTE STREET, FITZROY SQUARE, W.
Proprietor: Dr. E. Distin Maddick.

THE BRITISH TOPICAL COMMITTEE FOR WAR FILMS
request the pleasure of the company of Bearer and Friend on
THURSDAY NEXT, AUGUST 10th, at 11.30 a.m. prompt,
when they will present
OFFICIAL PICTURES
of the
"BATTLE of the SOMME,"
Taken by Special Arrangement with the
WAR OFFICE
and under their direction.

¶ No "Exclusive Rights" of this film will be granted.
Schedule of prices can be obtained from the sole booking director, W. F. JURY.

171 Invitation card to a screening of the film at the Scala Theatre, Charlotte Street, London, August 1916.

Battle of the Somme International Tour

IWM approached the Foreign and Commonwealth Office about screening the film overseas, and the take-up was enormous. It was screened on every continent excluding Antarctica, with audiences varying from several dozen to hundreds.

The British high commissions in Wellington and Ottawa, and the British embassies in Berlin and Dublin, screened the film accompanied by an orchestra. While the New Zealand and Canadian public are conscious of their countries' connection to the Somme, in Germany and Ireland the battle is less resonant. Commemoration of the First World War is not traditional in Germany, but the good relationship between the British Embassy and Berlin's Deutsches Historisches Museum made the museum a natural choice. Museum visitors catching the rehearsal, and guests for the evening event, were clearly very moved by the film. In Dublin the composer of the new orchestral score, Laura Rossi, attended the screening. With an increasing awareness of the role played by Irish soldiers at the Somme, this project was an important part of the British Embassy's commemorative work.

Often in conjunction with local groups, the film was screened around the world with a recorded soundtrack. Audiences included descendants of those who fought, veterans and serving military, diplomats and students, at embassies, cinemas and many other venues.

172 Jonathan Sinclair, British High Commissioner to New Zealand, introducing the screening at Wellington.

173 The orchestral performance in Newfoundland.

174 The atrium at the Deutsches Historisches Museum, Berlin, in readiness for the evening's orchestral screening.

Cynhaliwyd Gwasanaeth Coffa Cenedlaethol Cymru

Ymladdwyd un o frwydrau mwyaf gwaedlyd yr 38ain Adran (Gymreig) rhwng y 7fed a'r 11eg Gorffennaf 1916 yng Nghoedwig Mametz yn y Somme.

Ffurfiwyd yr 38ain Adran (Gymreig) ym mis Rhagfyr 1914 ac roedd ynddi ddynion a listiwyd o bob cwr o Gymru. Yn eu plith yr oedd y beirdd Siegfried Sassoon, Robert Graves a Llewelyn Wyn Griffith, a hefyd y bardd a'r arlunydd David Jones. Bu Griffith a Jones ill dau yn brwydro yng Nghoedwig Mametz.

Fore'r 7fed o Orffennaf, cychwynnodd y milwyr o Gymru am y goedwig yn wyneb tanio trwm y Gwarchodlu Prwsiaidd profiadol a oedd ar gyrion gogleddol a dwyreiniol y Goedwig ('the enemy front-fighters who shared our pains against whom we found ourselves by misadventure' – ys dywed David Jones yn *In Parenthesis*). Wrth i fwy a mwy o'r Cymry gael eu hanafu, ataliwyd yr ymosodiad tan y 10fed o Orffennaf pan wthiodd y milwyr yn eu blaen unwaith eto. Drannoeth, yn wyneb penderfyniad yr 38ain Adran (Gymreig) a'r pwysau cynyddol ar eu llinellau, ciliodd yr Almaenwyr, gan ddod â Brwydr Coedwig Mametz i ben. Anafwyd 4,000 o ddynion yr 38ain Gymreig, ond roedd yr ardal strategol allweddol ar faes y gad yn y Somme wedi'i hennill.

Cynhaliwyd Gwasanaeth Coffa Cenedlaethol Cymru ar y 7fed o Orffennaf 2016 yn ymyl cofeb drawiadol David Petersen i'r 38ain Adran (Gymreig) yng Nghoedwig Mametz. Trefnwyd y gwasanaeth gan gangen De Cymru o Gymdeithas Ffrynt y Gorllewin, gyda chefnogaeth Llywodraeth Cymru. Daeth 1,000 o bobl i'r gwasanaeth, gan gynnwys Prif Weinidog Cymru a phobl leol bwysig o Ffrainc a'r Almaen.

Ar y 30ain o Fehefin, ymunodd Cymru â gweddill y DU i nodi can mlynedd ers dechrau Brwydr y Somme drwy gynnal gwylnos yng Nghadeirlan Llandaf, gan orffen gyda gwasanaeth cyhoeddus wrth ymyl Cofeb Ryfel Genedlaethol Cymru am 7.30am ar y 1af o Orffennaf, sef yr amser y dechreuodd y Frwydr.

175 Y Cymry yng Nghoed Mametz 1916: Y Gwasanaeth Coffa Cenedlaethol, a gynhaliwyd ar safle'r Gofeb i'r 38ain Adran (Gymreig) yng Nghoed Mametz, Somme département, ar 7 Gorffennaf 2016. The National Service of Remembrance, held at the site of the Memorial to the 38th (Welsh) Division at Mametz Wood, Somme département, on 7 July 2016.

176 Y Gwir Anrhydeddus Carwyn Jones AC, Prif Weinidog Cymru, yn gosod torch ar Gofeb y 38ain Adran (Gymreig) yn ystod *Y Cymry yng Nghoed Mametz 1916: Y Gwasanaeth Coffa Cenedlaethol* yng Nghoed Mametz, Somme département, ar 7 Gorffennaf 2016. The Rt Hon. Carwyn Jones AM, First Minister of Wales, laying a wreath on the Memorial to the 38th (Welsh) Division during 'The Welsh at Mametz Wood 1916: The National Service of Remembrance', Mametz Wood, Somme département, 7 July 2016.

Welsh National Service of Remembrance

177 Y Gwir Anrhydeddus Carwyn Jones AC, Prif Weinidog Cymru, yn siarad yn ystod 'Y Cymry yng Nghoed Mametz 1916: Y Gwasanaeth Coffa Cenedlaethol' yng Nghoed Mametz, Somme département, ar 7 Gorffennaf 2016.
The Rt Hon. Carwyn Jones AM, First Minister of Wales, speaking during 'The Welsh at Mametz Wood 1916: The National Service of Remembrance' at Mametz Wood, Somme département, on 7 July 2016.

One of the bloodiest engagements of the 38th (Welsh) Division occurred between 7 and 11 July 1916 at Mametz Wood in the Somme.

Formed in December 1914, the 38th (Welsh) Division comprised recruits from across Wales. Among their ranks were the poets Siegfried Sassoon, Robert Graves and Llewelyn Wyn Griffith, and the poet and artist David Jones. Griffith and Jones both saw action at Mametz Wood.

On the morning of 7 July, Welsh troops advanced on the wood under a barrage of heavy fire by the elite Prussian Guard on the north and east sides of the wood ('the enemy front-fighters who shared our pains against whom we found ourselves by misadventure' – David Jones, *In Parenthesis*). With the Welsh casualty count increasing, the advance was held until a renewed push on 10 July. The next day, against the resilience of the 38th Welsh and under growing pressure on their lines, the Germans withdrew, signalling the end of the Battle of Mametz Wood. There were 4,000 casualties among the 38th Welsh, but the strategically key area of the Somme battlefield had been secured.

A Welsh National Service of Remembrance was held on 7 July 2016 at the site of David Petersen's striking Memorial to the 38th (Welsh) Division at Mametz Wood, arranged by the South Wales branch of the Western Front Association with support from the Welsh government. The event was attended by 1,000 people, including the First Minister of Wales and local dignitaries from France and Germany.

On 30 June Wales had joined the rest of the UK in marking the start of the Battle of the Somme with an overnight vigil at Llandaff Cathedral, culminating in a public service at the Welsh National War Memorial at 7.30am on 1 July, the time the battle began.

178 Cofeb y 38ain Adran (Gymreig) yng Nghoed Mametz, Somme département.
The Memorial to the 38th (Welsh) Division at Mametz Wood, Somme département.

First World War Memorials Programme

179 The Promenade de Verdun, Woodcote, Croydon, is part of a memorial landscape created in 1922 to cement the friendship between the English and French nations. Both the landscape (a registered park and garden) and the obelisk were listed as Grade II in 2016.

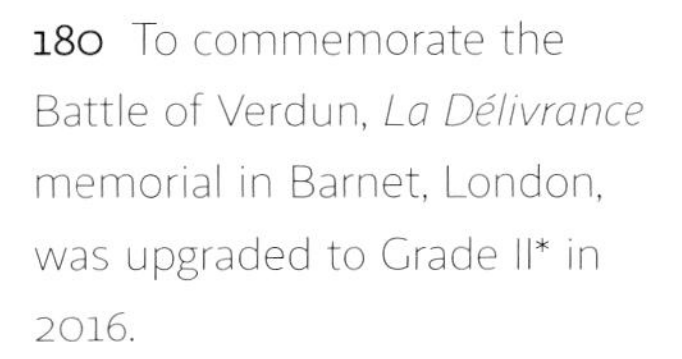

180 To commemorate the Battle of Verdun, *La Délivrance* memorial in Barnet, London, was upgraded to Grade II* in 2016.

In 2016 Historic England marked two of the bloodiest battles of the First World War – Verdun and the Somme – by protecting memorials associated with those battles. Verdun was the longest single battle of the war, and resulted in almost 400,000 French casualties. Historic England commemorated French losses at the battle by listing three French memorials. For Britain it was the Somme that was to prove the most deadly, and memorials at home indicate the terrible consequences for local communities. Fifteen memorials associated with the battle were listed or upgraded. Several of the memorials commemorate the Pals Battalions, the men who signed up as friends, then fought and died together and were commemorated together by their communities back home.

Many of the memorials erected by communities after the war were done so through public subscription. While this community effort adds to the special significance of memorials, it often means that few funds were put in place to ensure that they could continue to be maintained. During the centenary many memorials have been conserved that might have otherwise fallen into disrepair.

In 2016 War Memorials Trust and Historic England worked with the custodians of Bootle War Memorial on Merseyside to carry out extensive repairs. The custodians of the memorial were determined that it should continue to be a fitting tribute to the 1,007 members of the local community who died in the First World War. They also wanted to instil pride in the memorial and to engage the local community in their First World War heritage. To achieve this, specialist conservation was carried out to improve the legibility of the inscriptions, to repair stonework, and to clean and repair the bronze figures. War Memorials Trust also worked with the custodians to produce education materials and support local engagement. The successfully conserved memorial was unveiled in September 2016 after a grant of £86,660.

181 Detail of Sheffield War Memorial, South Yorkshire. Upgraded to Grade II* in 2016 to mark the centenary of the Battle of the Somme, it commemorates those who died in both world wars – including over 500 Sheffield Pals who were killed or injured on the first day of the Somme.

182 Preston War Memorial, Lancashire, designed by Sir Giles Gilbert Scott. It was upgraded to Grade I in 2016 to commemorate the centenary of the Battle of the Somme. Preston lost around 2,000 men during the First World War.

183 Detail of Bootle War Memorial on Merseyside. The inclusion of an airman is unusual for memorials of this period, as air warfare was still in its infancy. The memorial was upgraded to Grade II* in 2016 in recognition of this special significance.

14–18 NOW: 2016 Season

184 The Orchestra of Syrian Musicians reunited on stage at the Royal Festival Hall, London.

185 For *Dr Blighty*, powerful projections on the Brighton Royal Pavilion shone a light on the Indians who travelled across the world to fight during the First World War.

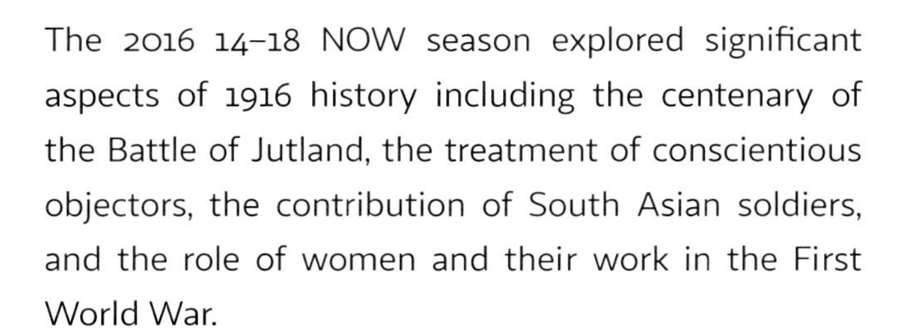

The 2016 14–18 NOW season explored significant aspects of 1916 history including the centenary of the Battle of Jutland, the treatment of conscientious objectors, the contribution of South Asian soldiers, and the role of women and their work in the First World War.

The season centred on 1 July, when the first day of the Battle of the Somme was marked by Jeremy Deller's powerful living memorial *we're here because we're here* (see pages 104-105). As part of the Norfolk and Norwich Festival, leading poets presented new poetry reflecting on the historic battle, while Simon Armitage created *Still*, a series of poems that responded to locations significant to the Somme offensive and were inspired by haunting aerial reconnaissance images of the battlefields.

The global impact of the war was explored with performances by the Orchestra of Syrian Musicians with Damon Albarn and guests, presented by Africa Express at the Royal Festival Hall, London. These performances drew attention to the millions of people across Europe who became refugees as a result of the First World War, by highlighting and celebrating the music and culture of Syria, a country from which refugees continue to be displaced 100 years later.

Through music, performance and spectacular video mapping, the ambitious large-scale installation *Dr Blighty*, created by Nutkhut for Brighton Festival, told the story of the hundreds of thousands of soldiers who came from India to fight for the Allies, and the experience of injured soldiers who came to be located in Brighton.

In *End of Empire*, a major new work at Turner Contemporary, artist Yinka Shonibare MBE explored how new alliances forged in the war changed British society forever and continue to affect us today, while Imran Qureshi's poignant outdoor artwork *Garden Within a Garden*, in a park in Bradford, was inspired by the often brutal experiences endured by Sikh, Muslim and Hindu soldiers from the British Raj on the Western Front.

The impact of the war on the role of women and women's fashion was the inspiration for the exhibition *Fashion & Freedom*, held at Manchester Art

186 Yinka Shonibare MBE, *End of Empire* installation view at Turner Contemporary.

Gallery and including pieces by Vivienne Westwood, Roksanda and other contemporary designers.

As part of the exhibition *The Body Extended: Sculpture and Prosthetics* at the Henry Moore Institute, which explored the impact the First World War had on our understanding of the body and the developments of prosthetics, the artist Rebecca Warren presented her large-scale sculpture *Man and the Dark*. A pair of striding legs is set upon a wheeled platform, reminiscent of vehicles used by amputee veterans after the war.

In Northern Ireland Anne Tallentire created *Shelter*. Inspired by the Nissen hut – the prefab structure invented in 1916 by Major Peter Norman Nissen – the work explores this familiar historic structure in the context of today's global humanitarian crisis.

187 *Fashion & Freedom* design by Sadie Williams.

188 *Garden Within a Garden* by Imran Qureshi at Lister Park, Bradford.

14–18 NOW: Poppies Tour 2016

In 2016 St Magnus Cathedral in Kirkwall, Orkney, was the first venue in Scotland to host Poppies: *Weeping Window*. The sculpture was installed on the exterior of the cathedral's west end, cascading down the building and on to the steps below.

Lincoln Castle became the second venue to present Poppies: *Wave*. Lincoln was a major centre for the manufacture of weapons and munitions during the First World War, and it was here that the world's first operational tank was invented. In this installation the poppies swept down from the castle's medieval curtain wall.

At the Black Watch Museum in Balhousie Castle, in the city of Perth in Scotland, Poppies: *Weeping Window* flowed from a second-floor turret window across the castle grounds. During the First World War 50,000 men saw service with the Black Watch, Scotland's premier Highland Regiment, in campaigns across the Western Front, Mesopotamia and Salonika. The Black Watch Castle and Museum became its regimental headquarters in 1962.

Poppies: *Weeping Window* then travelled to Caernarfon Castle, which was the first location in Wales to host the sculpture. Built in the Middle Ages, and home to the Royal Welch Fusiliers Museum, the castle hosted a number of First World War commemorative events during the years of the centenary, as part of the Cymru'n Cofio/Wales Remembers 1914–1918 programme.

189 St Magnus Cathedral, Orkney, was the first venue in Scotland to host Poppies: *Weeping Window*. The sculpture was installed on the exterior of the cathedral's west end.

190 Poppies: *Wave*, at Lincoln Castle.

191 Poppies: *Weeping Window*, at the Black Watch Museum, Balhousie Castle, Perth.

192 Poppies: *Weeping Window* at its first Welsh location, Caernarfon Castle.

National Railway Museum

In 2016, the National Railway Museum in York unveiled a new exhibition, *Ambulance Trains*, on the anniversary of the Battle of the Somme. Exploring the story of the trains that evacuated injured soldiers away from the conflict to receive medical help during the First World War, the exhibition proved extremely popular and is now a long-term feature of the museum's Great Hall.

The centrepiece of the exhibition is a recreated ambulance train carriage, transformed to evoke the intense atmosphere on board. Visitors can see a ward, pharmacy and a nurses' mess room, brought to life through digital projection, sound and historic images.

Rarely seen wartime letters, diaries, photographs and drawings reveal the stories of those involved in the ambulance trains war effort. Railway workers had to build these carefully designed trains at incredible speed, to keep up with demand. Medical staff worked tirelessly in claustrophobic conditions, and the wider public witnessed the grim reality of the Western Front when the trains pulled into British stations.

Accompanying the *Ambulance Trains* exhibition was a ten-year research project led by staff and volunteers from the museum's archive team to create the Fallen Railwaymen database. This records the 20,000 railway workers, young and old, who died during the First World War. Members of the public can search the results for free via a dedicated website: https://firstworldwar.nrm.org.uk/fallen-railwaymen

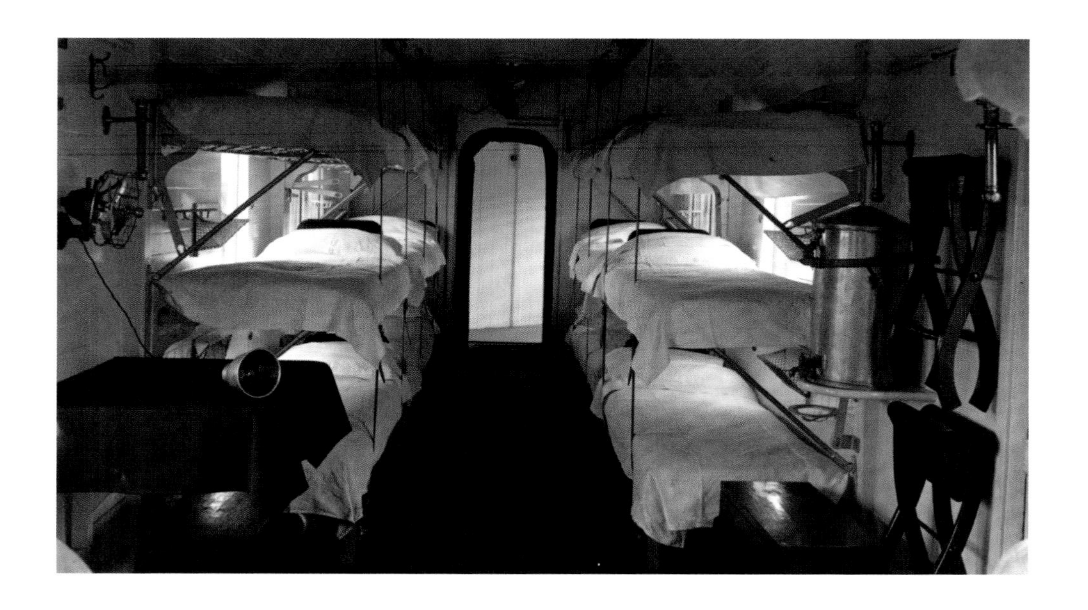

193 The recreated First World War 'hospital on wheels' train carriage.

194 Life on board the ambulance train is evoked through digital projection.

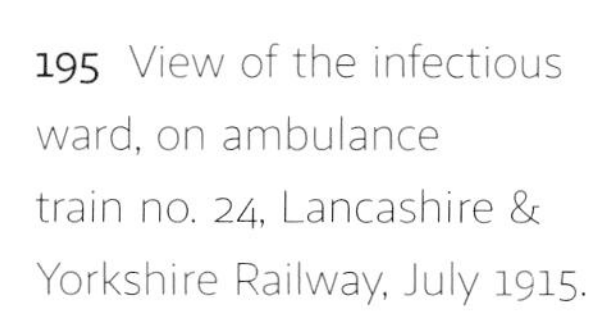

195 View of the infectious ward, on ambulance train no. 24, Lancashire & Yorkshire Railway, July 1915.

Science Museum

Exploring some of the medical innovations of the First World War through historic objects from the Science Museum Group Collection, *Wounded: Conflict, Casualties and Care* opened in 2016 to coincide with the centenary of the Battle of the Somme.

Featuring frontline equipment such as blood transfusion apparatus and portable X-ray machinery, as well as developments made back home in the treatment of facial wounds and the making of artificial limbs, the pioneering medical advances made during the war were central to the exhibition. Also displayed were medical techniques and technologies that were rediscovered, adapted and evolved through painful experience, as the scale of wounding created unprecedented demands on medical personnel.

From the immediate front line priorities to treat blood loss and infections, through to the emergence of new forms of wounding from poison gases and new levels of mental health wounds, the exhibition narrative then followed the wounded back to Britain. In the post-war period huge numbers of returning veterans were left with serious long-term care needs that required the creation of new medical and welfare organisations to cope with the physical and psychological costs of the war.

In the final part of the exhibition, the *Wounded* exhibition team worked closely with a group of recent veterans diagnosed with PTSD (post-traumatic stress disorder) to also reflect on military medical challenges faced today, drawing out parallels with the wounded of the First World war by sharing the personal experiences of soldiers wounded in more recent conflicts.

196 The jointed-pole trench stretcher was designed by George Herbert Colt, a London-based doctor, to help navigate the twists and turns of the trenches while carrying a patient.

197 View of the display cases showing First World War artificial limbs.

National Museum of the Royal Navy

198 HRH The Princess Royal at the official opening of the exhibition *36 Hours: Jutland 1916, The Battle That Won The War.*

199 Interior view of the exhibition. The display on the left honours VC recipient Major Francis John William Harvey RML. Moments before his death, he ordered his battle cruiser's storage of cordite to be flooded, preventing an explosion that could have killed over a thousand people.

To mark the centenary of the First World War, the National Museum of the Royal Navy (NMRN) launched their Great War at Sea campaign. As well as a war fought in the trenches of Northern Europe, the First World War was fought at sea around the globe. The NMRN invested over £23,000,000 in centenary projects to raise awareness of the immense naval contribution to the war. This included the conservation and opening of Gallipoli survivor HMS *M.33*, a conference held on the centenary of the Zeebrugge campaign, and an exhibition on the centenary of the Women's Royal Naval Service.

In May 2016, the NMRN opened *36 Hours: Jutland 1916, The Battle That Won The War* at Portsmouth Historic Dockyard, commemorating the largest naval battle in history. Although initial press reports in 1916 had suggested a German victory, within a few days perceptions shifted. While the British lost twice the number of seamen, their fleet maintained numerical supremacy – two dreadnoughts were damaged, leaving twenty-three dreadnoughts and four battlecruisers still able to fight, whilst the Germans had only ten dreadnoughts. So shaken were the Germans by the weight of the British response that they never again seriously challenged British control of the North Sea.

Working with the Imperial War Museums, the NMRN exhibition presented the battle as a tactical and strategic British victory. Alongside never-before-seen displays and immersive galleries, personal effects from men and women involved in the battle helped to tell the story.

Somme Vigil

The British high commission in New Delhi, working with Big Ideas, created a unique Vigil to mark the centenary of the Battle of the Somme on 30 June 2016 in the beautiful setting of the Delhi War Cemetery. This tropical garden contains the graves of more than one thousand British and Commonwealth soldiers from the First and Second World Wars. The Vigil took place at midnight with the cemetery bathed in marigold light, a reference to the marigold as the Indian flower of remembrance.

The event featured poignant readings – including the works of British, German and American war poets Rupert Brooke, Gerrit Engelke and Alan Seeger – and concluded with Indian Nobel Laureate Rabindranath Tagore's 'Parting Words', read by Squadron Leader Rana Chhina of USI of India.

200 Squadron Leader Rana Chhina of the Centre of Armed Forces Historical Research at USI of India reading from Rabindranath Tagore's 'Parting Words'.

201 Bhanu Sharma, baritone, and Sonal Sikka, keyboard, perform 'The Lads in Their Hundreds' under the War Memorial gates.

Lanterns were lit on the graves (despite the threatening monsoon), and at the end of the service baritone Bhanu Sharma sang 'The Lads in Their Hundreds' set to music by George Butterworth. Butterworth fought at the Somme with the Durham Light Infantry, and was killed by sniper fire on 5 August 1916. The performance was recorded and broadcast the next day on BBC Radio 3 to mark the centenary of the first day of the Somme.

Afterwards, guests including Indian Army veterans had the chance to sample some First World War army fare – trench cake and gunfire tea. The heavy fruit cake was baked by loved ones at home and sent to the troops at the front, while gunfire tea was an originally 19th-century British Army concoction of black tea and rum.

202 Guests were invited to lay flowers at the First World War headstones, lit with hurricane lamps.

London Transport Museum

203 Pupils of Northumberland Park Community School in Tottenham, as part of the *From Tottenham to the Trenches* research work, visited the Somme battlefields and located graves of soldiers whose stories they had learnt about.

On 18 November 2016 the museum's Battle Bus travelled to France for a commemorative tour of towns and villages along what had been the front line in 1916. It was also displayed at the Thiepval Memorial events on 1 July.

The Battle Bus learning project explored the role of underage soldiers and the heavy casualties of the war, working with three groups of young people to create a collaborative community exhibition: *From Tottenham to the Trenches*. The exhibition contained panels based on the findings of the first group, and videos that were produced by the second group. The third group produced poetry and spoken word, and performed at the opening of the exhibition.

National Memorial Arboretum

Marking the centenary of the end of the Battle of the Somme, on 18 November, a moving evening event in the Arboretum grounds included the symbolic installation of the final *Somme: En Masse* soldier. Created by Planet Art, *Somme: En Masse* commemorated the 19,240 lives lost on the first day of the battle with a wooden soldier (12 inches high) for each man who died. Two silhouettes were chosen, a Tommy and a Sikh solider. From 1 July to 18 November, the general public were invited to decorate one side of the soldiers, representing the individuality of those who served. The other side featured a uniform design representing the multitude. Rather than being simply a commemorative piece of art, it became an evolving memorial.

204 Detail of *Somme: En Masse*, showing the public's artwork.

205 *Somme: En Masse* artwork at sunset, National Memorial Arboretum.

The Tank Museum

On 15 September 1916 at the Battle of the Somme, the British Army sent tanks into action for the first time in history. The Tank Museum and the Royal Tank Regiment honoured the pioneering tank soldiers exactly 100 years later in London – a British First World War tank from The Tank Museum was displayed in Trafalgar Square, and then transported to Horse Guards Parade to join a British Army Challenger 2, crewed by members of the Royal Tank Regiment. This provided a unique opportunity to view the very first type of tank alongside the British Army's current main battle tank. Also in 2016, a new permanent exhibition, *Tank Men: The Story of the First Crews*, opened at The Tank Museum. Focusing on the experiences of eight men, it draws on surviving relatives' accounts as well as items in the collection.

206 The Royal Tank Regiment demonstrating 100 years of the tank, Horse Guards Parade, 15 September 2016.

207 View of the exhibition *Tank Men: The Story of the First Crews*.

Museum of Liverpool

The collections at the Museum of Liverpool pay homage to the servicemen and women – in particular members of the King's Regiment – who played such an important role in the First World War. Timed to coincide with the centenary of the Battle of the Somme, the exhibition *First World War: Charity and Liverpool's Home Front* explored the work of charity organisations established at the time.

The 20,000 British servicemen who lost their lives at the Somme are remembered in numerous memorials. Less is known about the 40,000 who survived, but suffered terrible injuries and trauma. Society had to learn how to deal with a generation of mentally and physically wounded people. Drawing on photographs, oral histories and case studies, with a particular focus on Liverpool, the exhibition examined how charities paved the way for better support for ex-servicemen. The charities included the Soldiers, Sailors and Airmen Families Association (SSAFA), the Royal British Legion and Blind Veterans UK.

208 Curator holding a flag pin for the Our Day charity. Street collectors gave these as a 'thank you' gift, to be worn on the lapel. By the end of the war, Our Day collections had raised more than £25 million, equivalent to £1.75 billion today.

2017
COMMEMORATIONS

ARMIES
ISH·EMPIRE
OD·HERE
4·TO·1918
OF·THEIR·DEAD
KNOWN·GRAVE

2017 INTRODUCTION

209 HM Royal Marines buglers sounding the Last Post at the Cross of Sacrifice, Tyne Cot Cemetery, at the Passchendaele event on 31 July 2017.

Following the major centenaries of 2016, attention turned in 2017 to the centenary of the Battle of Passchendaele – the Third Battle of Ypres. In many ways, this battle epitomised the true horror and suffering of war and the devastating impact of industrialised 'total' war. Industrialisation had brought about new technologies, leading to military operations being undertaken on a far larger scale than had ever been seen before.

210 At St Aldhelm's Church War Memorial, Doulting, Somerset, a conservator in-paints the inscription as part of war memorial repair work in 2017.

The government's 2017 commemorative events were delivered in partnership with Belgium, one of our close allies during the First World War, whose people have done so much since the war to keep alive the memory of the fallen. Reflected in many of the other commemorative projects in 2017 were the changing approaches to the waging of war that had become evident in 1917, together with changes on the home front to support the war effort.

The cultural and artistic elements of the centenary programme continued apace throughout 2017, as did many local projects, exhibitions and events. During this year a wide range of Heritage Lottery Fund grants were awarded, to deliver projects and to enable repairs to war memorials.

211 Milestone, at Christ Church in Greenwich, London, dating from the 18th century. After the First World War, a plate indicating the distance to Ypres and commemorating the battles was attached. The Grade II memorial was re-listed as part of Historic England's centenary commemorations in 2017.

Centenary of the Battle of Messines Ridge

The Battle of Messines Ridge was conducted by the British Second Army on the Western Front near the village now known as Mesen, about 6 miles south of Ypres (now Ieper). The battle started on 7 June 1917 and, following the harsh lessons learned on the Somme the previous year, was a strategic success. The taking of Messines Ridge preceded the Third Battle of Ypres (or Passchendaele).

To mark the centenary of the Battle of Messines Ridge, the Irish and UK governments delivered a joint commemoration at the Island of Ireland Peace Park in Belgium on 7 June 2017. The battle has considerable historic and symbolic significance for the UK and Ireland, as Messines was the first time that the 36th (Ulster) and 16th (Irish) Divisions fought alongside each other during the First World War.

The Island of Ireland Peace Park and Round Tower is dedicated to the memory of all those from the island of Ireland who fought and died in the First World War. It was erected by the Journey of Reconciliation Trust with the support of the people of Messines, and built in part by young people from cross-community groups in both Ireland and Northern Ireland. It was a hugely significant and symbolic location for the Messines event. This was the first time that the UK and Irish governments had designed and delivered a truly joint commemorative event, supported by a diverse group of partners and by both the Irish Defence Forces and 2nd Battalion, the Royal Irish Regiment.

The ceremony was attended by the Taoiseach Enda Kenny TD, HRH The Duke of Cambridge and Princess Astrid of Belgium. In an audience of almost 800 people, political representatives from Ireland and the UK sat alongside members of the British and Belgian royal families, Irish church leaders, senior military officers, civil society representatives, and relatives of

212 HRH The Duke of Cambridge, Princess Astrid of Belgium and Taoiseach Enda Kenny arriving for the joint Ireland/UK Messines centenary ceremony at the Island of Ireland Peace Park in Belgium.

many of those from the island of Ireland and beyond who had fought and died at Messines.

Following the ceremony, the Taoiseach, Princess Astrid and HRH The Duke of Cambridge visited Wytschaete Military Cemetery and met the families of some of those who are buried there. An act of remembrance took place at the 16th (Irish) Division Cross, as well as a symbolic handover of soil as part of the Flanders Field Memorial Project.

213 The Round Tower at the Island of Ireland Peace Park is dedicated to those from every part of the island who lost their lives in the First World War.

214 HRH The Duke of Cambridge and Taoiseach Enda Kenny TD laying wreaths during the Messines centenary ceremony at the Island of Ireland Peace Park.

215 The colour party, with the Round Tower behind them, at the centenary ceremony to commemorate the Battle of Messines Ridge.

FAUBOURG D'AMIENS CEMETERY, ARRAS

WW100 Scotland Centenary Service to Commemorate the Battle of Arras

The Battle of Arras began on 9 April 1917 and lasted until 16 May. Forty-four of the 120 battalions that made up the ten British assault divisions were Scottish, and a further seven were Canadian with Scottish heritage. Over 50,000 Scottish troops took to the field of battle, the highest concentration of Scottish troops in history, and more than the entire British forces at the Battle of Waterloo. Of the approximate total of 159,000 casualties at the Battle of Arras, around a third were Scottish, and of those Scots injured an estimated 18,000 lost their lives.

Seventy-two Scottish pupils – representing each local authority in Scotland – departed for France on

216 Scottish pupils visited Lijssenthoek Military Cemetery, the second largest CWGC cemetery in Belgium after Tyne Cot Cemetery. Lijssenthoek was the location for a number of casualty clearing stations during the First World War.

217 Representing each local authority across Scotland, the schoolchildren laid poppy crosses on the graves of those who died at the Battle of Arras.

7 April 2017 to participate in Scotland's international Battle of Arras commemorations. They were joined by a matching number of schoolchildren from France and Canada. During their three-day trip, the pupils visited First World War battlefields, cemeteries and memorials, reflecting on the magnitude of the loss suffered during the conflict.

On Sunday 9 April 2017, several hundred people joined the 9.30am service at Faubourg d'Amiens Commonwealth War Graves Cemetery, conducted by the Moderator of the General Assembly of the Church of Scotland, to commemorate the centenary of the first day of the Battle of Arras. That evening, the general public lined the streets and almost 15,000 gathered in the Place des Héros for a Beating Retreat conducted by the Pipes and Drums of the Royal Regiment of Scotland. On the same evening, in Edinburgh, a service was held in the Scottish National War Memorial, followed by a Beating Retreat by the Band of HM Royal Marines Scotland on Edinburgh Castle Esplanade.

218 In a symbolic gesture, a school pupil from Scotland and one from France laid a wreath together on behalf of the UK, French, Canadian, New Zealand, Australian and South African Allies who fought in the Battle of Arras.

219 Rt Hon. Nicola Sturgeon, First Minister of Scotland, meeting the schoolchildren in Place des Héros.

Centenary of the Bombing of Upper North Street School

On 13 June 1917, 20 German bombers were involved in a daylight raid on London. A bomb from a German Gotha aircraft hit Upper North Street School in Poplar, East London, killing 18 children (mostly aged between four and six years old) and injuring many more. This was one of the earliest examples of aerial bombing on urban targets. The unprecedented loss of young life outraged public opinion in the UK and around the world. In the East End, thousands of people lined the streets as the children were taken to their final resting place.

220 The Poplar Recreation Ground Memorial was built from public funds, raised by a shocked populace, to mark the loss of 18 children in Poplar when their school was hit by a bomb in June 1917. As part of their centenary programme, Historic England upgraded the memorial to Grade II* in 2017.

221 HM The Queen signs the visitor's book, while HRH The Duke of Edinburgh and headteacher Dee Bleech look at the school diary entry recording the day of the bombing in 1917.

Centenary events held in Poplar on 15 June 2017 to commemorate the 18 children who were lost were attended by HM The Queen and HRH The Duke of Edinburgh. In the morning, a multi-faith memorial service was held at All Saints Church in Poplar, where the funerals of 15 of the children had taken place in June 1917. Relatives of the children came together with the German Ambassador, local residents and community groups.

After the service HM The Queen unveiled a plaque bearing the names of the victims. The Queen and the Duke of Edinburgh then visited Mayflower Primary School, built in 1928 just up the road from the original Upper North Street School.

Continuing the theme of remembrance, solidarity and civic pride, a ceremony took place later that day at the Poplar Recreation Ground Memorial (known as the Angel Statue). The names of the children who died are inscribed on a marble column beneath an angel with spread wings. Flowers were laid by family members and dignitaries, and 18 posies were laid by schoolchildren to commemorate the children who lost their lives.

Other commemorative projects included a tree planted by the council in Poplar's Trinity Gardens, where the Upper North Street School originally stood, and the restoration of the children's graves (most were buried in a mass grave at East London Crematorium, but three had private burials).

222 Andrew Ashmore (in costume as headmaster Frank Denner) and Victoria Otter (in costume as Ms Watkins, infants teacher) at the Poplar Recreation Ground Memorial in 2017, as part of the centenary commemorations.

223 At Trinity Gardens, Poplar – the site of Upper North Street School – children from Mayflower Primary School helped plant a commemorative tree in memory of the children who died in the 1917 tragedy.

CWGC: Interns

224 CWGC centenary interns and staff at Tyne Cot. Left to right (starting top row): Andrew Williams, Jennifer Turner, Max Dutton (CWGC historian), Thomas Smith, Nick Bristow (CWGC historian), Andrew Brolly, Alisha Saleh, Calista Arthey, Scarlett Watkins, Jack Sibley, Louis Hunt-Cole, Daryl Smith, Victoria Maytom, Angus Urquhart.

225 Interns Katherine Crabb and Jack Owen lead guests through the Menin Gate, Ieper, April 2018.

226 Intern Megan Kelleher talks to guests during a Rugby Football Union visit on 24 April 2018, honouring rugby players who lost their lives in the First World War.

227 Intern Will Parkinson talks to visitors at the Menin Gate, April 2018.

In 2017 the CWGC marked its own centenary – 100 years of caring for the graves and memorials to those who died in the First World War.

Perhaps the biggest challenge a century later was not the physical maintenance of the cemeteries and memorials, but engaging with the hundreds of thousands of visitors to these special places, and helping them to better understand how they came to exist, why they are important, and the stories of those remembered there. It was with that in mind that CWGC launched the CWGC Centenary Internship. This was supported and funded for two years by a grant from the UK government.

Part of a programme continuing beyond the centenary years, the internships are a unique opportunity for young people to travel, live and work with the CWGC in France and Belgium. Following a period of training, the interns during the First World War centenary acted as paid guides at a number of iconic CWGC sites – including Tyne Cot Cemetery near Ieper (Ypres) in Belgium, and the Thiepval Memorial to the Missing in the Somme in France. They welcomed and guided visitors (both at the major centenary events and at the regular daily openings), and undertook research. From the perspective of people not much younger than many of those who died, they helped to offer context and clearer understanding of both the CWGC and the First World War.

The programme is now supported by the CWGC's new charity – Commonwealth War Graves Foundation (CWGF) – which has been specifically created to keep alive, for generations to come, the memory and the stories of those who died in the two world wars.

Centenary of Passchendaele – the Third Battle of Ypres: 30 July

228 The Menin Gate Memorial to the Missing, at Ypres (Ieper), is dedicated to British and Commonwealth soldiers who were killed in the Ypres Salient and have no known resting place. It was dedicated in 1927.

229 Kneelers with regimental insignia at St George's Memorial Church, Ieper (Ypres). The church has welcomed generations of those returning to the battlefields.

In 2017 thoughts turned to one of the most widely known battles of the Western Front – the Third Battle of Ypres, now referred to as the Battle of Passchendaele. Taking place between 31 July and 6 November 1917, the battle became infamous not only for the scale of casualties, but also for the terrible fighting conditions. During the war the town at the centre of the battle was known by its French name, Ypres. Today it is the Belgian city of Ieper. To the east of the city, the village of Passchendaele was close to a railway junction at Roulers, which was a vital supply network to the German army.

Marking the centenary, events were held in Belgium over two days on 30 and 31 July. The aim was to bring together allies and former enemies, now partners and friends, in reconciliation and peace, and to remember all those who served and died on the Ypres Salient during the First World War.

While the crowds gathered in Ieper's historic market square, 200 descendants whose ancestors' names are inscribed on the Menin Gate gathered at St George's Memorial Church. They were joined by serving soldiers and defence attachés from countries that had fought on the Ypres Salient.

The descendants and military personnel then joined a procession from St George's Memorial Church to the Menin Gate for the traditional 8pm Last Post ceremony. They were led by the Pipes and Drums of the Royal Irish

230 Representing every name inscribed on the memorial, 54,391 poppy petals cascaded from the top of the Menin Gate during the Last Post centenary ceremony.

Regiment and eight Standards provided by the Royal British Legion and eight Belgian Standards.

To commemorate the centenary of the eve of the Third Battle of Ypres, a specially extended Last Post Service took place at the Menin Gate. Attended by Their Majesties the King and Queen of the Belgians, TRH The Duke and Duchess of Cambridge, and the UK Prime Minister Theresa May, the service touched on the special relationship between Belgium and the UK during and after the war, and the role of the Belgian people in commemorating the huge losses sustained throughout the war.

As the National Youth Choir of Scotland sang the Ypres Hymn, 'O Valiant Hearts', 54,391 poppy petals cascaded from the top of the Menin Gate – one for each name inscribed on the memorial.

Later that evening, as darkness fell, a ground-breaking audio-visual public event was staged in

THE LAST POST AT THE MENIN GATE MEMORIAL

A moving ceremony takes place at the Menin Gate every night of the year, whatever the weather, as a tribute from the people of Ieper (Ypres) to the courage and self-sacrifice of those who fell in defence of their city. At 8pm the Last Post is played by the volunteers of the Last Post Association, followed by a minute's silence, and then the Reveille bugle call is played.

The Last Post has been sounded at the Menin Gate every night since 11 November 1929, with the exception of the four years of German occupation of Ypres from 20 May 1940 to 6 September 1944. During this period the ceremony took place in England at Brookwood Military Cemetery, Surrey.

231 Buglers played the Last Post on 30 July 2017 as part of a specially extended ceremony.

the market square. The event opened with Dame Helen Mirren reading 'In Flanders Fields', written by Canadian poet John McCrae, who served as a surgeon with the Canadian forces.

Using the exterior walls of the Cloth Hall, video projections of soldiers and testimonies of the battle formed a dramatic tribute to those who fought at Passchendaele. Footage included that of Harry Patch (known as the 'Last Tommy', who died in 2009 aged 111): 'Passchendaele when I knew it was flat ...

232 Crowds gathered in Market Square, Ieper (Ypres), in readiness for the evening's commemorations. The Cloth Hall, an iconic symbol of loss and recovery, played a key role in the event, providing a powerful backdrop to the performances and readings.

233 Footage of interviews with veterans, together with film clips, archival images and poignant phrases, were projected on to the clock tower and façades of the Cloth Hall.

everything was blown to pieces'; and of Private Jack Dillon, who described how the 'sweet smell' of death pervaded the battlefield.

The experience of civilians in and around Ypres during the war was evoked by a reading from the diary of Pastor Van Wallenghem, while journalist and broadcaster Ian Hislop, who co-wrote *The Wipers Times* stage production, told the story of the satirical newspaper which was founded in Ypres in 1916. A specially written *War Horse* story, with a focus on Ypres and Passchendaele, was performed by Michael Morpurgo and the UK's National Theatre.

As the crowds in 2017 dispersed, many were no doubt thinking of the events the next day, and the thoughts that must have occupied the troops the night before the offensive in 1917.

234 An extract from the play *The Wipers Times*, first staged in 2016 and touring across the UK in 2017, was performed as part of the evening's performance event.

235 and 236 The event closed with the Guard of Honour from the Irish Guards marching through the Menin Gate, just as their antecedents of 1917 had done, accompanied by a lone piper.

Centenary of Passchendaele – the Third Battle of Ypres: 31 July

The Allies launched a renewed assault on German lines in the Flanders region of Belgium on 31 July. The attack started the 100 days of fighting that became known as the Third Battle of Ypres. After an opening barrage of some 3,000 guns, Field Marshal Haig ordered nine British divisions, led by Sir Hubert Gough's 5th Army, to advance on the German lines near the village of Passchendaele; they were joined by six French divisions.

The British Expeditionary Force (BEF) incurred some 310,000 casualties, with German casualties reaching 260,000. The heaviest rainfall for 30 years produced a thick mud that clogged up rifles and immobilised tanks. It eventually became so deep that men and horses would drown in it, their bodies never to be recovered.

On the second day of the 2017 national events, 4,000 descendants congregated in the fields of Passchendaele Memorial Park, visiting exhibits in the Exhibition Field and meeting First World War reenactors, before heading to the CWGC's Tyne Cot Cemetery.

At the cemetery, guests were spread throughout the site, many standing among the approximately 12,000 graves of the fallen. In attendance were Their Majesties King Philippe and Queen Mathilde of the Belgians, HRH The Prince of Wales, TRH The Duke and Duchess of

237 Walking through the graves at Tyne Cot, guests included Their Majesties King Philippe and Queen Mathilde of the Belgians, TRH the Duke and Duchess of Cambridge, Vice Admiral Sir Timothy Laurence and UK Prime Minister Theresa May.

238 In 1918 three eminent architects of the day – Sir Edwin Lutyens, Sir Herbert Baker and Sir Reginald Blomfield – were appointed by the CWGC to design its cemeteries and memorials. The largest CWGC cemetery in the world, Tyne Cot, was designed by Herbert Baker.

CWGC TYNE COT CEMETERY

A barn named Tyne Cot (or Tyne Cottage) by the Northumberland Fusiliers stood near the level crossing on the road from Passchendaele to Broodseinde. Around it was a number of blockhouses or 'pillboxes', a few of which still remain. After the Armistice, Tyne Cot was established as a military cemetery under the auspices of the CWGC, with Herbert Baker as architect and designer. King George V visited Tyne Cot in 1922, and chose a blockhouse as the site on which the Cross of Sacrifice was to be placed.

Tyne Cot Cemetery is now the final resting place of 11,971 servicemen – 8,373 of whom are unidentified. In addition, 35,000 British and Commonwealth servicemen whose graves are not known are commemorated on the curved walls of the Tyne Cot Memorial. Many of those who fell on the Passchendaele battlefields are buried here. The first Commonwealth soldiers were buried at Tyne Cot during the closing weeks of the Allied offensive to take the Passchendaele ridge in autumn 1917. After the Armistice, the cemetery was considerably enlarged to accommodate graves from the battlefields of Passchendaele and Langemark.

Cambridge, British Prime Minister Theresa May and Vice Chairman of the CWGC, Vice Admiral Sir Timothy Laurence. They were joined by representatives from the former combatant nations at the battle – Australia, Canada, France, Germany, Ireland, Malta, New Zealand and South Africa. Also present were the Belgian defence minister, the Minister-President of Flanders and the Mayor of Zonnebeke, as well as around 250 other invited guests. The Royal British Legion and Belgian Standards lined the curved wall at the back of Tyne Cot Cemetery. This was a time to remember those who had served during the Third Battle of Ypres, and to connect with their stories and experiences.

The hour-long event was televised live for a wider audience beyond the former battlefields of Flanders and, appropriately, began with 'In Flanders Fields' performed by the National Youth Choir of Scotland. A British Guard of Honour was provided by Number 1 Company, The 1st Battalion Irish Guards, and the Belgian Guard of Honour was provided by the Regiment Carabiniers.

At the foot of the Cross of Sacrifice, HRH The Prince of Wales said that: 'The battle we know today as Passchendaele would last for over 100 days. We remember it not only for the rain that fell, the mud that weighed down the living and swallowed the

239 In their distinctive blue T-shirts, National Citizen Service (NCS) graduates assist guests at the ceremony at Tyne Cot.

240 HRH The Duchess of Cambridge, Her Majesty Queen Mathilde of the Belgians, and German Foreign Minister Sigmar Gabriel laid flowers at the graves of German soldiers buried at Tyne Cot.

241 About 70% of the graves in the cemetery mark those of unidentified British or Commonwealth servicemen. Their headstones are inscribed with the words 'Known unto God'.

242 The Belgian Air Force, in its poignant missing-man formation, in a flypast over Tyne Cot to conclude the commemoration ceremony marking the centenary of Passchendaele.

dead, but also for the courage and bravery of the men who fought here.'

Four German soldiers (three unidentified) are buried at Tyne Cot, their graves tended by the CWGC with the same devotion as all the others. HM Queen Mathilde of the Belgians and HRH The Duchess of Cambridge joined Sigmar Gabriel, German Minister for Foreign Affairs, in laying a tribute at their graves and standing side-by-side in a spirit of reconciliation. Readings included a letter from an unknown German soldier to his mother: 'You do not know what Flanders means. Flanders means endless endurance. Flanders means blood and scraps of human bodies. Flanders means heroic courage and faithfulness, even unto death.'

As part of the theme of connection with their ancestors, the descendants heard a 'Calling of the Names', as well as many personal stories of some of the thousands present at the battle, including nurses and stretcher-bearers. This was followed by the laying of wreaths at the Stone of Remembrance in the centre of the cemetery.

The ceremony culminated in the British and Belgian national anthems, followed by a spectacular flypast by the Belgian Air Force performing their 'Salute to the Missing Man' to symbolise those who fought and never returned.

Centenary Events in Passchendaele Memorial Park

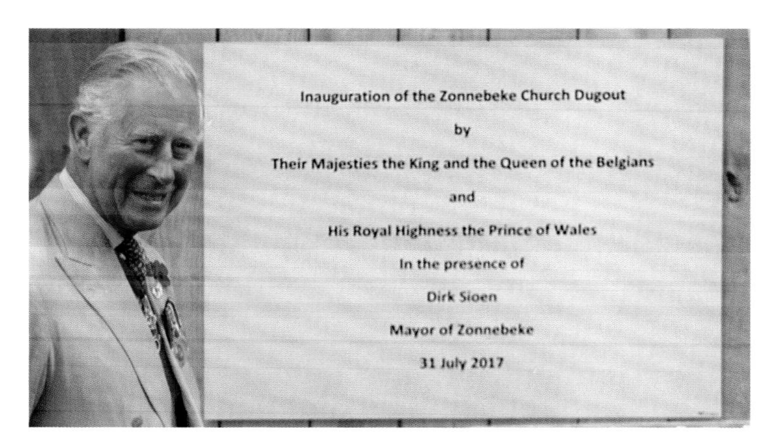

243 HRH The Prince of Wales at the official opening of the Zonnebeke Church Dugout, Passchendaele Memorial Park, 31 July 2017.

244 Guests to the Passchendaele centenary commemorative events visited the Exhibition Field at the Passchendaele Memorial Park and mingled with the re-enactors.

After the ceremony at Tyne Cot, HRH The Prince of Wales and the King and Queen of the Belgians returned to Passchendaele Memorial Park for further memorial events.

First was the official opening of the exceptionally well-preserved Zonnebeke Church Dugout. Built by the Allies in 1917 under Zonnebeke Church, the dugout comprises a main gallery – almost 29 metres long – as well as side corridors, five other rooms and two stairways. It was temporarily opened to the public from 31 July to 10 November as part of the Passchendaele centenary commemorations. The announcement of the opening followed a six-month feasibility study by engineers and scientists. Lying 5 metres underground, the dugout was drained as part of a joint project involving the Memorial

245 The annual WWI Living History event in the Exhibition Field held a special significance on 31 July 2017.

246 Re-enactors in the Exhibition Field at Passchendaele Memorial Park.

Museum Passchendaele 1917 and the municipality of Zonnebeke, supported by the Flemish government and the Flanders Heritage Agency.

Following the opening of the dugout, His Royal Highness and Their Majesties opened the nearby British Memorial Poppy Garden, and met some of the CWGC designers and gardeners who created the garden. The royal party then joined thousands of guests at the Exhibition Field to meet families and descendants of those who fought at Passchendaele, as well as schoolchildren learning about the history of the conflict.

Every year, the Memorial Museum Passchendaele 1917 organises a museum weekend with WWI Living History. In the centenary year of 2017, this was planned to coincide with the July commemorations. About 300 historical re-enactors, of many nationalities, spent the weekend in the grounds of the Zonnebeke Château. Using a large area of land converted to a terrain full of craters, bunkers, mud, gangways and tree stumps, scenes from 100 years ago were vividly recreated, with visitors able to view encampments, weapons, historical objects and demonstrations.

From 3 June to 15 November, the Memorial Museum Passchendaele 1917 staged the exhibition *1917, Total War in Flanders: Passchendaele, Landscape at War*. Looking at the crucial role of the devastated landscape during the battle, the exhibition explored how both armies were forced to adapt their tactics, methods of attack and logistical planning, and the enormous impact that this had on the servicemen, both physical and emotional.

Another centenary initiative organised by the Memorial Museum Passchendaele 1917 was the Tag for Remembrance project. From 1 July to 10 November anyone could leave a personal message of peace at the museum and the Research Centre. A selection of these messages was engraved on identity tags, and became a permanent work of art displayed in the Passchendaele Memorial Park.

247 The personal messages of peace and remembrance, written on poppies, were a moving tribute from the descendants of those who fought at Passchendaele.

Gwasanaeth Coffa Cenedlaethol Cymru

'Yn y man heddychlon hwn heddiw, mae'n anodd dychmygu erchyllterau'r rhyfel a wynebodd ein milwyr, a'r hir aros dirdynnol ymhlith y teuluoedd adref na fyddent, efallai, yn cael clywed am ffawd eu hanwyliaid am fisoedd maith.' Carwyn Jones AC, Prif Weinidog Cymru, 31 Gorffennaf 2017.

Roedd yr 38ain Adran (Gymreig) yn rhan o Frwydr Cefn Pilckem, sef cyrch cyntaf Passchendaele: Trydedd Frwydr Ypres, ar yr 31 o Orffennaf 1917. Ei hamcan oedd cipio tirnod y Groes Haearn. Ymladdwyd y frwydr enbyd dan amgylchiadau arswydus, a boddwyd dynion a cheffylau yn y gors. Ymhen ychydig ddyddiau o ddechrau Brwydr Cefn Pilckem, roedd 3,000 wedi'u clwyfo a channoedd wedi colli'u bywydau, gan gynnwys y bardd o Gymru, Hedd Wyn.

Ar safle Cofeb y Cymry yn Fflandrys y cynhaliwyd y Gwasanaeth Coffa Cenedlaethol ar yr 31ain o Orffennaf 2017. Yn bresennol yn y gwasanaeth yr oedd Ei Uchelder Brenhinol Tywysog Cymru, Prif Weinidog Cymru a phobl bwysig o'r DU; pobl o Wlad Belg yn cynrychioli'r Llywodraeth Ffederal, Llywodraeth Fflandrys a Bwrdeistref Langemark; a phobl o'r Almaen. Cynhaliwyd digwyddiadau eraill ym mynwent Artillery Wood gerllaw, ac yng Nghadeirlan Langemark.

248 Carwyn Jones AC, Prif Weinidog Cymru, yn siarad yng Ngwasanaeth Coffa Cenedlaethol Trydedd Frwydr Ypres, 31 Gorffennaf 2017.
Carwyn Jones AM, First Minister of Wales, speaking at the Third Battle of Ypres National Service of Remembrance, 31 July 2017.

249 Carwyn Jones AC, Prif Weinidog Cymru, ac Alun Cairns AS, Ysgrifennydd Gwladol Cymru, yn gosod torchau ym Mynwent Artillery Wood, Fflandrys.
Carwyn Jones AM, First Minister of Wales, and Alun Cairns MP, Secretary of State for Wales, laying wreaths at the Artillery Wood Cemetery, Flanders.

Welsh National Service of Remembrance

'In this peaceful spot today, it is hard to imagine the horrors of war faced by our soldiers and the agonising wait of families back home who might not know the fate of loved ones for many months.' Carwyn Jones AM, First Minister of Wales, 31 July 2017.

The 38th (Welsh) Division were engaged in the Battle of Pilckem Ridge, the first foray of Passchendaele: Third Battle of Ypres, on 31 July 1917. Their objective was to capture the Iron Cross landmark. The attritional battle was fought in appalling conditions, with men and horses drowning in the quagmire. Within a few days of the start of the Battle of Pilckem Ridge there were 3,000 casualties among their ranks and hundreds had lost their lives, amongst them the Welsh poet Hedd Wyn.

It was at the site of the Welsh Memorial in Flanders that the National Service of Remembrance was held on 31 July 2017. It was attended by HRH The Prince of Wales, the First Minister of Wales and dignitaries from the UK. Representatives from Belgium, including the federal government, the government of Flanders and the municipality of Langemark, and Germany also attended. Other events were held at the nearby Artillery Wood cemetery and at Langemark Cathedral.

COFEB GYMREIG

Yn 2014, gyda chymorth Llywodraeth Cymru, codwyd Cofeb Genedlaethol newydd gan Ymgyrch Cofeb y Cymry yn Fflandrys, sydd â'i haelodau yng Nghymru, a Chymdeithas Cofeb Genedlaethol y Cymry a Hedd Wyn, sydd â'i haelodau yn Fflandrys. Saif y Gofeb ar y Groes Haearn, lle syrthiodd Hedd Wyn, 'Er cof am bawb o dras Gymreig a gymerodd ran yn y Rhyfel Byd Cyntaf'. Fe'i dadorchuddiwyd gan Brif Weinidog Cymru a Maer Langemark yn ystod seremoni gysegru ar yr 16 o Awst 2014.

WELSH MEMORIAL

In 2014, a new National Memorial was erected by the Welsh Memorial in Flanders Campaign, based in Wales, and the Welsh National Memorial and Hedd Wyn Society, based in Flanders, with support from the Welsh government. The memorial is located at Iron Cross, where Hedd Wyn fell, 'In remembrance of all those of Welsh descent who took part in the First World War'. It was unveiled by the First Minister of Wales and the Mayor of Langemark during a dedication ceremony on 16 August 2014.

250 Cofeb y Cymry yn Fflandrys, canolbwynt Gwasanaeth Coffa Cenedlaethol Trydedd Frwydr Ypres.
The Welsh Memorial in Flanders, focal point of the Third Battle of Ypres National Service of Remembrance.

Centenary of the Death of Dr Elsie Inglis

In November 2017, two events were held in Edinburgh to commemorate the remarkable achievements of Dr Elsie Inglis and the Scottish Women's Hospitals during the First World War.

Qualifying as a doctor in 1892, Inglis set up a medical practice in Edinburgh and opened a maternity hospital. She was also an active member of the women's suffrage movement. With the outbreak of war, Inglis offered the British Royal Army Medical Corps a complete medical unit, staffed by qualified female practitoners. Her offer was rejected. Undeterred, she formed the Scottish Women's Hospitals (SWH) to

251 Wreaths were laid at the grave of Dr Elsie Inglis in Dean Cemetery, Edinburgh. Re-enactor Ailsa Clarke dressed in a replica of the uniform worn by doctors of the Scottish Women's Hospitals during the First World War.

252 The Military Band of the Royal Regiment of Scotland marched down from the Castle Esplanade to perform outside St Giles' Cathedral before the service.

253 During the centenary service of thanksgiving at St Giles' Cathedral, HRH The Princess Royal laid a wreath under the memorial plaque commemorating Dr Elsie Inglis.

254 The memorial plaque to Dr Elsie Inglis, by sculptor Pilkington Jackson, was erected in the north aisle of St Giles' Cathedral in 1922.

provide female-run relief hospitals for the Allied war effort. Denied funding by the Scottish Red Cross, Inglis started a fund with her own money which quickly grew thanks to the support of her associates in the suffrage movement.

SWH was welcomed by the governments of France, Russia and Serbia. Inglis went with the team to Serbia, where her pioneering work is remembered to this day. In total, 17 Scottish Women's Hospitals were set up across Europe, as well as a number of satellite hospitals and dressing stations, mainly treating soldiers. Of the nearly 1,500 personnel, only around 20 were men.

Tragically, Inglis did not live to see the end of the war. Suffering from cancer, she returned to Britain on 25 November 1917, and died the next day. Her funeral at St Giles' Cathedral in Edinburgh was attended by both British and Serbian royalty.

On Sunday 26 November 2017, a short service was held at her graveside in the Dean Cemetery, Edinburgh. It was attended by her relatives and by representatives of the medical profession, the armed forces and the Scottish and Serbian governments.

At 2pm on Wednesday 29 November, in the same location and at the same time as the funeral a century before, a Service of Thanksgiving was held at St Giles' Cathedral, in the presence of HRH The Princess Royal. Several hundred people from all walks of life attended the service, and large crowds lined the Royal Mile.

First World War Memorials Programme

255 View of Blackmoor War Memorial Cloister in Hampshire, designed by CWGC architect Herbert Baker. To mark the centenary of the CWGC, the memorial was upgraded from Grade II to Grade II*.

256 The central memorial at Westfield Memorial Village, Lancaster, designed in 1925 by art teacher Jennie Delahunt. To commemorate the centenary of Passchendaele, where many of those listed on it lost their lives, the memorial was upgraded to Grade II* in 2017.

The centenary of the First World War was also an opportunity to reflect on our shared war memorial heritage. Memorials are not only important in allowing us to remember those who made the ultimate sacrifice – they are also vital historical records of the First World War. A substantial programme of work was undertaken to ensure that the memorials are treated with the same care and respect as those they commemorate.

In 2017, Historic England listed many memorials which marked significant episodes of the conflict. In May, the centenary of the Commonwealth War Graves Commission (CWGC) was commemorated with 15 new and upgraded listings of memorials by one of the Commission's principal architects, Sir Herbert Baker. In July the nation's thoughts turned to one of the deadliest battles, that of Passchendaele. Historic England marked the centenary of the battle with 13 new and upgraded war memorial listings.

It was not just on the battlefield that lives were lost during the war. Developments in military technology led to many deaths on the home front, from explosions at munitions factories to Zeppelin attacks. The deadliest First World War air raid took place on 13 June 1917, when 18 Gotha heavy bombers hit London – 162 people were killed and more than 400 injured. Memorials were erected to mark these significant losses.

During the centenary many communities chose to clean and repair their local memorials so that they could continue to act as fitting tributes to those who died. War Memorials Trust helped many communities and memorial custodians to do this in a sensitive way. Taking a conservation approach to war memorials is important, as it allows communities to continue to remember those who made the ultimate sacrifice while preserving the unique historical nature of their war memorial. To support this, Historic England's conservation experts created technical guidance and advice to ensure that heritage professionals have the advice they need to care for the nation's war memorials.

257 In 2017 War Memorials Trust awarded a grant of over £7,000 to the custodians of Brookeborough war memorial in Northern Ireland, to support its cleaning and repair. As it did not have the names of the dead on it, War Memorials Trust worked with the custodians to add a plaque at the base of the memorial.

258 A specialist conservator in-painting the inscription on Portland Cenotaph. Throughout the centenary, Historic England worked to ensure that the right skills were available to care for memorials for many years to come.

14–18 NOW: 2017 Season

Continuing the five-year programme of extraordinary arts experiences connecting people with the First World War, 14–18 NOW commissioned many more projects in 2017.

Where are the Poppies Now was a global digital project to digitally reunite the 888,246 poppies from artist Paul Cummins and designer Tom Piper's 2014 installation, *Blood Swept Lands and Seas of Red* at the Tower of London. When the Tower of London installation was dismantled, the ceramic poppies were sold to the public to raise money for charity. Tracking the stories of poppy owners around the world, *Where are the Poppies Now* created a unique testament to those who lost their lives in the First World War.

The experiences from *we're here because we're here*, Jeremy Deller's living memorial to the Battle of the Somme that was enacted all over the UK in 2016, formed an exhibition that told the story of the work, and which toured to arts venues in 2017.

Following on from the immensely successful stage show *Young Men* – co-commissioned by Sadler's Wells and 14–18 NOW, with choreography by Iván Pérez and music by Keaton Henson – BalletBoyz Artistic Directors Michael Nunn and William Trevitt adapted the work from the stage to the big screen in their feature film debut, a moving silent drama that told the story of young men who fought in and are ultimately consumed by war.

259 This photograph, taken in Northern Ireland, formed part of the *we're here because we're here* exhibition that toured to arts venues across the UK in 2017–18.

260 Still from *Young Men*, a silent film adapted by BalletBoyz Artistic Directors Michael Nunn and William Trevitt from their successful stage production of the same name. The film was shot on location in northern France.

At the Barbican Simon McBurney directed a German cast in *Beware of Pity*, a pioneering collaboration between two of Europe's most innovative and exciting theatre companies, Complicité and the Schaubühne. The play is based on Stefan Zweig's 1939 novel, written just before the Second World War but looking back to the verge of the previous disaster. Also in theatre, the second part of the musical-theatre trilogy *The 306*, entitled *Day*, toured around Scotland. It followed the lives of three ordinary women fighting to be heard above the clamour of the First World War.

The year 2017 saw the world premiere of *Ceremony*, an extraordinary live film event that took place in Manchester on the centenary of the Russian Revolution. Artist Phil Collins brought a statue of Friedrich Engels from Ukraine and installed it in central Manchester, the city where Engels made his name. The second part of *Ceremony*, a film created from the footage produced in 2017, was launched the following year.

261 Performed in German at international venues such as London's Barbican and Taiwan's National Taichung Theater, *Beware of Pity* is a tense depiction of honour, love and betrayal during the disintegration of the Austro-Hungarian Empire and the rise of anti-Semitism.

262 Outside arts centre HOME in Manchester, artist Phil Collins staged *Ceremony*, a live film event around a Soviet-era statue of Friedrich Engels to mark the centenary of the Russian Revolution. Footage from the statue's journey across Europe was mixed with live coverage of its inauguration.

14–18 NOW: Poppies Tour 2017

Hull was the first city in 2017 to welcome Poppies: *Weeping Window*, when it was installed at the Maritime Museum. Next it went to Derby Silk Mill: Museum of Making, and then to the Senedd, home to the National Assembly for Wales. The final location in 2017 was the Ulster Museum in Belfast.

In April, Poppies: *Wave* was reconfigured at the Barge Pier in Shoeburyness, Southend-on-Sea, and then it travelled to the CWGC Plymouth Naval Memorial.

263 Poppies: *Weeping Window* at Hull's Maritime Museum. Much of Hull's fishing fleet was requisitioned in the First World War, and many crews served courageously.

264 Poppies: *Weeping Window* at Derby Silk Mill: Museum of Making. The building was used for two businesses in the war – one grinding corn, the other making medical supplies.

265 The Senedd in Cardiff hosted Poppies: *Weeping Window* in partnership with the Welsh Centre for International Affairs and its 'Wales for Peace' programme.

266 With its strikingly modernist extension dating from 1964, the façade of the Ulster Museum in Belfast provided a dramatic backdrop for Poppies: *Weeping Window*.

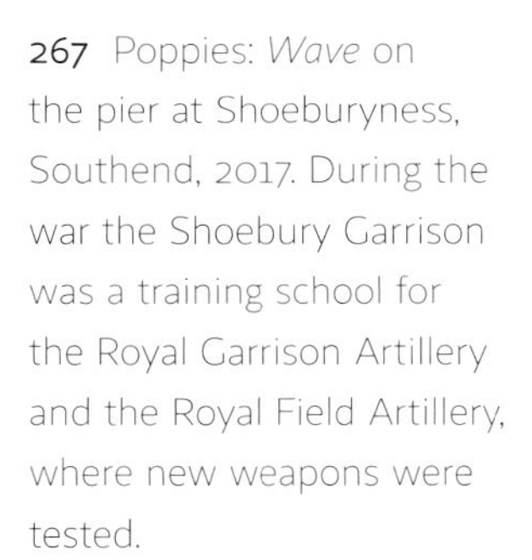

267 Poppies: *Wave* on the pier at Shoeburyness, Southend, 2017. During the war the Shoebury Garrison was a training school for the Royal Garrison Artillery and the Royal Field Artillery, where new weapons were tested.

268 Poppies: *Wave* at the CWGC Plymouth Naval Memorial, 2017. This was the first time the sculpture appeared on a war memorial.

Centenary Commemoration of the Sinking of SS *Mendi*

269 South African Minister in the Presidency Jeff Radebe speaking at the ceremony, 20 February 2017.

270 Attendees, in front of the flag of the Republic of South Africa, preparing to lay a wreath.

Carrying the last contingent of the South African Native Labour Corps bound for the Western Front (823 men of the 5th Battalion), SS *Mendi* set off on the final leg of her journey from Cape Town to France via England on 20 February 1917. To help avoid German submarines in the English Channel, she was escorted by Royal Navy destroyer HMS *Brisk*. In the early hours of 22 February, off the Isle of Wight, fog descended. Ignoring the conditions, SS *Darro*, a mail ship twice the size of SS *Mendi*, drove at full speed into SS *Mendi*. The troopship sank within 25 minutes. Almost 650 men lost their lives, comprising crew and hundreds of South Africans.

A memorial ceremony to mark the loss was held at Hollybrook Cemetery in Southampton on 20 February 2017. The site includes 600 of the casualties from SS *Mendi*. Dignitaries in attendance included HRH The Princess Royal, Vice Admiral Sir Timothy Laurence, South African Minister in the Presidency Jeff Radebe, the Chief of the South African Navy Vice Admiral Mosiwa Hlongwane, and UK Minister for the Middle East and Africa, Tobias Ellwood MP.

Royal Parks and Royal Parks Guild Partnership

Today, London's Royal Parks provide an oasis of calm in the busy city. In the First World War, however, they played a number of different (often top-secret) roles. To commemorate this, the Royal Parks charity and volunteer partner organisation the Royal Parks Guild joined together to research and present a series of events from spring 2017 to summer 2019.

In Kensington Gardens, a number of events took place in 2017. During the war, the park had been turned into a small slice of the Western Front to train soldiers in trench warfare. The Royal Parks and the Royal Parks Guild reconstructed the trench that was built 100 years ago, and ran 20-minute interactive tours led by a costumed soldier from the 10th Essex Living History Regiment. They also staged an exhibition about the Camouflage School, established by Solomon J. Solomon in 1916. The new use of aerial reconnaissance, and the close proximity of opposing trenches on the Western Front, greatly increased the need to conceal and observe while being unobserved. Solomon's cutting-edge camouflage techniques included observation posts disguised as war-torn trees.

Visitors could also explore war allotments, tended by a team of volunteers. During the war, growing your own vegetables provided a vital boost to a rationed diet, and Kensington Gardens had led the way with a 'model allotment'.

271 The reconstructed trench in Kensington Gardens, September 2017.

National Memorial Arboretum

To commemorate the centenary of the Battle of Passchendaele, the Arboretum staged *Passchendaele: Mud and Memory*, a solo exhibition by Stephen Dixon. The centrepiece was his large terracotta bust using the features of soldiers from six nations who fought and died at the battle – a representation of 'everyman'. Other works looked at the power of historical artefacts and the stories behind them.

Also in 2017, a replica above-ground trench was created in the grounds of the Arboretum. Thousands of visitors explored the trench, which featured firing steps, a latrine and an officers' dugout. Costumed interpreters and replica props within the trench helped bring history to life during weekends and school holidays.

272 Stephen Dixon's *Everyman* sculpture was created with clay from the Passchendaele region.

273 The Arboretum's above-ground replica trench.

MHCLG: Passchendaele at Home

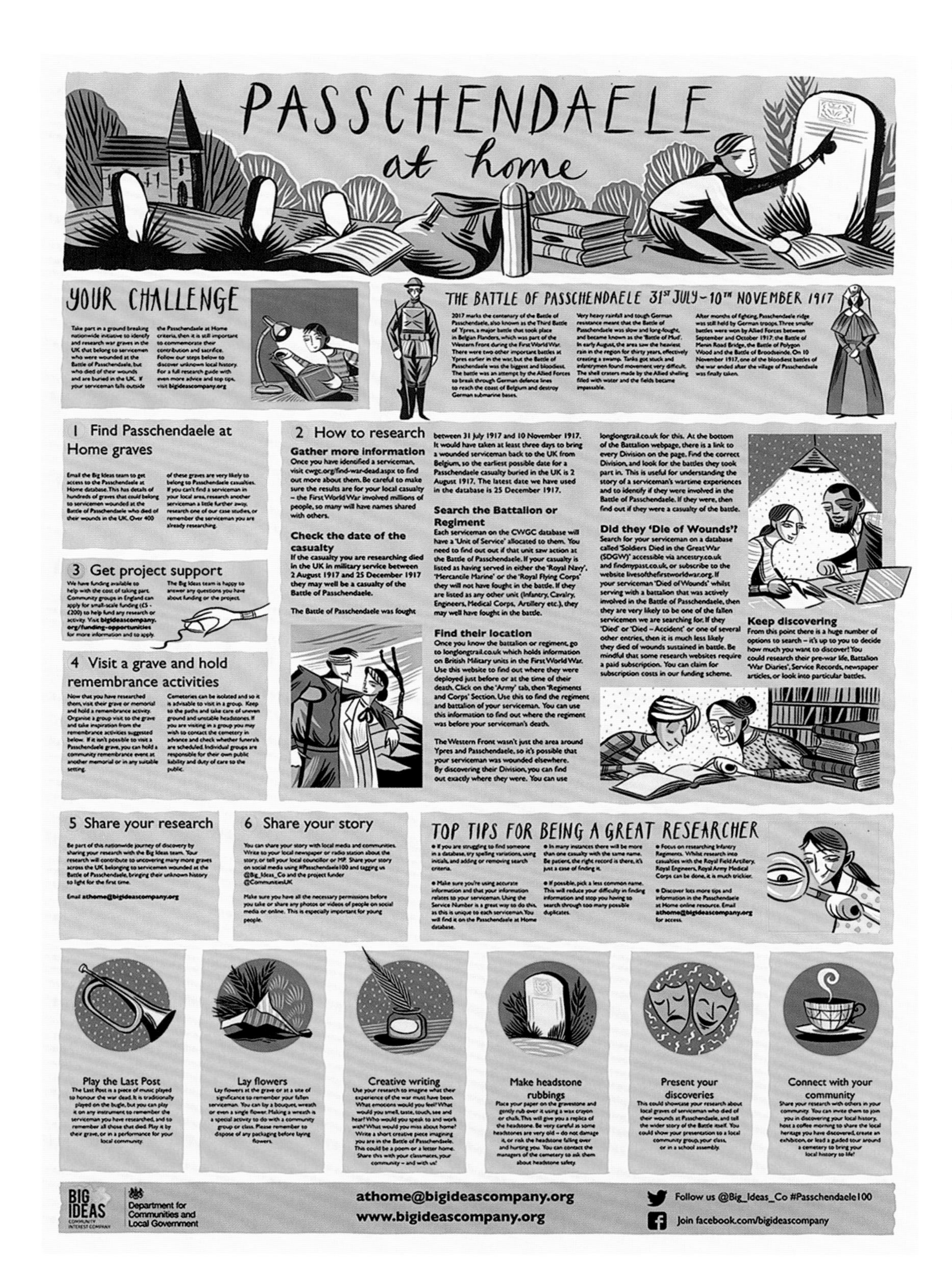

274 Poster issued by Big Ideas, for the Ministry of Housing, Communities and Local Government (MHCLG), outlining the project to research the graves of British soldiers injured at the Battle of Passchendaele who then died in the UK. Community groups and schools were invited to apply for funding (up to £200) towards the cost of their project.

Impressions Gallery

275 First World War photograph by Olive Edis. Commandant Johnson and members of the General Service Voluntary Aid Detachment Motor Convoy, Abbeville, France.

Impressions Gallery in Bradford, a charity helping people to understand the world through photography, staged *No Man's Land: Women's Photography and the First World War* in 2017. This touring exhibition, funded by Arts Council England, featured photographs made by three women during the conflict alongside artworks by three women a century later.

Ambulance driver Mairi Chisholm photographed life under fire at Pervyse in Belgium, while nurse Florence Farmborough depicted the horrors of war on the Eastern Front. Olive Edis, the UK's first female official war photographer, was commissioned by the Imperial War Museum to photograph the British Army's auxiliary services in France and Flanders.

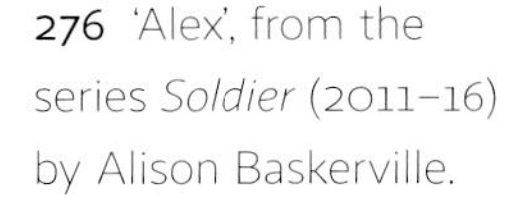

276 'Alex', from the series *Soldier* (2011–16) by Alison Baskerville.

Alison Baskerville took portraits of present-day women in the British Army, using a contemporary version of colour technology that had been pioneered by Olive Edis, while Dawn Cole was inspired by the diary of her great-aunt Clarice Spratling, a Voluntary Aid Detachment nurse. Chloe Dewe Mathews revisited the sites at which Allied soldiers were shot for desertion.

A companion Heritage Lottery project by New Focus, Impressions Gallery's young people's collective, enabled 16–25 year olds in Bradford to explore photographic archives and produce an innovative educational book to help young people engage with the First World War.

277 New Focus launch their book *No Man's Land: Young People Uncover Women's Viewpoints on the First World War*, 2017.

Centenary of the Battle of Cambrai

At the Battle of Cambrai, on 20 November 1917, the British advanced further in six hours than they had in three months at Passchendaele. It was a top-secret attack with no advance bombardment, using nearly 480 tanks – the largest tank force ever seen. Supported by artillery pieces, infantry and aircraft, the tanks smashed a 7-mile wide, 4-mile deep gap in the German defences. Exhausted by Passchendaele, however, the British could not build on their success. The enemy counter-attacked, and by 7 December the armies held the same amount of ground they had started with. Nevertheless, the new tactics were to shatter German defences on the Western Front in 1918.

Commemorating the courage and sacrifice of the world's first tank crews, many events took place in 2017. A Mark IV tank, given to the town in 1919 in recognition of impressive levels of wartime fundraising, was the focus for a remembrance service in Ashford on 17 November. In London, the annual Royal Tank Regiment march to the Cenotaph took place on 19 November. On 20 November, the regiment held a service at their home base in Wiltshire to mark the day of the battle.

The Royal Tank Regiment also took part in centenary commemorations in Cambrai, including the inauguration of the Cambrai Tank 1917 museum. There were ceremonies at French, Commonwealth and German cemeteries, and on Sunday 26 November the Mayor of Cambrai granted the Freedom of Cambrai to the regiment, handing the Town Gate key to commanding officer Lieutenant Colonel Simon Ridgway MBE.

278 On 19 November 2017, The Tank Museum's Mark IV replica joined the Royal Tank Regiment's annual march to the Cenotaph in memory of the Battle of Cambrai.

279 The Royal Tank Regiment parading through Cambrai after the Freedom to Cambrai ceremony on 26 November.

2018 COMMEMORATIONS

2018 INTRODUCTION

The year 2018 saw the culmination of the programme of centenary events and activities. While previous activity had focused on a specific battle or campaign, the challenge in 2018 was to tell a more nuanced story – how, after so many years of stalemate, the course of the war moved in a few months to the signing of the Armistice and peace. The appointment of Marshal Foch and the Battle of Amiens were key to this unfolding story. It was also important that commemorations in 2018 left the door open for opportunities to learn more about post 11 November developments, and to understand the uncertainty and turmoil which was faced around the world. This final year of the centenary also presented an opportunity to adopt a positive tone of thanksgiving – for peace, for the service of a generation, and for all those who returned to their families.

280 Prime Minister Theresa May at the St Symphorien Military Cemetery in Mons, on 9 November 2018, laying a wreath at the grave of Pte George Ellison of the 5th Royal Irish Lancers, the last British soldier to be killed before Armistice in 1918.

281 A volunteer preparing the Field of Remembrance at Westminster Abbey, with over 85,000 crosses commemorating the fallen British and Commonwealth soldiers of past conflicts. HRH The Duke of Sussex opened the 2018 Field of Remembrance on 11 November.

282 Dilys Armistice Fox, from West Sussex, receiving gifts and cards from local schoolchildren to celebrate her 100th birthday on 11 November 2018.

SS *Tuscania* and HMS *Otranto* Commemorative Events

On the small island of Islay, off the west coast of Scotland, events were held to remember Islay's contribution to the First World War and the loss of two British troop ships carrying American soldiers to fight alongside the Allies. Over 200 Islay and Jura men died during the war, while the sinking of SS *Tuscania* and HMS *Otranto* off the island's coast in 1918 saw around 700 US servicemen and British crew members lose their lives.

Carrying 2,500 British and US troops, SS *Tuscania* was torpedoed by a German U-boat. Most onboard were rescued by the Royal Navy, but more than 200 men were lost at sea, with many swept up on the shore of Islay. During a strong storm later that year, the *Otranto* crashed into HMS *Kashmir* while travelling in convoy. Many US troops were saved by HMS *Mounsey*, but those who could not escape the *Otranto* were swept toward an Islay reef that wrecked the ship. Around 470 men died.

On 4 May 2018, the commemorative events began with a re-dedication of the American Monument on the Mull of Oa. HMS *Raider*, USS *Ross*, FS *Andromede* and FGS *Lubeck* – ships representing Britain, America, France and Germany – marked the spot where SS *Tuscania* sank. Wreaths were laid at the monument.

283 On 3 May, during a service on board HMS *Raider*, a wreath was laid at sea by Lord Robertson of Port Ellen. His grandfather was the police sergeant on Islay who dealt with the aftermath of the sinkings in 1918.

284 A piper playing in front of warships that marked the spot where SS *Tuscania* sank.

Children from the island's schools carried US state flags, produced by the Islay Quilters, to the War Memorial in Port Ellen for the main commemorative service, attended by around 1,400 people. Descendants and locals were joined by dignitaries including HRH The Princess Royal; Fiona Hyslop MSP, Cabinet Secretary for Culture, Tourism and External Affairs; The Rt Hon. David Mundell MP, Secretary of State for Scotland; Robert Wood Johnson, United States Ambassador to the UK; M. Emmanuel Cocher, Consul General of France in Scotland; and Herr Jens-Peter Voss, Consul General of Germany. Along with readings and choir music, wreaths were laid and four Royal Marine buglers played the Last Post.

The Princess Royal later visited the town's Ramsay Hall to meet with islanders, dignitaries and descendants of those involved in the tragedies.

285 Children carrying flags for each of the US states, hand-made by the Islay Quilters in honour of the US servicemen who lost their lives off the coast of Islay.

286 The War Memorial in Port Ellen was the focal point for the commemorative service, attended by dignitaries, descendants and islanders, on 4 May 2018.

Centenary of the Appointment of Marshal Foch

Ceremonies were held in both the UK and France to mark the appointment of Marshal Ferdinand Foch as Supreme Allied Commander on 26 March 1918. This historically momentous switch to a single unified command occurred in response to the German spring offensives which threatened disaster on the Western Front.

British and French ministers, together with representatives from all the nations who fought on the Western Front in 1918, gathered in London to mark this historic anniversary at the statue of Marshal Foch. As the opening event of the UK government's 2018 commemorative calendar, it provided a focus and narrative context for the year's programme.

The focus of this commemoration was the strategic cooperation and friendship of the Allies, and honouring the impact on the war of a great soldier of France. Around 100 guests attended the ceremony, including Mme Geneviève Darrieussecq, French Minister of State for Defence with Responsibility for Remembrance and Veterans. The previous day

287 Statue of Marshal Ferdinand Foch by renowned French sculptor Georges Malissard, in Grosvenor Gardens, Victoria, London.

288 French Minister of State for Defence Geneviève Darrieussecq and UK Culture Secretary Matt Hancock laying wreaths during the centenary event marking the appointment of Marshal Ferdinand Foch as Supreme Allied Commander.

289 The Band of the Irish Guards marched from nearby Wellington Barracks accompanied by the Guard of Honour of the French Republic, provided by the 35e Régiment d'Artillerie Parachutiste from Tarbes (Marshal Foch's birthplace).

she had taken part in commemorations in Doullens, the Somme town where the unified command was agreed. At the London event, music was performed by the Band of the Irish Guards and Les Fauristes, a London-based French chamber choir.

In the opening address the Rt Hon. Matt Hancock MP, Secretary of State for Digital, Culture, Media and Sport, described how the decision to coordinate military strategy under Marshal Foch's leadership enabled the Allies to withstand the German spring offensives and to make their own successful advances later in 1918. He paid tribute to 'the significant contribution made by Marshal Foch to the outcome of the war'.

Mme Geneviève Darrieussecq and the Rt Hon. Matt Hancock laid wreaths at the statue, followed by Éric Bécourt-Foch (Foch's great-grandson) and Lord Astor of Hever (grandson of Field Marshal Douglas Haig), as well as representatives of the other Allied nations who fought under Marshal Foch on the Western Front in 1918. Following their contribution to the Passchendaele commemorations of 2017, graduates of the National Citizen Service programme acted as wreath bearers.

The national anthems of France and the UK closed the event, before guests attended a reception at the nearby Guards' Museum.

Centenary of the Battle of Amiens

290 Crowds gathered on 8 August 2018 outside Amiens Cathedral, in anticipation of the commemorative event marking 100 years since the Battle of Amiens.

The Battle of Amiens followed Allied success at the 2nd Battle of the Marne. Representing a decisive moment that saw the British and Allied forces push the German forces back, it is often seen as a turning point in the war. The battle is less well known than other major battles of the First World War, and one of the key aims of the centenary event was to highlight its historical significance.

The event on 8 August 2018 at the historic Amiens Cathedral was delivered by the UK government in partnership with the governments of Australia, Canada, France and the USA, supported by the Préfecture de la Somme and the City of Amiens. Continuing the theme of coalition and reconciliation with former enemies, the focus of this event was on new military tactics including the contribution of the Royal Air Force.

Commemorating the centenary of the Battle of Amiens and the start of the subsequent Hundred Days Offensive that would lead to the end of the war, the

291 The National Youth Choir of Great Britain singing at Amiens Cathedral during the centenary event.

292 HRH The Duke of Cambridge and Prime Minister Theresa May attended the event at Amiens Cathedral.

event was designed to convey a more positive tone, moving away from a focus on loss and remembrance and towards a spirit of thanksgiving for victory and the care of those who returned. It also acted as an important precursor to the Armistice commemorations, by helping to explain how the course of the war changed after so many years of bloodshed and stalemate. The event was broadcast live in the UK on BBC One and Sky News and in France on France 3, reaching over 1 million viewers in the live TV slot and more than 75,000 on catch-up services or online. The event was also covered extensively on social media.

Outside the cathedral, dignitaries from the UK and international partners arrived to the sight of military personnel from each of the participating nations. A joint Guard of Honour was provided by the Royal Anglian Regiment and the 2nd Hussars Regiment from the French Army, whose antecedent regiments had fought in the battle. Along with a band from the French Army, the Central Band of the RAF provided a musical welcome, reflecting both the important role played by air power during the battle, and the significance of 2018 as the centenary of the RAF.

The event was attended by French Defence Minister Mme Florence Parly, HRH The Duke of Cambridge, and British Prime Minister the Rt Hon. Theresa May MP. The coalition nations were represented by the Australian and Canadian Veterans' Ministers, the American Deputy Head of Mission and the Irish Ambassador. Former President Joachim Gauck represented Germany.

293 French Defence Minister Mme Florence Parly and HRH The Duke of Cambridge laid wreaths in the Chapel of the Allies at Amiens Cathedral.

294 Mme Florence Parly, Prime Minister Theresa May and HRH The Duke of Cambridge outside Amiens Cathedral after the centenary event.

Following a welcome address from the Bishop of Amiens, a selection of accounts were read from those who witnessed events in Amiens in August 1918 – from each of the nations that participated in the battle. It included the orders given by Allied commanders in the hours before the battle began, eyewitness accounts of soldiers, and a recollection by the Mayor of Amiens in 1918 read by the current Mayor of Amiens, Brigitte Fouré. The event was attended by 500 British descendants of those who served, and a number of them had an opportunity to meet HRH The Duke of Cambridge and the Prime Minister.

Dating back to the 13th century, Amiens Cathedral escaped relatively unscathed during the war while the city itself suffered heavy damage. The cathedral is now home to a number of memorial tablets commemorating the fallen of the Allied nations, including the first of many memorial tablets to the men of Great Britain and Ireland installed in the 1920s and 1930s by the Imperial War Graves Commission at cathedrals across France and Belgium. At the event, young people from each of the Allied nations, accompanied by a young person from the city of Amiens, laid wreaths beneath their nation's tablet to honour and remember the fallen.

At the cathedral's Chapel of the Allies, senior dignitaries paid their respects and reaffirmed the bonds of friendship between the Allied nations, Germany and the city of Amiens.

Music for the event was provided by a multinational ensemble of musicians from the Allied nations and the National Youth Choir of Great Britain. There was also a powerful arrangement of the Last Post, performed by trumpeters from all the nations who fought at the Battle of Amiens. In the square outside the cathedral, a special viewing area enabled the people of Amiens to watch the arrivals of dignitaries and to see the military bands performing, and included a large screen to show the ceremony.

Alongside the event, UCL Institute of Education (University College London) delivered an International Student Programme supported by the Department for Digital, Culture, Media and Sport (DCMS). Young people from each of the nations that had fought in the Battle of Amiens spent a number of days together visiting the battlefields and attending lectures by leading historians. They exhibited their work at a special event attended by senior representatives from each of the Allied nations.

295 Flags being carried out of Amiens Cathedral after the centenary event that commemorated a decisive turning point in the First World War.

Centenary of the Armistice: The National Service of Remembrance

Throughout the UK, Remembrance Sunday takes place every year on the Sunday closest to Armistice Day. It not only commemorates the fallen of the British and Commonwealth forces in the First World War, but all those in subsequent conflicts too.

In 2018, 11 November fell on a Sunday, presenting the challenge of ensuring that the commemorations for the centenary of the Armistice did not overshadow or detract from traditional acts of remembrance for all those lost in conflict since that time. Out of respect for the living veterans of more modern conflicts, the National Service of Remembrance in 2018 followed traditional lines.

296 Aerial view of the Remembrance Sunday service at the Cenotaph on 11 November 2018.

297 TRH The Earl of Essex, The Duke of York, The Duke of Sussex and The Duke of Cambridge, with the President of the Federal Republic of Germany, His Excellency Frank-Walter Steinmeier, at the Cenotaph.

298 HRH The Prince of Wales laid a wreath at the Cenotaph on behalf of HM The Queen as well as his own wreath.

299 President Frank-Walter Steinmeier lays a wreath at the Cenotaph.

THE CENOTAPH

The Cenotaph on London's Whitehall began as one of a number of temporary structures erected for the London Victory Parade on 19 July 1919, marking the formal end of the First World War on the signing of the Treaty of Versailles a month earlier.

The location chosen on the parade route along Whitehall was between the Foreign Office and Richmond House. During the parade, those saluting the temporary cenotaph included Allied commanders General John J. Pershing, Marshal Ferdinand Foch, Field Marshal Douglas Haig and Admiral David Beatty. For some time after, the base of the memorial was covered with flowers and wreaths by members of the public. Pressure mounted to retain it, and it was decided that a permanent memorial should replace the wooden version and be designated Britain's official national war memorial.

Designed by Edwin Lutyens, the permanent structure was built from Portland stone between 1919 and 1920. Lutyens's Cenotaph design has since been reproduced elsewhere in the UK and in other countries, including Australia, Canada, New Zealand, Bermuda and Hong Kong.

The memorial was unveiled by King George V on 11 November 1920. The unveiling ceremony was part of a larger procession bringing the Unknown Warrior to be laid to rest in his tomb nearby in Westminster Abbey. The funeral procession route passed the Cenotaph, where the waiting King laid a wreath on the Unknown Warrior's gun-carriage. He then unveiled the memorial, which had been draped in large Union Flags.

300 Postcard of the Cenotaph, Whitehall, London, c.1920

The Nation's Thank You

On the morning of 11 November 2018, 10,000 invited members of the public from all over the UK gathered on The Mall to watch the National Service of Remembrance on large screens. Following the traditional Royal British Legion's Veterans' Parade, they then processed along The Mall and onto Whitehall. Led by civilian bands from around the UK, the procession passed the Cenotaph in an act of thanksgiving – the Nation's Thank You.

Many of those taking part brought wreaths to be laid at the Cenotaph. For many this was a tribute to family members who served during the war, while for others it was an opportunity to pay tribute to a whole generation.

301 Getting ready for the Nation's Thank You procession, the 10,000 members of the public lined The Mall.

302 As part of the Nation's Thank You, a Queen's Scout laid wreaths from participants in the procession.

303 The Cenotaph on 11 November 2018, exactly 100 years after the First World War Armistice.

Bell Ringing

304 The Central Council of Church Bell Ringers' Ringing Remembers programme supported the 11 November bell-ringing. As some 1,400 bell ringers were killed in the war, Ringing Remembers set out to recruit 1,400 new ringers to commemorate Armistice – and ended up with nearly double that number.

At precisely 12.30pm on 11 November 2018, just prior to the start of the Nation's Thank You, the bells of Westminster Abbey and Big Ben rang out, providing a moving backdrop as the procession made its way towards the Cenotaph. The bells in the immediate vicinity of the Cenotaph were joined by many from across the UK and around the world, as bell-ringers were called to 'look to' and participate in the commemorations.

The ringing of bells mirrored the outpouring of relief in 1918 which greeted the news of the signing of the Armistice. It also helped to mark a change in the tone of the day, from one of remembrance in the morning to one of thanksgiving in the afternoon.

Overall bells were rung at over 2,500 separate events around the world. Cathedrals, parish churches, town halls, ships and other organisations took part in events covering the whole of the UK from the Isles of Scilly to St Magnus Cathedral in Orkney. Bells were rung at St George's Memorial Church in Ypres, at Passchendaele church and at Amiens Cathedral, all sites of HM Government's previous First World War centenary commemorations. In Germany, bell-ringing was supported by the German government and included the participation of Berlin's iconic church, the Kaiser-Wilhelm-Gedächtniskirche.

Many British embassies and high commissions around the world also held their own Armistice commemorations and coordinated bell-ringing events in their host countries. Bells also rang out at St Peter's Basilica in the Vatican in Rome and the World Peace Gong in Vientiane, Laos, was sounded.

In Australia, bell towers across the country complemented the work of the Australian and New Zealand Association of Bellringers (Anzab) in marking the centenary. In New Zealand, starting with the Rangimarie peace bell of the National War Memorial Carillon, bells created a 'Roaring Chorus' on land and sea to mark the centenary. In Canada, the 'Bells of Peace' initiative encouraged Canadian communities to ring bells at sunset ceremonies, recalling the sense of relief and joy that the end of four long years of war had brought to Canada and the Dominion of Newfoundland. As part of the US's Bells of Peace programme, the Centennial Bell in Philadelphia was tolled to mark the centenary of the Armistice. The Liberty Bell, silent in her enclosure nearby, stood witness to the commemoration as the Honorary Bell of Peace.

305 Christopher O'Mahony, President of the Central Council of Church Bell Ringers (CCCBR). The CCCBR compiled the Roll of Honour that established that some 1,400 bell ringers lost their lives in the First World War.

A Service to Mark the Centenary of the Armistice

On 11 November 1918, in Marshal Foch's private train in a railway siding in Compiègne, France, the Armistice between the Allies and Germany was agreed at 5am Paris time. The cessation of hostilities came into force at 11am. Exactly 100 years later (6am London time), a lone piper played the traditional Scottish lament 'Battle's O'er' at the Grave of the Unknown Warrior in Westminster Abbey, in concert with 1,000 other pipers at locations across the UK.

Westminster Abbey was also the setting for the final event of the day – the service commemorating the centenary of the Armistice at 6pm. Marking the end of fighting on the Western Front, the service of thanksgiving was the culmination and state finale of the government's four-year programme of commemorative events for the centenary of the First World War. It was broadcast live on BBC television and watched by millions.

Following the Remembrance Sunday service in the morning, the royal family and dignitiaries from around the world attended the abbey for the evening commemoration. Other guests included individuals and organisations who had been nominated for their

306 The Westminster Abbey choir process past the Grave of the Unknown Warrior.

307 Prerna Acharya, Michaela McKay, Baljodh Singh, Rebecca Dunning, Lauren King, Elmer Djassi, Jhonattan Goncalves, Zach Opere-Onguende and Morgan McArthur lay flowers at the Grave of the Unknown Warrior.

308 Jasleen Singh, Rebecca PInkerton and Joel Williams-Modeste, seen here in the congregation, read prayers during the service.

contributions, at both national and local level, to the four years of centenary commemorations.

HM The Queen and His Excellency Frank-Walter Steinmeier, President of the Federal Republic of Germany, laid fresh flowers at the Grave of the Unknown Warrior, in symbolic recognition of the hope arising from the sacrifices of earlier generations. Completing the floral arrangement at the grave were young people who had been inspired to commemorate the First World War through visits to war graves and memorials, through their own research, through the writing of poetry, and through playing and composing music.

The service included moments of reflection on the differing responses to news of the Armistice in 1918. Sophie Okonedo read an extract from the diary of social reformer Beatrice Webb, describing the rejoicing in the streets of London and commenting that 'Berlin, also, is reported to be elated, having got rid not only of the war but also of its oppressors', while John Simm read from the memoirs of Private John Jackson: 'I think we were slow to believe it could really be true after the long years of fighting.' Simon Russell Beale read an extract from the memoirs of Winston Churchill, describing the great responsibility felt by the victorious nations.

Prime Minister Theresa May, HRH The Prince of Wales and President Steinmeier read passages from the Bible, the latter reading in German. Prayers were said by young people, asking God for peace and reconciliation, and entreating future generations to remember the fallen. The Westminster Abbey choir sang an anthem, 'The True Light', composed for the occasion by Master of the Queen's Music, Judith Weir,

309 Sophie Okonedo reading from Beatrice Webb's account of Armistice Day in 1918.

310 John Simm reading an extract from John Jackson's *Private 12768: Memoir of a Tommy*.

and commissioned by the Department for Digital, Culture, Media and Sport (DCMS).

As the service ended, the bells of Westminster Abbey rang out and the Government's formal commemorative programme drew to a close. After one hundred years, the nation and beyond had come together to honour all those who served, to learn from their experiences, and to rededicate themselves to ensure that 'their name liveth for evermore'.

311 At the beginning of the service, HM The Queen shook hands with the President of Germany, His Excellency Frank-Walter Steinmeier, in a symbolic gesture of peace, friendship and hope for the future.

312 TRH The Duke and Duchess of Cambridge and The Duke and Duchess of Sussex at the end of the service.

14–18 NOW: *Pages of the Sea*

On the centenary of Armistice, tens of thousands of people took part in *Pages of the Sea*, commissioned by 14–18 NOW and delivered with partner organisations across the UK. Filmmaker Danny Boyle invited people to gather on 32 UK beaches for a nationwide gesture of remembrance to honour the men and women who left their home shores during the First World War.

Large-scale portraits, designed by sand artists Sand In Your Eye, were drawn into the sand and then washed away as the tide came in. Representing a small selection of the millions who gave their lives to the war, the portraits were chosen by Danny Boyle to represent a range of stories – ordinary people from doctors and poets to munition workers, privates and majors.

313 Around the main sand portrait, the public were invited to use stencils to create silhouettes of soldiers totalling the number of lives lost to the local community.

314 The sand portrait of Walter Tull, on Ayr Beach, Scotland. Walter Tull found fame as one of Britain's first black footballers, and became the first ever black officer to command white troops.

315 Sand portrait of First World War poet Wilfred Owen at Sunny Sand Beach, Folkestone.

Visitors to the beaches were asked to join in by creating silhouettes of people in the sand, remembering the millions of lives lost or changed forever by the conflict. The community near each beach personalised their own event, tailored to reflect the sacrifices of their local community. Many people had taken part in community projects in the preceding weeks, discovering their local history. In Swansea, hundreds of white kites were decorated and flown as the waves washed away the face of Dorothy Watson, a munitions worker who was killed in an explosion aged 19. In Ayr, Walter Tull, the first black officer to serve in the British Army, was remembered to the sound of pipers. Perranporth in Cornwall saw horses, flags and dancing by young people, with lanterns lit along the shore as the night closed in.

Poet Carol Ann Duffy was invited by Danny Boyle to write a poem to mark the centenary. Her sonnet, 'The Wound in Time', was read by individuals, choirs, families and communities as they gathered on the beaches. The poem was printed on cards featuring over 14,000 different images of casualties from the First World War.

Aerial photographs of the sand portraits became one of the outstanding symbols of the Armistice centenary, as the pictures were circulated around the world through the press and social media. The day's events engaged more than 25 million people in the UK, showing the relevance of commemorations in today's society.

Coffáu Canmlwyddiant y Cadoediad yng Nghymru

316 Y Gwasanaeth Cenedlaethol o Ddiolchgarwch yn cael ei gynnal yn Eglwys Gadeiriol Llandaf, 11 Tachwedd 2018.
The Welsh National Service of Thanksgiving taking place at Llandaff Cathedral, 11 November 2018.

317 Aelod o'r Gwarchodlu Cymreig yn gosod Llyfr Coffa Cenedlaethol Cymru ar y drymiau catrodol. Mae'r Llyfr yn rhestru enwau bron i 40,000 o filwyr Cymreig a laddwyd yn y Rhyfel Byd Cyntaf.
A Welsh Guardsman placing the Welsh National Book of Remembrance on the regimental drums. The Book lists the names of the approximately 40,000 Welsh servicemen killed in the First World War.

318 Archesgob Cymru, Y Parchedicaf John Davies, a Deon Llandaf, Y Tra Pharchedig Gerwyn Capon, â'u Huchelderau Brenhinol Iarll ac Iarlles Wessex, y tu allan i Eglwys Gadeiriol Llandaf.
The Archbishop of Wales, the Most Reverend John Davies, and the Dean of Llandaff, the Very Reverend Gerwyn Capon, with TRH The Earl and Countess of Wessex outside Llandaff Cathedral.

Yn 2018, roedd digwyddiadau coffa'r Rhyfel Byd Cyntaf yng Nghymru wedi troi eu sylw at nodi can mlynedd ers llofnodi Cadoediad Compiègne ar 11 Tachwedd 1918 a ddaeth â'r rhyfel athreuliol i ben. Achosodd y Rhyfel hwn laddfa na welwyd ei thebyg o'r blaen ar faes y gad yn Ewrop. Roedd Cymru yn rhan o hynny hefyd – lladdwyd bron 40,000 o Gymry ar faes y gad mewn ardaloedd cyn belled â Ffrynt y Gorllewin, Gallipoli, Gaza a hyd yn oed Tsingtao yn Tsieina.

Yng Nghymru, dechreuwyd y digwyddiad i goffáu'r canmlwyddiant drwy hoelio sylw ar goffáu a chofio yn ystod Gwasanaeth Sul y Cofio a gynhaliwyd ger Cofeb Ryfel Genedlaethol Cymru yng Nghaerdydd am 11am. Am 12:30pm ymunodd Cymru â gweddill y DU a gwledydd eraill i ganu clychau i nodi can mlynedd ers diwedd y Rhyfel.

Yn hwyrach yn y prynhawn, adlewyrchu a diolch oedd naws y digwyddiad gyda Gwasanaeth Cenedlaethol o Ddiolchgarwch yn cael ei gynnal yn Eglwys Gadeiriol Llandaf am 3pm. Ymunodd y Gwir Anrhydeddus Carwyn Jones AC, Prif Weinidog Cymru â'u Huchelderau Brenhinol Iarll ac Iarlles Wessex, a gwŷr pwysig eraill o Gymru yn y gwasanaeth. Yn ystod y gwasanaeth, traddodwyd yr anerchiad gan Archesgob Cymru, y Parchedicaf John Davies, a chlywodd y gynulleidfa darlleniadau gan Nia Hâf ac Ethan Williams o Urdd Gobaith Cymru a chan Mari Wyn Jones o Ysgol Maes Garmon, yr Wyddgrug.

Cymerodd Cymru ran ym mhrosiect *Tudalennau'r Môr* a arweiniwyd gan y cyfarwyddwr a'r cynhyrchydd o fri, Danny Boyle. Cynhaliwyd y digwyddiadau teimladwy hyn yn Ynyslas, Ceredigion; Bae Colwyn, yn y Gogledd; Freshwater West, Sir Benfro; ac Abertawe.

319 Gwirfoddolwyr yn creu portread yn y tywod fel rhan o brosiect *Tudalennau'r Môr* y cyfarwyddwr Danny Boyle.
Volunteers participating in director Danny Boyle's *Pages of the Sea* project by creating a sand portrait.

Wales's Commemoration of the Centenary of the Armistice

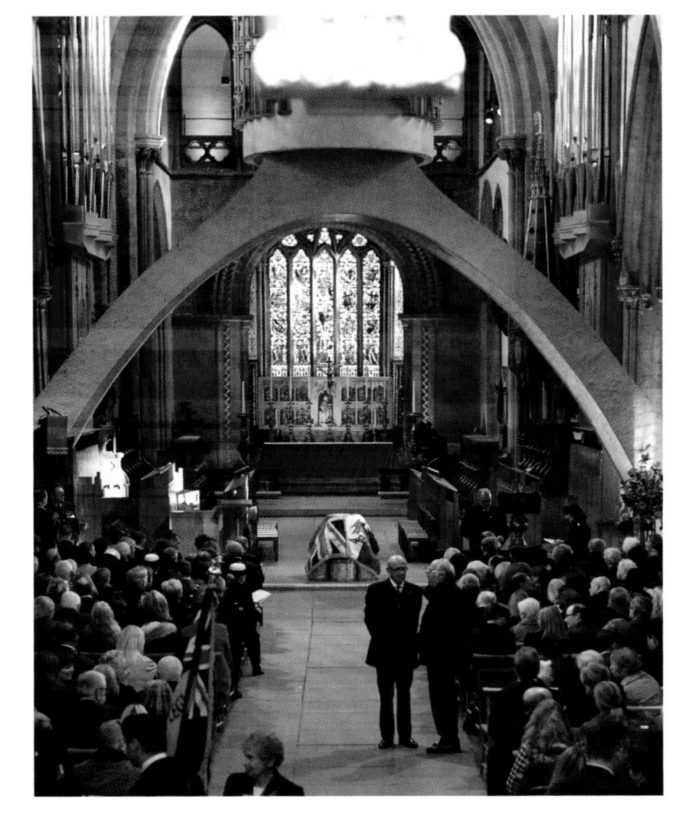

320 Gwesteion yn ymgynnull yn Eglwys Gadeiriol Llandaf ar 11 Tachwedd 2018.
Guests assembling at Llandaff Cathedral, 11 November 2018.

In 2018 the focus of Wales's First World War commemorations turned to the centenary of the signing of the Armistice of Compiègne on 11 November 1918, bringing to an end the attritional war that had resulted in unprecedented carnage on the battlefields of Europe. Wales was no exception – nearly 40,000 Welshmen had been killed on battlefields as far afield as the Western Front, Gallipoli, Gaza and even Tsingtao in China.

Wales's commemoration of the centenary of the signing of the Armistice began with a focus on commemoration and remembrance during the Remembrance Sunday service held at the Welsh

321 Y Gwir Anrhydeddus Carwyn Jones AC, Prif Weinidog Cymru, Eu Huchelderau Brenhinol Iarll ac Iarlles Wessex a gwahoddedigion pwysig eraill yn y gwasanaeth.
The Rt Hon. Carwyn Jones AM, First Minister of Wales, joined by TRH The Earl and Countess of Wessex and other dignitaries at the service.

322 Y Gwir Anrhydeddus Carwyn Jones AC, Prif Weinidog Cymru yn darllen darn o araith a wnaed gan y Prif Weinidog David Lloyd George.
The Rt Hon. Carwyn Jones AM, First Minister of Wales, reads an excerpt from a speech given by Prime Minister David Lloyd George.

National War Memorial in Cardiff at 11am. At 12.30pm Wales joined the rest of the UK and countries farther afield in the ringing of bells to mark the centenary of the end of the war.

Later in the afternoon the tone changed to one of reflection and thanksgiving, with the National Service of Thanksgiving taking place at Llandaff Cathedral at 3pm. The Rt Hon. Carwyn Jones AM, First Minister of Wales, was joined by TRH The Earl and Countess of Wessex, and Welsh dignitaries. During the service the Address was given by the Archbishop of Wales, the Most Reverend John Davies, and the congregation heard readings from Nia Hâf and Ethan Williams from Urdd Gobaith Cymru and Mari Wyn Jones from Ysgol Maes Garmon in Mold.

Wales also took part in the *Pages of the Sea* project led by the renowned director and producer Danny Boyle. These poignant events were held at Ynyslas, Ceredigion; Colwyn Bay, north Wales; Freshwater West, Pembrokeshire; and Swansea.

323 Portread ar draeth Ynyslas o Richard Davies, morwr yn Llynges Frenhinol y Rhyfel Byd Cyntaf, o bentref y Borth gerllaw. Rhan o ddigwyddiadau *Tudalennau'r Môr* ar Ddydd y Cadoediad.
Giant sand portrait on Ynyslas beach of Richard Davies, a First World War Royal Navy sailor from nearby Borth village – created as part of the *Pages of the Sea* event on Armistice Day.

Centenary of the First Armistice

Of the 700,000 Scots who joined the armed forces, the estimated total of those who died in the First World War is between 100,000 and 148,000. The war subjected those at home to considerable suffering and grief – nearly every village, city and town in Scotland has a memorial displaying the names of their war dead.

On 11 November 2018, events took place all over Scotland to mark 100 years since the end of the First World War. In Edinburgh, a wreath laid by First Minister Nicola Sturgeon was one of over a hundred wreaths laid for servicemen and women at the Stone of Remembrance outside the City Chambers. Hundreds of people, including senior military, serving members of the forces, veterans and cadets, gathered on the Royal Mile. Military bands played as parades were formed ahead of the two-minute silence, marked by a gun fired from Edinburgh Castle.

At 4pm in Glasgow Cathedral, the Scotland Commemorative Service for the Centenary of the First Armistice took place. HRH The Princess Royal and Vice Admiral Sir Timothy Laurence were joined by First Minister Nicola Sturgeon and over 1,000 other guests in attendance, including military personnel,

324 Lord Provost Frank Ross and First Minister Nicola Sturgeon outside the City Chambers, Edinburgh, on the 100th anniversary of the signing of the Armistice.

325 J.J. Chalmers, narrator of the WW100 Scotland Commemorative Service for the Centenary of the First Armistice.

326 HRH The Princess Royal signing the visitors book at the conclusion of the service at Glasgow Cathedral.

327 The Revd Professor Norman Drummond, chair of WW100 Scotland, and Cara Lucas – the 'passing of the torch' to the next generation.

dignitaries and descendants of those who served in the war.

Featuring young people and representatives from the Commonwealth, and including First World War songs as well as traditional hymns, the service was broadcast live on BBC One Scotland. It reflected on four themes that evoked the mixed emotions felt at the Armistice 100 years before: sadness and relief (sadness for the loss of life, but relief that war was near an end); joy and victory (joy of returning home from war and for the sense of victory despite all the odds); seeds of change (life could never be the same again); and courage for the future (the need to hold on to values and to hope in uncertain times).

328 HRH The Princess Royal meets Gurjit Singh Lalli and Amy Hawthorn, both of whom participated in the service.

329 The cast of *Far, Far from Ypres*.

To mark the centenary of the First Armistice, Professor Norman Drummond, chair of WW100 Scotland and the Scottish Commemorations Panel, had composed a commemorative prayer. It was read at the service by three generations of a German/Scottish family, along with representatives from Canada, Australia and New Zealand.

In the run-up to the Armistice centenary commemorations, the critically acclaimed musical production, *Far, Far from Ypres* – based on words, songs and verse from the trenches – was performed in ten venues across Scotland. The final performance took place in the Usher Hall, Edinburgh, on the evening of 11 November 2018.

Far, Far from Ypres follows the war through the experiences of one young Scottish soldier, chronicling the transition from the excitement of joining-up to the realities of trench warfare, and to ultimate victory. A memorable and moving production, devised and produced by Ian McCalman, the show played to large audiences and standing ovations. The tour was a joint project between WW100 Scotland, Royal British Legion Scotland, Poppyscotland and the production company, and was supported by Creative Scotland and by CYBG (Clydesdale and Yorkshire Banking Group) among others. *Far, Far from Ypres* was subsequently awarded the BBC Alba Traditional Music Event of the Year Award.

Armistice Centenary Service at St Anne's Cathedral, Belfast

To mark the centenary of Armistice Day, a service of commemoration took place at St Anne's Cathedral in Belfast. It was led by the Dean of the Cathedral, Rt Revd Stephen Forde, and organised by the Northern Ireland First World War Centenary Committee.

The service was attended by HRH The Duke of York, representing HM The Queen. Also in attendance were Rt Hon. Karen Bradley MP, Secretary of State for Northern Ireland, Damien English TD, the Minister for Housing and Urban Development, as well as senior politicians, members of civil society, representatives of veterans groups and 600 guests drawn from across the island of Ireland.

The Cathedral choir sang a new piece especially composed for the centenary entitled 'Flower of Youth', and Belfast poet Michael Longley read his work 'Ceasefire'. The sermon was given by the Roman Catholic Archbishop of Armagh and Primate of All Ireland, Eamon Martin, who reflected on his journey of discovery about the First World War as well as its significance to all the people of Ireland.

The service culminated in a moment of reflection where the Memorial Books of the Dead, containing the names of all Irish men and women killed in the war, were laid at the altar. At a memorial to 2nd Lt Edmund de Wind, posthumous recipient of the Victoria Cross in 1918, his great-great nephew placed a candle.

330 Servicemen lining the steps of St Anne's Cathedral, Belfast, before the centenary service on 11 November 2018.

331 HRH The Duke of York giving a reading at the service in St Anne's Cathedral.

332 The commemorative service for the centenary of the Armistice at St Anne's Cathedral.

Pages of the Sea in Northern Ireland

On 11 November, tens of thousands of people took part in *Pages of the Sea*, created by filmmaker Danny Boyle. It was delivered in Northern Ireland and in County Donegal by the Nerve Centre and National Trust, in partnership with Big Telly Theatre Company, Stendhal Festival, UV Arts, Artlink and Live Music Now.

On Murlough Beach, near Dundrum, County Down, the portrait of Rifleman John McCance emerged from the sand at sunrise. John McCance was born in Dundrum, enlisted in Downpatrick and died at Passchendaele. Music was provided by Mourne Community Choir.

On Portstewart Strand in County Londonderry, Big Telly Theatre Company invited members of the public to help them create an artwork in the sand using stencils of portraits. The day finished on Downhill Beach with a large 30-metre square portrait of First World War nurse, Rachel Ferguson. She died on 26 June 1918 at Bordighera, Italy, whilst working for Queen Alexandra's Imperial Military Nursing Service. Members of the public had a spectacular view of the portrait from Mussenden Temple and Downhill Demesne, with Stendhal Festival and Live Music Now providing music.

333 Sand portrait of Rifleman John McCance at Murlough Beach.

334 A costumed First World War nurse looking down at the sand portrait of nurse Rachel Ferguson at Downhill, County Londonderry.

RAF100 in Northern Ireland

On 29 April 2018, an evening service of celebration and thanksgiving was held at St Anne's Cathedral, Belfast, to commemorate the centenary of the Royal Air Force (RAF). At this unique event, the RAF's Chief of the Air Staff, Air Chief Marshal Sir Stephen Hillier, was joined by his counterpart from the Irish Air Corps, Brigadier General Sean Clancy. Both air forces have their roots in the Royal Flying Corps and the early days of the Royal Air Force. In 1922, when the Irish Army Air Corps was established, the original 15 pilots had all flown in the First World War, serving in the Royal Flying Corps. Combining with the Royal Naval Air Service, the Royal Flying Corps became the Royal Air Force in April 1918. The Irish contribution to the early development of the RAF dates from before the First World War.

The centenary service at St Anne's Cathedral recognised these historic links between the formation of the RAF and the Irish Air Corps. In his words of welcome, the Dean of Belfast, the Very Revd Stephen Forde, said that the presence of both Air Chief Marshal Sir Stephen Hillier and Brigadier General Sean Clancy was particularly significant 'because those pioneer

335 Air Chief Marshal Sir Stephen Hillier, left, and Irish Air Corps Brigadier General Sean Clancy, right, outside St Anne's Cathedral in Belfast.

336 Air Chief Marshal Sir Stephen Hillier laying a wreath at an altar in St Anne's Cathedral commemorating all those, from the very earliest days of flight, who lost their lives in war.

337 *RAF100 Mural*, on the Donegall Road, Belfast.

aviators of the RAF in the final months of the First World War included those drawn from across the whole island of Ireland'.

Leading political and civic figures from Northern Ireland attended the service, including Parliamentary Under-Secretary of State Shailesh Vara MP and Lord-Lieutenant of Belfast Mrs Fionnuala Jay-O'Boyle. Veterans and relatives of those who fought in both world wars also attended, including Robin Murray Brown, great-grandson of William Robert Gregory. In 1916, as a fighter pilot with 40 Squadron Royal Flying Corps, Gregory was credited with eight victories and became one of the first Irish pilots to achieve the status of wartime ace. He was awarded the Military Cross for gallantry and also became a Chevalier of the Legion d'Honneur (the highest French order of merit). He died aged 36 when his plane came down over Italy in January 1918. At the service, Robin Murray Brown read the poignant W.B. Yeats poem, 'An Irish Airman Foresees His Death', which was written by the poet in 1918 in honour of Gregory.

The centenary service was part of a wider programme of RAF100 events in Northern Ireland, including the launch of a major artwork. The *RAF100 Mural* focuses on the aircraft that were built locally under licence during the First World War, and the pilots from throughout the island of Ireland who flew for the Royal Flying Corps and its successor, the Royal Air Force. Occupying a huge rear wall of the City Hospital on Belfast's Donegall Road, the wall art project was facilitated by Pete Bleakley and the Shared History Workshop, along with the Greater Village Regeneration Trust and Archer Advertising Limited. The mural was unveiled by Northern Ireland's most senior RAF officer – Air Vice-Marshal David Niven CB CBE – on 25 August 2018.

IWM: *Making a New World*

From July 2018 to March 2019, IWM marked the end of the First World War centenary with *Making a New World*. This season of five major exhibitions, alongside an innovative programme of immersive events, performances and public debates, set out to discover how the First World War has shaped today's society.

338 Commissioned by the British War Memorial Committee to document the war, John Singer Sargent went to the Western Front in 1918. His painting *Gassed*, showing a line of wounded soldiers walking towards a dressing station, was completed in March 1919.

339 John Akomfrah's *Mimesis: African Soldier* combines archival sources with newly filmed material, artistic reflections and tableaux reconstructions to reveal how the First World War affected the history of Africa and its inhabitants.

Opening the season, *Lest We Forget?* at IWM North explored how commemoration of the First World War has endured for a century – from a national monument made permanent by popular demand to poppies sewn into football shirts. Exhibition highlights included John Singer Sargent's iconic painting *Gassed*, back in the UK after a two-year international tour, and an original Joey puppet from the National Theatre production of *War Horse*.

Four exhibitions spanning photography, film and sound opened at IWM London in September. *Mimesis:*

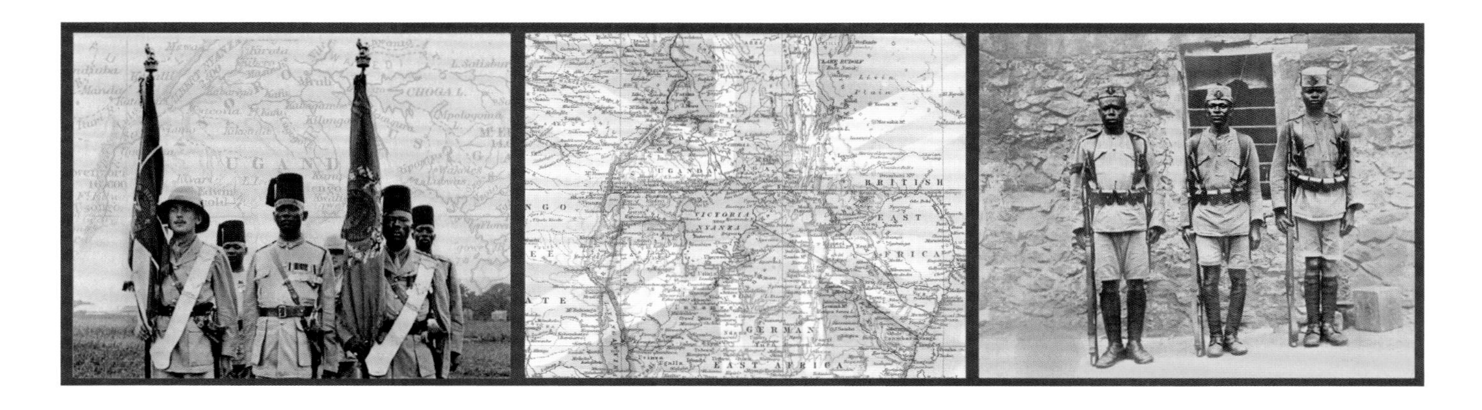

340 Celebrating the Armistice in Birmingham, this image was one of over 130 photographs exploring the impact of the war in *Renewal: Life After the First World War in Photographs*.

341 In its exploration of remembrance, *Moments of Silence*, created by 59 Productions, includes two-minute silences from the depths of the ocean to the heights of Everest.

African Soldier, a new multi-screen installation by artist John Akomfrah, remembered the millions of African men and women who served in the First World War. *Renewal: Life After the First World War in Photographs* highlighted the ways in which lives, landscapes and national identities evolved in the aftermath of war through a display of over 130 black-and-white photographs. Two immersive installations, *Moments of Silence* and *I Was There: Room of Voices*, brought together personal testimonies reflecting on the Armistice and how we choose to remember.

A series of live events complemented the exhibition programme, with highlights including *Contagion*, a new dance piece exploring viral infection and the Spanish flu performed by Shobana Jeyasingh Dance at IWM North, and a performance at IWM London by Frantic Assembly's 2018 Ignition Company, made up of young men aged 16–20. The IWM Remembrance Lecture at IWM London – 'Why are we silent when conflict is loud?' – brought together a panel of artists, historians and psychologists to challenge and discuss the role that organised silences play in 21st-century remembrance. IWM's annual Short Film Festival included a *Making a New World* award category, inviting filmmakers from around the world to respond to themes explored in the season.

Alongside *Making a New World*, the iconic poppy sculptures Poppies: *Wave* and Poppies: *Weeping Window*, by artist Paul Cummins and designer Tom Piper, were presented at IWM on the final stage of their 14–18 NOW UK-wide tour. Poppies: *Wave* was at IWM North and Poppies: *Weeping Window* was at IWM London. The sculptures became part of IWM's permanent collection at the end of the UK tour.

First World War Memorials Programme

During the course of the centenary, Historic England, with its partners Civic Voice, IWM and War Memorials Trust, worked with communities and schools throughout the UK to ensure that war memorials across the country are cared for and protected. Over £2 million in grant funding was distributed to over 400 memorials across Britain to ensure that they remain standing in the best possible condition in remembrance of those who paid the ultimate sacrifice. Many of these grants were small, such as the £150 awarded to Balsham war memorial in Cambridgeshire for mortar repairs. Yet the funding also allowed large, complex memorial structures to be cared for. The Isle of Lewis Memorial was awarded over £130,000 for structural repairs. Memorials come in many forms, and many of the nation's more unusual memorials received funding, including bells, clocks and stained-glass windows.

Over 2,500 war memorials were newly listed or upgraded on the National Heritage List for England. This not only protects them from insensitive changes, to both their structure and surroundings, but it recognises the crucial role of memorials as part of our

342 The largest grant of the First World War Memorials Programme (over £132,000) was awarded to the Isle of Lewis Memorial outside Stornoway. The tower commemorates the 1,151 lives lost from the island during the First World War.

343 In the village church at Berkeley, Gloucestershire, the treble and second bells were provided by the Gloucester and Bristol Diocesan Association of Change Ringers in memory of those who lost their lives in the First World War. A repair grant of £16,500 was awarded.

344 This unusual memorial, to Captain Eric Lubbock who was shot down over Belgium in 1917, was newly listed at Grade II in 2018 to commemorate the centenary of the formation of the RAF.

345 St Peter's Church war memorial, Cheltenham, undergoing cleaning and conservation work. Technical support from conservation professionals, and the dedication of local communities and memorial custodians, ensure that memorials stand for many years to come.

First World War heritage. Some listings were carried out in commemoration of significant events during the war, including the 14 war memorials dedicated to airmen which were newly listed and upgraded in April 2018 to mark the centenary of the Royal Air Force.

The vast majority of memorials that were protected were small local memorials, some of which were put forward as candidates by members of the towns and villages themselves. This community support for memorials echoes the collective efforts that went into their construction over 100 years ago, when communities came together to find ways to honour the dead and to help make sense of their loss. Such community support, along with the technical support of professional bodies, will ensure that the nation's war memorials continue to stand for the next 100 years.

14–18 NOW: 2018 Season

The final season of 14–18 NOW's programme was experienced by 35 million people. It culminated on Armistice Day, which marked the end of the war 100 years before.

Throughout the year, and in the lead-up to Armistice, a number of other significant centenaries provided the inspiration for artists and arts projects. On 6 February 1918, the Representation of the People Act gave the first British women the right to vote, a landmark for women's equality and British democracy. One hundred years later, tens of thousands of women processed through the streets of Belfast, Cardiff, Edinburgh and London, wearing green, white and violet scarves (the colours of the suffragettes) and carrying handmade banners in the mass-participation artwork *PROCESSIONS*, produced by arts organisation Artichoke.

Women's changing roles were also celebrated with the first ever sculpture of a woman in Parliament Square – that of suffragist leader and social campaigner Millicent Fawcett, created by Gillian Wearing. At Yorkshire Sculpture Park, Katrina Palmer presented *The Coffin Jump*, a piece inspired by the work of the all-female First Aid Nursing Yeomanry, who rescued wounded men directly from the battlefields.

By the end of the First World War over 100

346 An aerial view of *PROCESSIONS* in London, showing the ribbon of colour formed by the participants.

347 Peter Jackson's extraordinary film *They Shall Not Grow Old* used state-of-the-art technology to bring the experiences of the First World War to life.

348 *The Head and the Load*, by William Kentridge, told the story of the millions of African porters and carriers who were involved in the First World War.

countries were involved in the conflict, and 14–18 NOW's 2018 season sought to bring attention to wartime stories from around the world that had often gone unheard. In a blend of Indian classical dance with contemporary choreography, Akram Khan's *XENOS* told the tale of an Indian colonial soldier in the first modern conflict. Artist William Kentridge created an epic stage performance, *The Head and the Load*, to tell the story of the millions of African porters and carriers who were involved in the war, a subject that was also explored by John Akomfrah's film installation *Mimesis: African Soldier*. Numerous other commissions, such as Suzanne Lacy's *Across and In-Between*, Raqs Media Collective's *Not Yet at Ease* and *SS Mendi Dancing the Death Drill* by Isango Ensemble, also explored the global and human impact of the world at war.

Celebrated film director Peter Jackson created *They Shall Not Grow Old*, using original footage from the Imperial War Museums' film archive. Jackson's astonishing new movie, colourised and transformed with modern production techniques, presented contemporary viewers with a new perspective on the human realities of the conflict.

The season concluded with *Pages of the Sea* on Armistice Day – in which filmmaker Danny Boyle invited thousands of people to gather on beaches around the UK to say a personal thank you to the millions of men and women around the world who left their home shores, many never to return.

14–18 NOW: Poppies Tour 2018

The final year of the tour began with Poppies: *Weeping Window* at Hereford Cathedral. Young men recruited into the Herefordshire Regiment landed in Gallipoli in August 1915 before being transferred to the Western Front. Carlisle Castle in Cumbria, the headquarters of the King's Own Royal Border Regiment from 1873 to 1959, was next to host Poppies: *Weeping Window*, where the poppies flowed in a dramatic arch from the top of the castle's keep. It then travelled to Middleport Pottery in Stoke-on-Trent – the city had provided the clay from which the poppies were created.

349 Hereford Cathedral was the first location for Poppies: *Weeping Window* in 2018. In the war Herefordshire produced munitions and supplied horses and food to the front.

350 Poppies: *Weeping Window* at Carlisle Castle. A total of 23,000 recruits passed through the castle during the First World War. It also served as an HQ for the Volunteer Training Corps, and provided accommodation for the Labour Corps.

351 Close-up of Poppies: *Weeping Window* pouring down the exterior of the bottle-shaped kiln at Middleport Pottery in Stoke-on-Trent.

352 Poppies: *Weeping Window* at the Royal Armouries Museum at Fort Nelson, Hampshire, one of a large ring of forts built to defend the naval base of Portsmouth.

353 Dramatically cascading down the 19th-century portico, Poppies: *Weeping Window* concluded its four-year tour at IWM London.

Wave was presented at the Royal Armouries Museum at Fort Nelson in Hampshire, which housed part of Herbert Kitchener's volunteer army during the war.

The tour concluded in the autumn with the simultaneous presentation of Poppies: *Weeping Window* at IWM London and Poppies: *Wave* at IWM North, after which the works became part of the Imperial War Museums collection.

354 Poppies: *Wave* swept over Daniel Libeskind's iconic IWM North building in its final presentation of the tour.

Wilfred Owen Festival, Oswestry

355 Bronze sculpture of Wilfred Owen, Oswestry.

This festival of commemoration and remembrance ran from 15 September to 17 November 2018, to coincide with the centenary of the death of war poet Wilfred Owen, who was killed in action a week before the Armistice. The festival was a fitting tribute to Owen in the town of his birth, and to all those who lost their lives in the war. A wide range of events and performances took place, including poetry, drama, music, lectures, re-enactment, films, an artist's trail, exhibitions and more.

Designed by sculptor Tim Turner, a life-size bronze statue of Wilfred Owen was unveiled on the morning of 20 October. Commissioned by Oswestry Town Council, it stands in Cae Glas Park and is adorned with the words of Owen, handwritten by local primary schoolchildren, along with five original poems, contributed by pupils from local schools.

Royal Parks and Royal Parks Guild Partnership

Research by the Royal Parks Guild during its centenary programme revealed a wealth of information about how government authorities used the London parks to aid the war effort. Regent's Park was the location of the Home Depot. This huge wooden building covered four acres, and was subsequently extended to just over five. Every single item of post sent to members of the British Army from across the UK went through the Home Depot. It was sorted by thousands of postal workers, mostly women. By 1918, 12 million items were being handled every week.

In May 2018, a pop-up mail-sorting office was set up as an immersive experience to evoke the stories of the 2,500 people who worked at the Home Depot. Visitors could even work a shift, as part of an interactive session led by the Postal Museum. Activities, talks and exhibitions demonstrated the vital, and often very personal, role of the Home Depot during wartime Britain.

356 Talks and activities as part of the postal immersive experience in May 2018 paid homage to the thousands of workers at the Home Depot.

The Tank Museum: *Victoria Cross Exhibition*

Four Victoria Crosses were awarded to members of the Tank Corps in the First World War. All four medals were brought together, for the first time ever, in this remarkable exhibition at The Tank Museum. The museum owned the VC awarded to Cecil Sewell; Lord Ashcroft loaned the VC awarded to Richard West; the family of Richard Wain loaned his VC; and the VC awarded to Clement Robertson was secured through an appeal.

At Passchendale, Tank Corps officer Clement Robertson spent three days in no-man's-land, under heavy fire, marking out routes for his tanks to follow for an advance on 4 October 1917. Despite his marked routes, on the day he worried the tanks might lose their way and get bogged down – and so he led them on foot. Refusing to take cover he was shot and killed, but his self-sacrifice led to a successful attack.

On 20 November 1917, at the Battle of Cambrai, Captain Richard Wain was seriously injured when his tank was hit, but shunned a stretcher, climbed out with a Lewis gun and attacked the enemy. Capturing a strong point, taking prisoners and allowing the infantry to advance, he continued shooting at the retreating Germans until he received a fatal shot to the head.

Cecil Sewell was awarded his VC for two linked actions on 29 August 1918. After seeing one of his fellow Whippet tanks fall into a shell-hole and catch fire, he leapt from his own tank and dug the mud away so the men could escape. He then saw that his own tank driver was wounded and rushed to help. As he ran across open ground he was shot several times. Administering first aid he was shot again, fatally.

Richard West was an experienced soldier when the war started. His VC was awarded for two actions in 1918. The first was leading men to their objective after having two horses shot from beneath him. The second was on 2 September when, as a Lieutenant-Colonel attached to the Tank Corps and in command of the 6th Light Battalion and their Whippet tanks, he feared a retreat from his infantry due to an enemy counter-attack. He rode on horseback up and down the line, encouraging them to fight and defend their position. He was shot and killed, but his words and actions inspired the men and the attack was defeated.

357 Relatives of the four VC recipients attend the exhibition opening. Left to right: Ian Robertson (Clement Robertson), Peter Harbinson (Richard Wain), Wendy Shaw (Cecil Sewell) and Kitty Morris (Richard West).

London Transport Museum

Of the nearly 3,000 B-type buses built, only four remain. All four buses were bought to the London Transport Museum for a day to mark the end of the war. B340, owned by the museum, carried wounded troops in London during the war, and was the first bus set aside for preservation. B2737 was restored to commemorate the buses and transport workers' sacrifice, while B1609 was recently restored in its London service livery. B43 became a mobile war memorial in 1920, and was presented to the Imperial War Museum in 1977.

The learning project focused on commemoration, with volunteers of all ages working together. Uncovering stories of wartime transport workers, their research formed an exhibition in October 2018. In a fitting final tribute, Battle Bus and B340 participated in the Nation's Thank You in Westminster on Armistice Day 2018.

358 The last four surviving B-type buses outside the London Transport Museum, Covent Garden.

National Army Museum

For the final year of the First World War centenary, the National Army Museum presented *Alfred Munnings: War Artist, 1918*, developed by the Canadian War Museum (Ottawa) in partnership with the Munnings Art Museum (Dedham, UK). Munnings' wartime art had not been seen in the UK in its entirety since 1919.

The Canadian War Memorials Fund commissioned Munnings as an official war artist in 1918. His first work was a portrait of General Jack Seely, commander of the Canadian Cavalry Brigade, on his horse Warrior. Over 40 paintings by Munnings were shown at the exhibition, along with items relating to General Seely.

359 Alfred Munnings, *Major-General The Right Honourable J.E.B. Seely*, 1918.

Centenary of the Zeebrugge Raid

The centenary of the Zeebrugge Raid was marked on both sides of the Channel. At the daring raid on 23 April 1918, two British blockships were scuttled in the Bruges Canal, to block German U-boats leaving the port, while a submarine rammed the viaduct to the harbour. The British suffered 583 casualties, the Germans 24. Just a few days later, the Germans had re-opened the canal. Although the raid failed, the participants' bravery was hailed by the Admiralty and eight VCs were awarded.

On 21 April 2018, HRH The Princess Royal, Vice Admiral Timothy Laurence and other dignitaries from Britain, Germany and Belgium attended a commemoration in Zeebrugge. At Blankenberge Cemetery a memorial was dedicated to Lt Cdr George Bradford, VC. The day closed with a concert by a combined British-Belgian-German military band.

360 HRH Princess Anne and a representative of the German president laying wreaths at the St Georges Day Monument, Zeebrugge.

361 A member of HMS *Somerset*'s guard at the dedication ceremony, Blankenberge Cemetery.

362 Memorial to Lt Cdr George Bradford, VC, at Blankenberge Cemetery, who jumped into the line of fire to secure his storming party's boat at Zeebrugge harbour.

At St James's Cemetery, Dover, where a mass funeral of participants had taken place a century earlier, a service of remembrance on 23 April included wreath-laying by a German naval representative and counterparts from Belgium, Australia and New Zealand. After a military parade, the Mayor of Dover struck the Zeebrugge Bell, which is rung annually at noon on the anniversary of the Zeebrugge Raid. At Wirral, Merseyside, a wreath-laying service on the Mersey and a centenary service at the Zeebrugge Memorial Stone at the Seacombe Ferry Terminal were followed by a parade along Wirral's promenade by HM The Royal Marines. In the 1918 raid, Mersey ferries were used to carry large numbers of servicemen in the shallow waters at Zeebrugge.

War Horse, National Theatre

363 Silk poppies falling during the special commemorative performance on 11 November 2018.

In November 2018 *War Horse* returned to the National Theatre for the first time in 11 years to mark the centenary of Armistice Day. On Sunday 11 November, a special commemorative performance in the Lyttelton Theatre was introduced by *War Horse* author Michael Morpurgo.

The performance included a specially staged moment of remembrance performed by the acting company, with bells rung across the auditorium to mark the moment when, on 11 November 1918, the guns fell silent. Silk poppy petals fell from the lighting rig as the bells rang, and the cast were joined by more than 800 audience members in observance of a tribute to the human and animal lives lost during the First World War. The audience included veterans and servicemen and women.

The day ended with a projection on the theatre's fly tower – a sketch of blood red poppies designed by the production's designer, Rae Smith.

Commemoration of the Chinese Labour Corps

364 Students from local schools take part in a service commemorating six CLC labourers buried in Shorncliffe Military Cemetery, with the Royal Gurkha Rifles from Shorncliffe Station in attendance.

365 A child learning Chinese calligraphy at a workshop in Folkestone.

As part of the First World War centenary, Chinese cultural heritage group the Meridian Society highlighted the role of the Chinese Labour Corps (CLC) in the war. To provide essential logistical support in Europe, 96,000 men were recruited by Britain. They worked 10-hour days building roads and docks, assembling equipment and digging trenches. When the war on the Western Front was over, the CLC were made to stay on to clear mines, bury the dead and restore battle-scarred fields to agricultural land. It was not until 1920 that most of them returned home. At least two thousand had died from shellfire or disease.

The Meridian Society worked closely with key commemorative organisations – such as the Commonwealth War Graves Commission, the Western Front Association, the Royal British Legion, the Imperial War Museum, the National Archives and the Heritage Lottery Fund – to create a virtual memorial in honour of the CLC. The CLC travelled to France in 1917, mostly via Canada and England. Some never made it; over a dozen lie buried in Liverpool, Plymouth and Folkestone. In 2018, commemoration services took place in these three cities, as well as workshops with schools and communities, and a touring exhibition of photographs, documents and artefacts. As a result of this work, a series of dedicated webpages on the Meridian Society website was launched, creating an educational resource and a lasting memorial to the CLC.

2014–18
PROGRAMMES

Centenary Planning: Scotland

The Scottish Commemorations Panel was appointed by the Scottish government to recommend a programme of events to commemorate the centenary of the First World War. The 12-strong panel consisted of experts from the military and veterans communities, community leaders, clergy, media, historians and education specialists.

From marking the impact on Scottish communities of major battles such as Jutland and the Somme, to discovering less well-known stories about the people affected by the conflict, WW100 Scotland set out to inform people about Scotland's unique contribution to the First World War. The commemorations were a chance to remember the sacrifices made and to reflect on what we can, and should, learn from the war which was meant to end all wars.

The three main aims of WW100 Scotland were Education, Genealogy and Legacy – each theme helping people to discover the effects of the war on their local communities, and its lasting impact on life in Scotland today.

As part of the Education Programme the voices of many across Scotland – from professors to poets, from children to councillors, from servicemen and women to those faithfully serving the community in other ways – were recorded as a broadcast archive, for the use of those teaching History and Modern Studies in schools and colleges across Scotland, as well as for research purposes in the future.

At 1.48am on New Year's Day 2019, a gathered invited party kept vigil on shore at the Iolaire Memorial above the Beasts of Holm, marking 100 years to the moment since HMY *Iolaire* went aground. Out of a ship's company of 280 returning home after the war, 201 servicemen were lost. Later that day, at 12 noon, there was a short commemorative service at the memorial, attended by hundreds from across the Western Isles and beyond, reflecting the international diaspora of the descendants.

The centenary programme concluded in 2019 with a WW100 Scotland exhibition exploring the wide-ranging achivements of the programme. All 32 local authorities across Scotland were invited to provide a sample of their First World War commemorative activity, with artefacts and human interest stories very much to the fore.

366 On 30 June 2016 an overnight vigil was held at the National War Memorial in Edinburgh to mark the centenary of the Battle of the Somme.

367 The memorial to HMY *Iolaire*, above the Beasts of Holm near Stornoway on the Isle of Lewis, was restored for the 2019 centenary of the tragic sinking of the ship.

368 Unveiled on the morning of 1 January 2019, this newly commissioned sculpture to commemorate the loss of HMY *Iolaire* features a coiled 'heaving line', a rope used to rescue sailors.

Adolygiad o Ddigwyddiadau'r Canmlwyddiant: Cymru

DAVID LLOYD GEORGE

We shall descend into the valleys again; but as long as the men and women of this generation last, they will carry in their hearts the image of those mighty peaks whose foundations are not shaken, though Europe rock and sway in the convulsions of a great war.

—araith David Lloyd George yn Queen's Hall, Westminster, Llundain, ar 19 Medi 1914 i gefnogi'r ymgyrch recriwtio.

—David Lloyd George (Queen's Hall Speech to the London Welsh in support of the recruiting campaign, Westminster, 19 September 1914)

369 Cartŵn gan J M Staniforth o'i gymeriad enwog Mam Cymru. Yn 'Equal to the Occasion' mae Mam Cymru, fel perchennog y siop, yn derbyn archeb gan Lloyd George am 40,000 o filwyr Cymreig.
Cartoon by J.M. Staniforth with his famous character Dame Wales (Mam Cymru). In 'Equal to the Occasion', Dame Wales in the role of a shop owner takes an order from Lloyd George for 40,000 Welsh soldiers.

Cafodd y Rhyfel Byd Cyntaf ddylanwad dwys ar Gymru. Effeithiodd colled yn agos at 40,000 o ddynion ar bron pob cymuned, gyda chanlyniadau pellgyrhaeddol. Er hynny, bu i'r rhyfel hefyd sbarduno newidiadau mawr yn y gymdeithas, yr economi a gwleidyddiaeth, a cyflymodd y newidiadau hynny yn ystod y degawdau dilynol.

Pwrpas rhaglen fframwaith coffa Cymru, Cymru'n Cofio Wales Remembers 1914–1918, oedd meithrin gwell dealltwriaeth o'r rhyfel ymysg pobl o bob oedran a chefndir. Mae'r enghreifftiau a ganlyn yn rhoi blas o'r digwyddiadau coffa a gynhaliwyd yng Nghymru a thu hwnt.

370 Cymru'n Cofio Wales Remembers 1914–1918, y Rhaglen Fframwaith ar gyfer coffáu'r Rhyfel Byd Cyntaf yng Nghymru. Cymru'n Cofio Wales Remembers 1914–1918, the Framework Programme for the commemoration of the First World War in Wales.

Ar 4 Awst 2014, fe wnaeth Cymru a gweddill y Deyrnas Unedig goffáu dechrau'r Rhyfel Byd Cyntaf. Ymunodd y Prif Weinidog â Eu Mawrhydi'r Dug a Duges Caerloyw ac Archesgob Cymru bryd hynny, Dr Barry Morgan, mewn gwylnos yng ngolau canhwyllau yn Eglwys Gadeiriol Llandaf.

Gwae fi fy myw mewn oes mor ddreng,
A Duw ar drai ar orwel pell;
O'i ôl mae dyn, yn deyrn a gwreng,
Yn codi ei awdurdod hell.

Why must I live in this grim age
When, to a far horizon, God
Has ebbed away, and man, with rage
Now wields the sceptre and the rod?

Dyma eiriau Hedd Wyn, efallai bardd rhyfel gorau Cymru, a laddwyd yn Pilckem Ridge, Passchendaele, ar 31 Gorffennaf 1917. Bu farw dim ond chwe wythnos cyn ennill y wobr uchaf i fardd o Gymru sef Cadair yr Eisteddfod Genedlaethol. Â lliain du drosti, daeth y Gadair Ddu, fel y'i henwyd o'r amser hynny ymlaen, yn symbol o'r miloedd o gadeiriau gwag mewn cartrefi ledled y wlad a'r genhedlaeth o ddynion ifanc a fu farw.

Prynwyd cartref Hedd Wyn, yr Ysgwrn, yn 2012 gan Awdurdod Parc Cenedlaethol Eryri â chymorth ariannol gan Gronfa Goffa'r Dreftadaeth Genedlaethol a Llywodraeth Cymru. Defnyddiwyd grantiau ychwanegol wedyn i'w ailddatblygu fel canolfan dreftadaeth. Fe'i hail-agorwyd i'r cyhoedd yn 2017.

Yn 2013, defnyddiwyd technegau argraffu 3D arloesol i greu copi o'r Gadair Ddu. Cafwyd cymorth ariannol gan Lywodraeth Cymru a chymorth technegol gan ei phartneriaid.

Drwy gydol y canmlwyddiant, trefnwyd rhaglen arloesol o arddangosfeydd, digwyddiadau, darlithoedd a gweithgareddau i bobl ifanc gan Lyfrgell Genedlaethol Cymru ac Amgueddfa Genedlaethol

371 Yr Ysgwrn, cartref teuluol y bardd Rhyfel Byd Cyntaf Hedd Wyn, a ail-agorwyd fel canolfan dreftadaeth yn 2017.
Yr Ysgwrn, the ancestral home of Welsh First World War poet Hedd Wyn, which was reopened as a heritage centre in 2017.

Cymru. Roedd y rhaglen yn cynnwys arddangosfa'r Llyfrgell: *Lloyd George: y Dewin, yr Afr a'r Dyn enillodd y Rhyfel* ac arddangosfa'r Amgueddfa: *Ymdrechion a Delfrydau: Printiau'r Rhyfel Byd Cyntaf.* Yn ogystal, buont yn cydweithio i ddatblygu adnoddau addysgol fel rhan o Brosiect Addysg y Rhyfel Byd Cyntaf, â chymorth ariannol gan Lywodraeth Cymru.

Rhoddodd Adran Addysg a Sgiliau Llywodraeth Cymru grantiau hyd at £1,000 i bob ysgol uwchradd yng Nghymru ymgymryd â gweithgareddau coffa i nodi'r canmlwyddiant. Mae'r myfyrwyr wedi cynnal amrywiaeth o brosiectau diddorol, gan gynnwys trefnu arddangosfeydd, peintio murluniau, ymweld â meysydd brwydr, ac ymchwilio i storïau milwyr lleol. Cewch weld y rhain ar wefan Cymru'n Cofio: http://www.cymruncofio.org/projects/

Cafodd y prosiect Cymru dros Heddwch ei reoli gan Ganolfan Materion Rhyngwladol Cymru a'i ariannu gan Gronfa Dreftadaeth y Loteri. Fe ddaeth â chymunedau ac ysgolion ledled Cymru at ei gilydd i ddysgu am y bobl, y mudiadau a'r straeon sydd wedi helpu i lywio hunaniaeth Gymreig.

Bob blwyddyn, cynhaliwyd nifer o ddigwyddiadau arbennig; ceir detholiad eu cynnwys yma. Yn 2014, trefnodd Amgueddfa'r Ffiwsilwyr Brenhinol Cymreig a'i phartneriaid yn yr Almaen, Gwlad Belg a Ffrainc ddigwyddiad yn Frelighien ac arddangosfa i nodi canmlwyddiant Cadoediad y Nadolig yn 1914. Drwy eiddo personol a storïau milwyr, roedd yr arddangosfa'n myfyrio ar effaith ddynol y rhyfel. Teithiodd yr arddangosfa i wledydd y partneriaid ac i wahanol rannau o Gymru.

Yn 2015, datblygodd Amgueddfa'r Ffiwsilwyr Brenhinol Cymreig, ar ôl ymgynghori â'r gymuned Dwrcaidd, arddangosfa deithiol ar rôl yr 53ain Is-adran (Gymreig) yn Ymgyrch Gallipoli. Datblygodd yr Amgueddfa adnoddau addysgol, arddangosfa ar-lein a llyfryn coffa. Teithiodd yr arddangosfa i chwe lleoliad yng Nghymru sydd â chysylltiadau â dynion a gymerodd ran yn y frwydr yn Gallipoli.

Yn 2017, cydweithiodd Llywodraeth Cymru â Llywodraeth Fflandrys, Llenyddiaeth Cymru a phartneriaid yn Iwerddon i drefnu cyfres o ddigwyddiadau llenyddol i goffáu canmlwyddiant marwolaeth Hedd Wyn. Cynhaliwyd *Barddoniaeth Colled* ym Mrwsel a fu'n canolbwyntio ar waith Hedd Wyn, gwaith y bardd Gwyddelig Francis Ledwidge (a laddwyd hefyd yn Pilckem Ridge ar 31 Gorffennaf 1917), ac ar farddoniaeth Fflemaidd y Rhyfel Byd Cyntaf. Roedd digwyddiadau eraill yn cynnwys cyfnodau i

372 Poster Cynllun Addysg Y Rhyfel Byd Cyntaf 1914-1918.
Poster of the First World War Education Project 1914–1918.

lenorion weithio yng Ngwlad Belg a Chymru, gweithdai barddoniaeth yn Nulyn dan arweiniad Ifor ap Glyn, Bardd Cenedlaethol Cymru, ac uwchgynhadledd yng Nghaerdydd o'r enw *Fflandrys a Chymru: y Rhyfel Byd Cyntaf*. Ar 9 Tachwedd, cynhaliwyd digwyddiad yn y Senedd lle cyfnewidiwyd anrhegion gan bobl Cymru a Fflandrys rhwng Llywydd Cynulliad Cenedlaethol Cymru a Llefarydd Senedd Fflandrys i goffau'r hanes a rennir o'r Rhyfel Byd Cyntaf.

Mae'r blynyddoedd o goffáu wedi dangos diddordeb dwfn yn nigwyddiadau'r Rhyfel Byd Cyntaf a'r effaith a gafodd ar y wlad. Trwy gydol cyfnod y coffáu mae gweithgareddau a digwyddiadau wedi eu cynnal ledled Cymru, ar lefel leol a chenedlaethol. Mae gwaddol digidol ac addysgol yn cael ei sefydlu i sicrhau fod cenedlaethau'r dyfodol yn medru dysgu mwy am y rhyfel dychrynllyd hwn, a sut y cofiodd Cymru.

373 Disgyblion Ysgol Uwchradd Fitzalan, Caerdydd yn cyfarfod â pherfformiwr ail-greu mewn ffos replica o'r Rhyfel Byd Cyntaf a wnaethant helpu i'w ddylunio a'i adeiladu.
Pupils at Fitzalan High School, Cardiff, meeting a re-enactor in a replica First World War trench that they had helped to design and build.

Review of Centenary Events: Wales

The First World War had a profound impact on Wales. The loss of almost 40,000 men affected nearly every community, with long-term consequences. The war also stimulated major changes in society, the economy and politics, which accelerated in the decades ahead.

Wales's commemorative framework programme, Cymru'n Cofio Wales Remembers 1914–1918, was designed to foster a better understanding of the war among people of all ages and backgrounds. The following gives a flavour of the commemorative events held in Wales and beyond.

On 4 August 2014, Wales and the rest of the UK commemorated the start of the First World War. The First Minister joined TRH The Duke and Duchess of Gloucester and the Archbishop of Wales, Dr Barry Morgan, at a candlelit vigil in Llandaff Cathedral.

374 Cynnau cannwyll yn ystod yr wylnos i nodi canmlwyddiant dechrau'r Rhyfel Byd Cyntaf yn Eglwys Gadeiriol Llandaf ar 4 Awst 2014.
The lighting of a candle during the candlelit vigil to mark the centenary of the start of the First World War, Llandaff Cathedral, 4 August 2014.

Gwae fi fy myw mewn oes mor ddreng,
A Duw ar drai ar orwel pell;
O'i ôl mae dyn, yn deyrn a gwreng,
Yn codi ei awdurdod hell.

Why must I live in this grim age
When, to a far horizon, God
Has ebbed away, and man, with rage
Now wields the sceptre and the rod?

These are the words of Hedd Wyn, perhaps Wales's greatest war poet, killed at Pilckem Ridge, Passchendaele, on 31 July 1917. He died just six weeks before being awarded the highest honour bestowed on a Welsh poet, the National Eisteddfod Bardic Chair. Draped in a black cloth, the chair would henceforth be known as The Black Chair, and represent the thousands of empty chairs by hearths across the nation, symbolising a lost generation of young men.

Hedd Wyn's home, Yr Ysgwrn, was purchased by the Snowdonia National Park Authority with financial assistance from the National Heritage Memorial Fund and the Welsh government in 2012 and redeveloped with further grants as a heritage centre, reopening in 2017.

In 2013 a replica of Y Gadair Ddu (The Black Chair) was created using innovative 3D printing techniques, with Welsh government funding and technical support of partners.

Throughout the commemoration, an innovative programme of exhibitions, events, talks and activities for young people was arranged by the National Library of Wales and Amgueddfa Cymru – National Museum Wales. This included the library's *Lloyd George: The Wizard, the Goat and the Man Who Won the War* exhibition, and the museum's *Efforts and Ideals: Prints of the First World War* exhibition. In addition, both collaborated on developing educational resources as

375 Y Gwir Anrhydeddus Carwyn Jones AC, Prif Weinidog Cymru, gyda Mr Gerald Williams, nai'r bardd Hedd Wyn, yng nghegin Yr Ysgwrn yn ystod yr ail-agoriad swyddogol ar 6 Medi 2017.
The Rt Hon. Carwyn Jones AM, First Minister of Wales, and Mr Gerald Williams, nephew of the poet Hedd Wyn, in the kitchen of Yr Ysgwrn on its official reopening on 6 September 2017.

part of the First World War Education Project, with funding from the Welsh government.

The Welsh government Department for Education and Skills provided grants of up to £1,000 for every secondary school in Wales to undertake centenary activities. The students undertook a variety of fascinating projects, including arranging exhibitions, painting murals, trips to the battlefields, and researching the stories of local servicemen. These have been captured on the Wales Remembers website: http://www.walesremembers.org/projects/

The Wales for Peace project was managed by the Welsh Centre for International Affairs and supported by the Heritage Lottery Fund. It brought together communities and schools across Wales to explore people, movements and stories which have shaped Welsh identity.

Each year a number of special events took place, and a selection are included here. In 2014, the Royal Welch Fusiliers Museum together with partners in Germany, Belgium and France organised an event at Frelinghien and an exhibition to mark the centenary of the 1914 Christmas Truce. Using personal belongings and soldiers' stories, the exhibition explored the human effect of war. It toured in the partner countries and in different parts of Wales.

In 2015 the Royal Welch Fusiliers Museum, in consultation with the Turkish community, developed a travelling exhibition on the role of the 53rd (Welsh) Division in the Gallipoli campaign. The museum developed educational resources, an online exhibition and a commemorative booklet. The exhibition toured six locations in Wales with links to Welshmen who served at Gallipoli.

In 2017 the Welsh government collaborated with the government of Flanders, Literature Wales and Irish partners to arrange a series of literary events to mark the centenary of the death of Hedd Wyn. *Poetry of Loss* was held in Brussels, and focused on the work of Hedd Wyn and the Irish poet Francis Ledwidge (both killed at Pilckem Ridge on 31 July 1917) and Flemish

376 Replica o'r Gadair Ddu yng Nghanolfan Ymwelwyr Y Beudy Llwyd yn Yr Ysgwrn.
Replica of the Y Gadair Ddu (The Black Chair), displayed at the Beudy Llwyd Visitor Centre, Yr Ysgwrn.

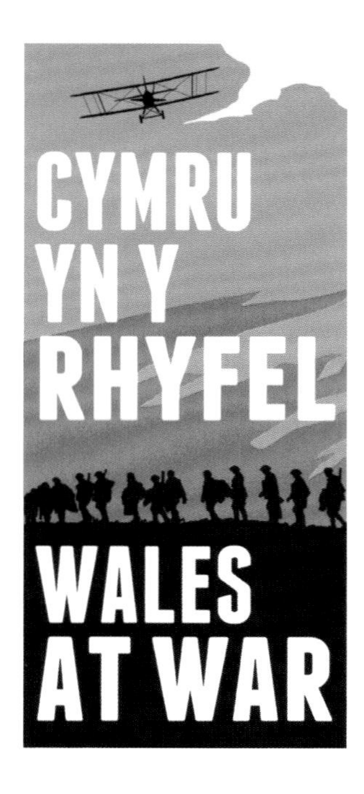

377 Poster prosiect Cymru yn y Rhyfel.
Wales at War project poster.

378 Crëwyd pabïau cochion papur gan ddisgyblion Ysgol Uwchradd Fitzalan, Caerdydd fel rhan o raglen addysg y Rhyfel Byd Cyntaf.
Pupils at Fitzalan High School, Cardiff made tissue paper poppies as part of the First World War educational programme.

First World War poetry. Other events included literary residencies in Belgium and Wales, poetry workshops for schoolchildren with Ifor ap Glyn, the National Poet of Wales, and a symposium, 'Flanders and Wales' in Cardiff. On 9 November, at an event in the Senedd, the Speaker of the Flemish Parliament and the Presiding Officer of the National Assembly of Wales exchanged gifts between the peoples of Wales and Flanders to mark their shared history during the First World War.

The years of commemoration demonstrated a deep interest in the events of the First World War and the impact it had on the nation. Throughout the period of the commemoration activities and events took place across Wales, at both a local and national level. A digital and educational legacy is being established to ensure that future generations can learn more about this terrible conflict, and how Wales remembered.

Review of Centenary Events: Northern Ireland

379 Covers of graphic novels produced by Creative Centenaries. The project included innovative new learning resources such as 2.5D parallax animations, interactive iBooks and graphic novels, all of which could be accessed for free.

The Creative Centenaries project, led by the Nerve Centre in Derry-Londonderry, serves as a hub for information and resources around the Decade of Centenaries in Northern Ireland, highlighting and contributing to the work of the creative sector in commemorating events such as the First World War. Taking a unique, creative approach, the project produced a series of graphic novels focussed on the real life actions of people from across Ireland caught up in the global events of the early 20th century. *The Battle of the Somme* tells the story through the experiences of Victoria Cross winner William McFadzean; *The Sinking of the Lusitania* explores the story through the collections of a family in north-west Ulster; the story of Francis Ledwidge touches on the role of Irish Nationalists fighting for Britain; *The Battle of Messines* recalls the shared experiences of soldiers in both the 16th (Irish) and 36th (Ulster) Divisions; and the story of Lady Londonderry explores the role of women during wartime. The graphic novels were linked to the curriculum with background information and suggested classroom tasks.

National Museums NI (NMNI) provided a diverse and ambitious 'Remembering 1916' programme to mark the key centenaries around 1916. The programme was underpinned by a range of partnerships spanning universities to community groups. The centrepiece of the programme was a dedicated temporary exhibition at the Ulster Museum produced in conjunction with the Living Legacies 1914–18 First World War Engagement Centre. The aims of the programme included acknowledging the importance of the Battle of the Somme and the Easter Rising as distinct events, encouraging visitors to make new connections and

380 Keith Lilley, Director of Living Legacies 1914–18, and William Blair, Director of Collections at National Museums NI, in the *Remembering 1916: Your Stories* exhibition at the Ulster Museum, Belfast.

381 In the Garden of Remembrance at Belfast City Hall, 3,775 miniature shrouded figures were laid out to form Rob Heard's poignant *Shrouds of the Somme* exhibition.

appreciate the impact of war and revolution on wider society, and showcasing what has been achieved in working with the community to explore, interpret and record the legacies of the First World War.

A powerful piece of commemorative art, the *Shrouds of the Somme* exhibition formed a major part of Belfast City Council's Decade of Centenaries programme. It was installed in the grounds of City Hall from 23 August to 16 September 2018, marking the centenary of the end of the First World War. The exhibition was created by artist Rob Heard, who hand-cut and stitched 3,775 figures – each representing a serviceman from the Ulster or Irish regiments, or from Belfast, who died in the Battle of the Somme and has no known grave. The exhibition appeared in different forms in other locations across the UK.

As part of a UK government First World War centenary campaign, commemorative paving stones were laid at the birthplaces of every Victoria Cross (VC) recipient of the First World War. There were eight stones for recipients born in what is now

Ireland. Thirty-two stones were also provided for the VC recipients from across the island of Ireland, which were unveiled in stages at Glasnevin Cemetery in Dublin. The UK provided the paving stones and offered local councils or community groups the opportunity to create events with themes of reconciliation and shared history. A service was held in the Presbyterian Church of Ireland Assembly Buildings on 30 September 2018 to remember those Irishmen who received the Victoria Cross between 1914 and 1918. Attendees included family members, veterans' groups, the armed services, and government and political representatives including the Tánaiste Simon Coveney TD.

The Bellanaleck Local History Group in County Fermanagh undertook original research entitled 'Making it Home', to tell the story of local servicemen who survived the war. The Irish Land (Sailors and Soldiers) Act 1919 provided money from the Treasury to provide homes for ex-servicemen. The Bellanaleck Local History Group pieced together the story of eleven veterans who were provided with farm holdings on Cleenish, a beautiful but relatively isolated island in Upper Lough Erne. The Ulster Historical Foundation produced two publications, *Ballymena and the First World War* and *Ballymacarrett and the First World War*, born out of programmes undertaken with young Catholics and Protestants from ordinary backgrounds in East Belfast and Ballymena. They helped to document the commonality of suffering and encourage a better understanding of the war.

382 In May 2017 TRH The Prince of Wales and The Duchess of Cornwall unveiled four new Victoria Cross paving stones in Glasnevin Cemetery, Dublin, in honour of four Irish-born soldiers who were awarded the Victoria Cross in 1917.

383 Map of the island of Cleenish, showing the 11 holdings of between 26 and 42 acres that were given to ex-servicemen after the war.

Farm 2: Thomas Bannon - 31 acres
Farm 3: Clements Cluff - 27 acres
Farm 4: Henry Carrothers - 33 acres
Farm 1: Humphrey Boyd - 42 acres
Farm 5: Frank Brennan - 27 acres
Farm 10: John Balfour - 33 acres
Farm 9: Thomas McAloon - 26 acres
Farm 6: Alex Boyd - 36 acres
Farm 8: Thomas Dickson - 37 acres
Farm 11: James McNally - 35 acres
Farm 7: Francis Suttle - 39 acres

HLF: Restoring First World War Heritage

384 Replica of The Tank Museum's Mark IV built for the *War Horse* film. It was acquired by The Tank Museum, and is seen here at a museum event in 2017.

Funding from the Heritage Lottery Fund (HLF) during the centenary helped restore some of the most iconic heritage of the First World War. People in the UK today can experience elements of the war on land, sea and in the air, and visit places associated with both the ordinary experience and the unique.

Already a well-established museum of armoured warfare, The Tank Museum in Dorset was able to mark the centenary with a new exhibition: *Warhorse to Horsepower*. This explored the role played by cavalry in the early days of the conflict, and how the stalemate of trench warfare rendered the horse far less effective and led to a new British invention, the tank. A highlight of the exhibition was a working replica of the Mark IV tank, alongside other armoured vehicles from the period. Part of a £2.5 million investment by HLF in the museum, the exhibition featured live displays of cavalry, tanks and aircraft. It opened at the time that the blockbuster film *War Horse* was arriving in cinemas, adding greatly to the public interest.

In 2012 funding was secured to restore HMS *Caroline*, the last surviving British warship to take part in the Battle of Jutland. The National Heritage Memorial Fund (NHMF) – which was set up in 1980 to commemorate those who gave their lives in conflict for the UK through saving our most-loved treasures

from being lost forever – awarded £1 million to the National Museum of the Royal Navy (NMRN) to enable urgent repair works. Thanks to a grant of £15 million from HLF, HMS *Caroline* is now permanently docked in Belfast as a major tourist attraction.

HMS *Caroline* was a light cruiser launched in 1914; she also undertook convoy protection duties and continued to serve throughout the Second World War. The vessel's historic interior spaces – the living quarters of the captain, officers and ratings, as well as the signal school, engine room, sick bay and galley – have been recreated to look as they did in 1914. State-of-the-art multi-screen video experiences reproduce the sounds and drama of the biggest naval battle ever fought. Interactive installations have ensured that the historic ship and her incredible story have become an integral part of Belfast's Titanic Quarter.

The NHMF was also instrumental in saving a near-complete example of a First World War aerodrome, untouched and largely forgotten: Stow Maries aerodrome in rural Essex. Thanks to a grant of £1.5 million, Stow Maries Great War Aerodrome Trust acquired the site and, in 2017, with substantial

385 Based in Belfast's famous Titanic Quarter, HMS *Caroline* is the last survivor of the Battle of Jutland still afloat.

386 Historic spaces on the ship have been recreated to look as they did in September 1914.

387 One of the surviving wartime structures at Stow Maries Great War Aerodrome, near Maldon, Essex.

388 An airshow and fly-in took place at Stow Maries aerodrome to mark its centenary. A BE2c biplane performed at the event, an aircraft that would have been seen at the aerodrome 100 years ago.

funding from HLF, it set about further restoration in order to open it to a much wider public.

Stow Maries was established by the Royal Flying Corps in 1916, and played a pivotal role in defending London and the British mainland from German Zeppelin airships and Gotha bombers. At the end of the war, the site reverted to agricultural use, leaving behind a unique collection of two-dozen historic buildings still in their original form. Stow Maries fell into disrepair until local historians and military aviation enthusiasts recognised its importance. Once complete, the project will create a visitor attraction as a unique memorial to the earliest days of military flying, with buildings fitted out as they would have been at the time alongside an operational airfield featuring replica First World War aircraft.

The NHMF and the HLF also combined to save a very special place in Wales for future generations: Yr Ysgwrn, the home of Hedd Wyn, war poet and soldier, who was killed in 1917 on the first day of the Battle of Passchendaele. With a grant of £350,400 from the NHMF, and £388,000 from the Welsh government, Snowdonia National Park Authority acquired the house in 2012. It opened to the public for the first time on the centenary of the Battle of Passchendaele, after a full restoration funded by a grant of £2.8 million from HLF and other funding. This safeguarded the future of the Grade II* listed building, and the heritage and legacy of this iconic First World War soldier and Welsh-language poet.

Among the most famous poems of Ellis Humphrey Evans, whose bardic name was Hedd Wyn, are 'Rhyfel' (War) and 'Yr Arwr' (The Hero), the latter earning him the Eisteddfod chair awarded posthumously six weeks after his death. His story and his work represent a generation of young Welshmen killed in the conflict, while his former home, which remains largely unchanged since he lived there, provides an insight into life in rural Wales a century ago. The landscape surrounding Yr Ysgwrn inspired several of Hedd Wyn's most well-known poems and continues to inspire people from all over the world who are fascinated by the poet's story and the site's extraordinary heritage.

389 Yr Ysgwrn, the Grade II* listed farmhouse of Welsh poet, Hedd Wyn, who lost his life in the First World War. The door is always left open for visitors, as it was in Hedd Wyn's day.

390 The old cowshed behind the farmhouse is now the Beudy Llwyd Visitor Centre, with views of the landscape that inspired young shepherd Ellis Humphrey Evans to become a poet and take the bardic name Hedd Wyn ('blessed peace').

HLF: Community Projects

391 Still from *Shot at Dawn: Lest We Forget*, a film created by the Central Youth Theatre in Wolverhampton that explored stories of soldiers executed for cowardice during the First World War.

392 1st Menai Bridge Scout Group finding out about the scout leaders who went to fight in the First World War.

393 Inspired by the stories of women who worked in mustard gas factories in Bristol during the First World War, community theatre Acta researched and produced the play *Gas Girls*.

Across the UK hundreds of communities and organisations, large and small, came together to explore, conserve and share the heritage of the First World War in more than 2000 projects supported by the National Lottery through the Heritage Lottery Fund.

Thousands of young people have been actively involved. Wolverhampton-based Central Youth Theatre produced a film and exhibition telling the story of the 306 soldiers executed for cowardice but who were subsequently pardoned once so-called shell shock was better understood. Fifteen young people aged nine to twenty-three carried out the research and interviewed descendants of executed soldiers and of firing squad members for *Shot at Dawn: Lest We Forget*. So inspired were the young researchers that they went on to produce a second film detailing the campaign for the pardons.

Meanwhile, members of a north Wales scout group decided to discover what became of local scouts and scout leaders who had gone off to fight in the war. The 1st Menai Bridge Group was especially interested to learn about Anglesey scout John Fox Russell, who was awarded both the Victoria Cross and the Military Cross. One of the 17-year-olds involved in the project commented: 'Going through old papers and documents makes it so real, and it's scary to think that one of us now could just go to war ...'

In Bristol, community theatre Acta researched female workers in a factory producing mustard gas. The group uncovered facts about the so-called 'gas girls' that were hidden because of the secret nature of their work. In August 2014, as part of 'No

394 Olive Edis's camera being conserved at Sheringham Museum for an exhibition in 2018 about the pioneer inventor and first official female war photographer. She documented British women's services and the battlefields of France and Belgium between 1918 and 1919.

395 An exhibition of food for the heritage project How the Pershore Plum Won the War!

Game for Girls', a large crowd watched players from Coventry City Ladies Football Club recreate a game of football played in 1917 between women from Coventry's munitions factories. The Royal College of Nursing digitised nurses' scrapbooks from its archives and made them available online, while the Scottish Women's Hospital WW1 Memorial Group researched the lives of Dr Elsie Inglis (see page 148) and other women who set up hospitals in Serbia. Norfolk Museums put on exhibitions about Olive Edis, the first woman to work as an official war photographer.

Pershore Heritage and History Society looked at how schoolchildren, prisoners of war, Belgian refugees and boy scouts all had a part to play in preventing the nation from starving by picking plums, looking after chickens and digging potatoes. A group of prisoners at HMP Low Moss explored stories of conscientious objectors, producing drawings which developed into *Charcoal War*, a film now used at Remembrance Day services. Larger projects looked at the impact of the war across a whole county.

It was important to reflect the contribution to the war of people from what was the Empire but is now the Commonwealth. In Empire, Faith and War, the United Kingdom Punjab Heritage Association energised the British Sikh community with some 850 people volunteering on activities such as a roadshow exhibition reaching 38 venues. A young participant in Black on Both Sides in London said of exploring archives and making a film, 'It was so much fun being part of the project, just like a family. Black people from Africa fought for Britain, France and Germany in World War One'.

A unique project, Meeting in No Man's Land, led by Age Exchange, brought British and German descendants together in Germany to share their family histories of the war. They showed each other artefacts, letters and diaries. The powerful film of the project is available in an app for schools to inspire students to create their own interpretation and response through art, poetry, animation, performance and film.

396 Citizen historians researching their own connections to those who fought and lived through the First World War as part of the Empire, Faith and War project.

397 Handmade postcard using bark, moss, flowers etc. sent home by Christel Berger's grandfather from the Russian Front. Berger was a participant in the Meeting in No Man's Land project.

Many projects undertook conservation work to war memorials and remembered the soldiers who did not come home. Powys War Memorials project in Wales identified and mapped all the memorials in the county and conserved those most in need. Poppyscotland took the story of the poppy around the country to ensure sacrifices made during the conflict are recognised today. Other projects looked at the way veterans were treated. Bellanaleck Local History Group in Northern Ireland made a film about men settled on Cleenish Island in Upper Lough Erne, who faced untold hardships. With Writing on the Wall, families in Liverpool's black community explored documents highlighting the plight of black servicemen, workers and seafarers 'abandoned' in Liverpool after the war, including the impact of the 1919 race riots.

Alongside traditional forms of commemoration, millions of people contributed through projects such as these to a rich new citizen history of the First World War. This local community activity has had a profound impact on individuals and has increased our collective knowledge, enriching our heritage for present and future generations.

IWM: Centenary Programming

398 On 30 June 2016, the eve of the centenary of the Battle of the Somme, IWM London hosted a late-night event of film screenings, live music, immersive theatre and poetry, exploring the themes of love, fear, hope and courage.

The sheer breadth of involvement in the centenary of the First World War was remarkable – from high-profile national commemorations to community-led initiatives, and academic researchers to community historians. Millions engaged with the national story, as well as researching and sharing their own personal and community histories.

As the UK's national museum for war and conflict, IWM was an obvious resource for commemorating the centenary of the First World War. Across three of the sites – IWM London, IWM North and IWM Duxford – a huge range of activities, tours, performances, talks and screenings accompanied the exhibitions programme. In addition, IWM was aware of its critical role in leading the wider cultural heritage sector in commemorating the centenary. To create the greatest impact for the millions of individuals and organisations involved, IWM's programme for the centenary needed to extend beyond its sites.

To ensure that there was a clear way for organisations to work alongside national commemorations,

399 Cover of the Centenary Partnership branding guidelines. Membership was open to not-for-profit organisations worldwide, and included the right to use the Centenary Partnership logo.

400 The Lives of the First World War website enabled people from all over the world to discover and contribute to the histories of those caught up in the First World War.

401 Detail of a digital page from the War Memorials Register. The register ranges from small plaques to large town memorials across the UK. It includes details such as the type of memorial, the conflict it commemorates and its Ordnance Survey reference.

to create high-quality projects with a lasting legacy, IWM established and led the First World War Centenary Partnership, with support from Arts Council England.

IWM also launched Lives of the First World War, in partnership with Findmypast. This initiative was a fitting acknowledgement of the founding vision for IWM – that all those who contributed their 'toil and sacrifice' during the First World War would be represented.

Further contributing to preserving the memory of those who lost their lives in wartime service, by 2018 over 77,000 UK war memorials from the First World War onwards were available for people to search online using the War Memorials Register.

By 2018, over 4,000 organisations from over 60 countries had joined the Centenary Partnership, and over 2.2 million facts, anecdotes and images had been added to Lives of the First World War.

Millions of people across the world engaged with Partnership activity, creating a lasting legacy in the form of increased knowledge and coordination across the UK alongside permanent digital records.

MEMORIAL DETAILS

Memorial type	Board / Plaque / Tablet
District	Wigan
Town	Goose Green
County	Greater Manchester
Country	England
Commemoration	First World War (1914-1918)
Lost	Not lost
WM Reference	45320

Current location

ST PAULS CHURCH
St Pauls Av
Goose Green
Wigan
Greater Manchester
WN3
England

OS Grid Ref: SD 560 030
Denomination: Church of England

View location on Google Maps ›

IWM: First World War Centenary Partnership

From 2014 to 2018 the First World War Centenary Partnership, led by IWM and supported by Arts Council England, helped thousands of organisations and millions of people across the world to commemorate the centenary of the First World War.

The Partnership was a digital community which existed to share, support, develop and coordinate First World War activity. By 2018, over 4,000 not-for-profit organisations had joined, representing over 60 countries. All marked the centenary in their own way. The membership included an enormous variety of organisations, including national governments, embassies and cultural institutes; museums, libraries, archives and galleries; theatre and music groups; charities; universities, colleges and schools; community groups and local history societies.

Members joined a digital community with its own website – 1914.org. By 2018, IWM had digitised over 300 photographs and film clips from their First World War archives, all of which were available to members for free. As well as digital resources, the Partnership directly supported members to develop their activity

402 IWM banners at the London Remembers event, 1 September 2018, which honoured the last 100 days of the London units fighting in the First World War.

403 Attendees participate in a workshop at the Cymru'n Cofio: Wales Remembers Partnership Conference, Aberystwyth University, January 2016.

404 Photograph by Horace Nicholls of a female coke-heaver at the South Metropolitan Gas Works, Old Kent Road, London, overlaid with the logo from the Women's Work 100 campaign.

and to ensure a legacy for commemorations. This activity could be online through information packs, marketing and social media support, or at regular Partnership events.

From 2014 to 2018 Arts Council England (ACE) funding enabled 20 regional events, bringing together hundreds of organisations from across the country. IWM also supported yearly events with the Welsh government's Wales Remembers programme for hundreds of organisations in Wales, as well as events in Ireland, Northern Ireland and Scotland. The Partnership provided a platform for organisations to reach new people and to tell new stories.

To coincide with the centenary of the Representation of the People Act (6 February), in 2018 the First World War Centenary Partnership presented Women's Work 100, an international programme of activity that explored the working lives of women in the First World War. This included events and exhibitions, and a vibrant digital campaign: #WomensWork100. In October and November the Partnership shared stories of the 'remarkable women of the First World War you've never heard of', including the suffragette surgeons of Endell Street Military Hospital, and women who defied convention to fight on the front line. Partnership film screenings, featuring archive footage from IWM of women at work in the First World War, took place at around 50 venues across Europe.

405 Photograph of three female War Office workers, taken on the roof of the offices of the Department of Information, 8 Buckingham Gate, London. From left to right: an outdoor messenger, an indoor messenger and a supervisor.

406 A half-length portrait of Rajkumar Hira Singh of Panna, of the Indian Army, overlaid with the logo from the Armistice 100 Days project.

Through Women's Work 100, IWM was also able to share its unique Women's Work Collection, a collection closely linked with the establishment of IWM in 1917. Almost immediately after IWM's creation, plans were put in place to ensure that the role of women would be recognised and recorded. Against the backdrop of a political campaign for female suffrage, IWM formed a committee tasked with collecting material that recorded women working in new roles.

Coinciding with the centenary of the Hundred Days Offensive and the Armistice of 11 November 1918, the Centenary Partnership commissioned a literary project – Armistice 100 Days. One hundred volunteer writers from the not-for-profit organisation 26 were connected with 100 members of the Centenary Partnership. From this collaboration, each writer created 100 word piece (a centena) based on an individual who experienced the First World War. One centena was shared every day online from 5 August to 12 November.

Armistice 100 Days encouraged members of the Centenary Partnership, and the wider public, to engage with personal stories of the First World War, and to find out more about organisations who commemorated the centenary. The digital campaign #Armistice100Days, including a Twitter Q&A, brought these stories to new audiences, and reinvigorated interest in the commemoration of the centenary in 2018.

In 2018, IWM worked with members of the First World War Centenary Partnership and the composer Laura Rossi to screen the 1917 film *The Battle of the Ancre and Advance of the Tanks* (1917) to audiences across the world. This little-known masterpiece of British non-fiction cinema documents the autumn and winter stages of the Somme campaign, including the first ever scenes of tanks in battle. The film was screened from August to December 2018 to coincide with the centenary of the Hundred Days Offensive and Armistice.

407 A regimental cook eating a meal in the Ancre Valley, 1916. The autumn and winter stages of the Somme campaign were documented in the film *The Battle of the Ancre and Advance of the Tanks* (1917), screened in 2018 to audiences across the world.

IWM: Lives of the First World War

Launched on 12 May 2014, in partnership with Findmypast, Lives of the First World War quickly became an incredibly rich resource of stories about those who contributed to the British war effort. Millions of facts, anecdotes and images were added, and over 7,000 communities were also created, linking individuals who were part of the same family, workplace, sports team and so on. From factory workers to the armed forces, medics to conscientious objectors, more than 7.6 million stories were pieced together. These milestones could not have been achieved without the support and dedication of the many Lives of the First World War members.

The Lives of the First World War project also had an active outreach role, from being a key part of the BBC World War One At Home Tour in 2014 – where activities, performances and interactive sessions helped people to explore their relatives' links to the war – to hosting family history shows and teachers' events. Social media feeds on Twitter and Facebook doubled the number of those engaging in these events.

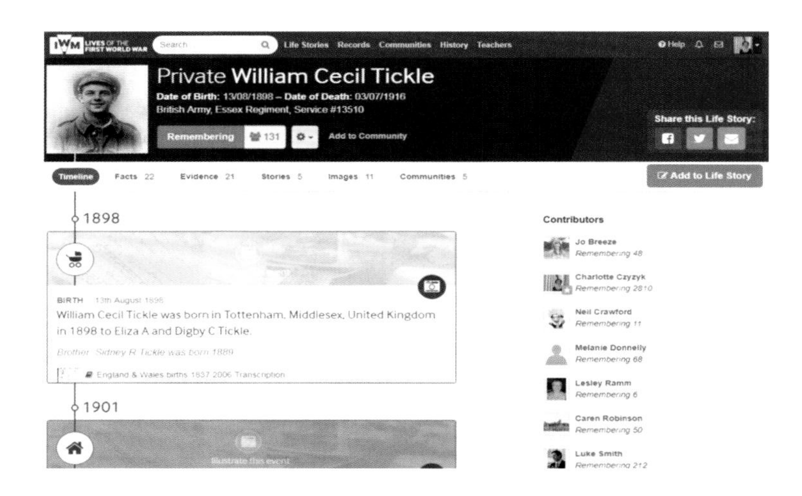

A team of 25 dedicated remote volunteers, who offered their skills and knowledge to assist other members wherever possible, helped to drive the project forward. They also promoted the site to other community groups. Their incredible achievements were recognised through a RememberWW1 Award in 2016, and an IWM Volunteer Award in 2017.

An online Teachers' Hub was set up to help schools engage with real-life stories from the First World War.

408 Detail of a digital page from the Lives of the First World War website.

409 A party of British troops with guns and shovels at Fleurbaix, *c.*1916. Millions of images like this were added to the Lives of the First World War website as users contributed their family stories and archives.

410 The Lives of the First World War team giving a presentation at the Somme Conference, Stonyhurst College, 2016.

Key themes such as the Home Front, Remembrance, Trench Warfare and Conscription were linked to the Lives of the First World War website via individual stories, from a munitions worker to a Victoria Cross recipient, a tunneller digging under the German trenches to a conscientious objector. One teacher commented: 'It is a really engaging way to teach historical interpretation. A fantastic resource!'

Lives of the First World War remained live and active until 18 March 2019, after which IWM became the custodian of the millions of incredible public contributions that were made over the five years. This permanent digital memorial will always remain free and accessible – helping to shape our understanding of the First World War both now and in the future.

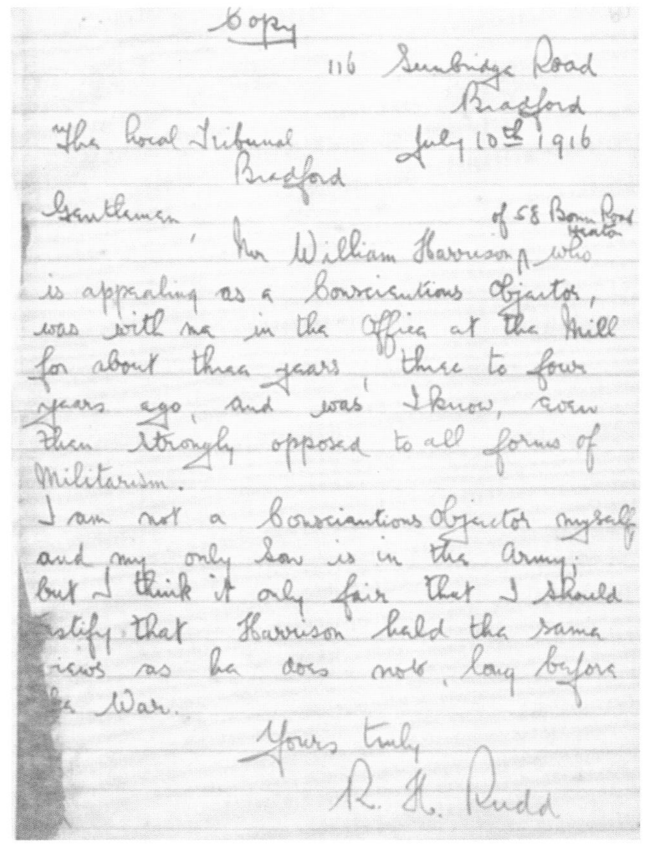

Copy

116 Sunbridge Road
Bradford

The Local Tribunal
Bradford
July 10th 1916

Gentlemen,

Mr William Harrison of 58 [illegible] Road Heaton who is appealing as a Conscientious Objector, was with me in the Office at the Mill for about three years, three to four years ago, and was I know, even then strongly opposed to all forms of Militarism.

I am not a Conscientious Objector myself and my only Son is in the Army, but I think it only fair that I should testify that Harrison held the same views as he does now, long before the War.

Yours truly
R. H. Rudd

411 The Teachers' Hub offered suggested themes and classroom packs. It included this letter, written in 1916 as part of court evidence confirming that conscientious objector William Harrison was opposed to 'all forms of militarism' before the war broke out.

MHCLG: Centenary Projects 2014

The aim of the Ministry of Housing, Communities and Local Government (MHCLG) throughout the centenary was to engage communities at all levels to understand the First World War in its fullest sense – highlighting everyone from the bravest in battle to those who cooked, cleaned, carried and cared for the soldiers on the front line.

As a visible reminder of the contribution made by local people, a commemorative paving stone was placed in the birthplace of every Victoria Cross recipient. The first (posthumous) recipient of the VC during the First World War was Lieutenant Maurice Dease VC, 4th Battalion Royal Fusiliers, born in 1889 in Gaulstown, County Westmeath, Ireland. Machine-gun officer of his battalion at the Battle of Mons, he was in command of guns protecting the crossing of Canal Bridge at Nimy. On 23 August 1914 he was wounded several times, and ultimately he and nearly all the machine gun detachment were killed. On the centenary of his death, his was the first paving stone to be laid, at Glasnevin Cemetery, Dublin.

Throughout the centenary, MHCLG strove to ensure that communities commemorated the contribution made by men and women from across Africa, Asia and the Caribbean. The year 2014 saw the start of work to restore the unique First World War Muslim burial ground at Horsell Common near Woking in Surrey, which was transformed into the Peace Garden. Revealing to people that their forefathers served in the war not only shows that people of all nationalities and religions played their part on the global stage, but also establishes a shared history and heritage that is too often forgotten.

The Curzon Education programme of 50 lectures in 2014 highlighted the Commonwealth contribution to the First World War, such as that of Colour Sergeant George Williams, from the King's African Rifles – a Sudanese soldier with an English name. Already a Distinguished Conduct Medal holder, in 1915 Williams, under heavy enemy fire, extricated the remainder of his platoon after one officer was killed and the other seriously wounded. He personally carried away the platoon machine gun after the crew were killed or wounded. Williams was recommended for a Victoria Cross, and received a Bar to his Distinguished Conduct Medal.

In 2014, *A Soldier's Tale* was launched, telling the fictional story of Walter Carter through social media as if it were happening today. His tweets captured the imagination of 13–18 year-olds right up to Armistice. The online 'Show and Tell' scheme with Imperial War Museums enabled people to share their artefacts, while the Last Post Project supported communities across the UK to remember through music by playing

412 The design for the commemorative First World War VC paving stones was by Charlie MacKeith, an architect who studied the material, form and lettering of CWGC memorials. Here we see the vinyl process for transferring the inscription onto the paving stones.

the Last Post on any instrument. Among many creative responses, the performance of the Last Post on Chinese and Indian heritage instruments paved the way to explore a new voice in commemoration that was both in step with tradition and reflected a wider heritage

Remember World War One was an initiative that encouraged people to mark the contribution that others made in the First World War by giving 100 minutes of their time to community work.

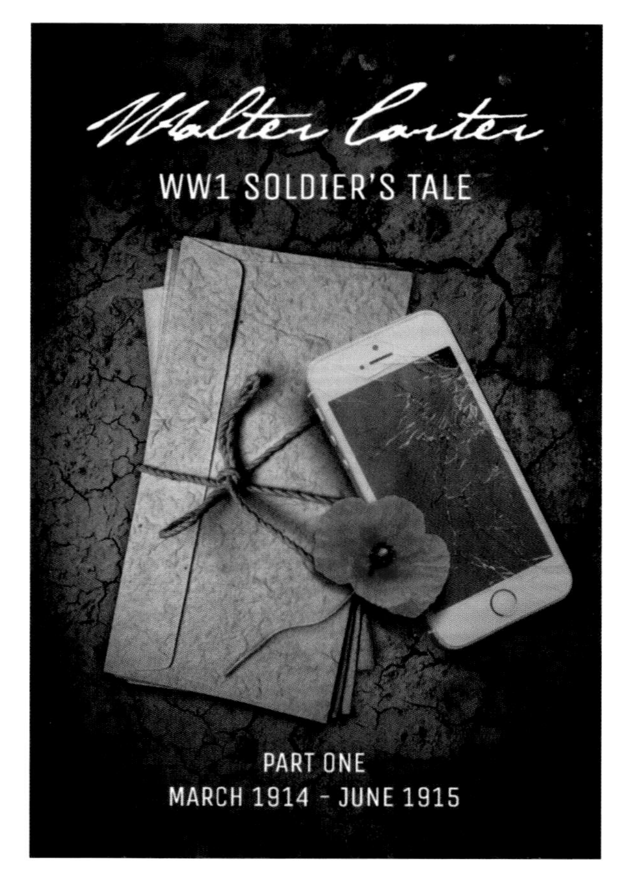

413 In 2014, a memorial garden in honour of Muslims who fought for Britain was opened by the Earl of Wessex. The Muslim Burial Ground Peace Garden in Woking, Surrey, is on the site of a former Grade II-listed cemetery where 27 Indian soldiers were buried.

414 In *A Soldier's Tale*, a character named Walter Carter told his experience of the First World War through social media. Young people across the country followed his story 100 years on from the day it happened.

MHCLG: Centenary Projects 2015

415 St Michael's Youth Project performing First World War music and the Last Post in London, as part of the Last Post Project in 2015.

416 Taking part in the Last Post Project Gallipoli, Cameron Chin See performed the Last Post at the National Memorial Arboretum to remember his great grandfather who fought at Gallipoli.

The Last Post Project continued in 2015, engaging in two years with over 450 groups across the UK. The project's success led to the use of the same format to commemorate Gallipoli. Paul Sartin and Cigdem Aslan brought together the experience of everyone involved with Gallipoli by creating a new version of the traditional song of mourning, 'Çanakkale Türküsü'. Groups across the UK performed this moving tribute to those who lost their lives at Gallipoli.

The power of music in commemoration was also at the heart of Lest We Forget, Ron Dawson's brain child. This centenary programme of learning and music involved hundreds of British schools, building up to a mass choir concert in Birmingham for the Armistice Centenary year.

MHCLG launched their partnership with Big Ideas Community Interest Company and the Commonwealth War Graves Commission in 2015 by piloting an innovative approach to community commemoration – the Living Memory pilot. They worked together to shine a light on the existence of 300,000 war graves within the British Isles, and to develop thought-provoking activities. This allowed schools to connect the story of the war to the graves in their local cemeteries.

Victoria Cross paving stones continued to be laid in 2015, including a stone for Jewish soldier Lance Corporal (later Lieutenant) Leonard Keysor of the 1st Battalion, Australian Imperial Force, who received the

award for noticeable bravery at Lone Pine, Gallipolli, on 6 August 1915. Born in London, he enlisted in the Australian Imperial Force when war broke out, having emigrated to Australia just three months earlier. Rabbi Major Reuben Livingstone, Principal Jewish Chaplain to HM Forces, said words of remembrance and prayers at the ceremony. The Lord Mayor of Westminster, Councillor Christabel Flight, unveiled the paving stone.

In addition, 146 Victoria Cross paving stones in honour of foreign-born Victoria Cross recipients were laid at the National Memorial Arboretum, and bronze memorial plaques were placed in the high commissions of Australia, New Zealand, Canada, India, Pakistan, Sri Lanka and South Africa.

417 Memorial service on 7 July 2015 at the VC paving stone for Lance Corporal Leonard Keysor, Victoria Embankment Gardens, Westminster.

418 In 2015, Birmingham's ten First World War VC recipients were honoured in a new memorial, the Walk of Heroes. VC paving stones were also laid, including that of Lieutenant Colonel James Neville Marshall VC, who died while leading his men in bridge repairs at the Sambre-Oise Canal, France.

MHCLG: Centenary Projects 2016

419 Members of the Bristol Sikh Association visiting war graves at Greenbank Cemetery in Bristol, as part of the Living Memory project.

420 Pupils from Manchester Academy making rubbings of war grave headstones at Manchester Southern Cemetery for the Living Memory project in 2016.

For the Centenary of the Battle of the Somme, MHCLG worked with Big Ideas on the Living Memory project, delivered throughout the British Isles. With a war grave within three miles of every British community, Living Memory groups researched those graves of men injured at the Somme who had died in hospitals in the UK. They identified more than 100 graves.

Schools and community groups in Brent held a Living Memory event attended by HRH The Duke of Cambridge at Willesden New Cemetery. St Michael's Youth Project, a steel pan band, played the Last Post by the local Cross of Sacrifice.

421 On 10 November 2016, HRH The Duke of Cambridge walked with Michaela McKay, aged 14, from St Michael's Youth Project, to lay a floral tribute at Willesden New Cemetery in London, where he viewed the work of Living Memory.

MHCLG: Centenary Projects 2017

422 Launching 'The Unremembered' project in 2017, South African Diaspora Singers, Chichester Community Choir and pupils from St John's Cathedral Catholic Primary School sang the Xhosa song 'Lizalis idinga lakho', commemorating the South African Native Labour Corps.

The anniversary of the sinking of the SS *Mendi* in 2017 kickstarted the creation of 'the Unremembered' project, honouring the role of Labour corps in the First World War including the South African Native Labour Corps and the Chinese Labour Corps.

'The Unremembered' also initiated the Remember Together programme, exploring diverse and shared heritage. MHCLG supported the Nubian Jak Community Trust in creating a memorial to African and Caribbean men and women who served in both world wars. Shaped in the form of two obelisks – one horizontal, to represent the fallen, and the other vertical, to represent their descendants – the memorial is sited in Windrush Square, Brixton.

423 Britain's first memorial to African and Caribbean servicemen and women was unveiled in Brixton on 22 June 2017, in a ceremony that was attended by Defence Secretary Michael Fallon and Mayor of London Sadiq Khan.

MHCLG: Centenary Projects 2018

For the final year of the centenary, MHCLG supported Remember Together to offer a range of innovative projects highlighting the forgotten stories of the war. The Big Lottery Fund extended this project to include the Home Nations.

As part of 'The Unremembered' project, community groups made 'Unremembered' wreaths to remember the Labour Corps from around the world. They were invited to take part in the People's Procession on the centenary of the Armistice, and lay their wreaths at the Cenotaph alongside traditional poppy wreaths. Reflecting community identity with recycled sarees, knitted flowers, mosaics, archive photographs and beach debris, among the many materials chosen, their creative, striking and moving tributes remained at the Cenotaph for several days afterwards for the public to view.

MHCLG supported the Golden Tours Foundation to launch a travelling exhibition in an open-top bus on the role of Indian soldiers during the war. The First World War was the first time that soldiers from various parts of undivided India were recognised as 'Indian' soldiers and not as 'Jats', 'Marathas', 'Hindus', 'Muslims' or 'Sikhs'.

The first black heritage infantry officer in the British Army in modern times was Walter Tull. Born in Folkestone in 1888, he was the son of a local woman and a carpenter from Barbados. He joined the Footballers' Battalion in 1914 and served in the Army

424 'Unremembered' wreaths laid for the Labour Corps at the Cenotaph, Armistice Day 2018.

425 Community groups walking in the People's Procession on Remembrance Sunday 2018 with 'Unremembered' wreaths for the Labour Corps.

426 Participants in a street soccer tournament in Townhead, Glasgow, commemorating Walter Tull with a poster identifying barriers to overcome in their community.

until his death in March 1918. Tull was commissioned an officer in 1917, despite an explicit ban on men who were not of 'pure European descent'. Following an exceptional mission in the Battle of Piave early in 1918, Tull was recommended for the Military Cross. This was never awarded. At his death, fellow officers wrote to his family about his courage in action. His story was the basis for Tull100 – Football Remembers, a project to inspire social inclusion and celebrate diversity supported by the Premier League, the Football Association and the English Football League.

Trailblazers: World War One's Inspirational Women marked the centenary of the Representation of the People Act. Starting with the stories of Elsie Inglis and Sofia Duleep Singh and dozens of other ground-breaking women from the period, schools and community groups developed engaging activities for young people, and identified inspirational and trailblazing women in their communities today.

On Mothering Sunday the Motherhood, Loss and the First World War project was launched, exploring bereavement – a universal experience of the war that is somewhat side-lined in British commemorative culture. Local stories of British mothers who had lost sons inspired communities to discover and share their stories. Unique commemorative activities included music by composer Clare Connors giving a 'voice' to Susan Owen, mother of Wilfred Owen, and community playground equipment evoking the relationship of mothers and sons.

MHCLG was approached by the Royal Air Force Centenary team to engage new audiences at a local level. Remember RAF100 was aimed at primary schools, and included the *Name Your Plane* exhibition. Schools and visitors to RAF100 air shows decorated 4,805 individual paper planes with the names of the 4,805 men and women who are buried and commemorated in First World War air service war graves in the UK. The Remember RAF100 schools pack included poems by children's author Jim Eldridge, with the difference between remembering your packed lunch and remembering war dead described as: 'Remember is of the past / Remembrance is for the future.'

427 A selection of resources available for those taking part in Trailblazers: World War One's Inspirational Women.

428 *Name Your Plane* artwork decorated by a pupil from Farsley Farfield Primary School near Leeds, commemorating F.E. Burton – one of the 4,805 RAF air personnel listed on the Remember RAF100 database.

The Great War Debate

429 Students had the opportunity to put their questions directly to the panel at each event. This photo was taken at The Great War Debate in Cambridge, chaired by BBC *Newsnight*'s Mark Urban.

A nationwide series of interactive events, The Great War Debate was an initiative organised by Hopscotch Consulting and the Department for Education, forming part of the government's wider First World War centenary commemorations. From 2016 the debate series brought a new dimension to GCSE and A-level students' history studies, and showed how the Great War played a key role in shaping life as we know it today. With studies indicating an increasing detachment between young people and the world wars, the series was created to develop young people's engagement with the First World War as a subject together with an appreciation of its lasting legacy.

The series covered a broad range of themes, from looking at the extent to which the First World War can be seen as an essential catalyst for social change, to questioning if Europeans went willingly to war in 1914 and considering if the roots of today's Middle Eastern instability lie in the First World War. As well as representatives from BBC *Newsnight*, the Science Museum, the National Archives and the Imperial War Museums, the series benefitted from valuable contributions from historians such as Professor Sir Hew Strachan, Professor Alison Fell, Professor John Horne and Professor Gary Sheffield.

Each event opened with an object-handling session led by a military historian, allowing students to get up close to real artefacts from the First World War and to consider the significance of their purpose and impact during the war itself. This session also encouraged the students to note their local war memorial – and to

430 A military historian led an interactive object handling session using artefacts from the First World War, ranging from military uniforms to inert grenades and gas masks.

stop and take a moment to remember people from all walks of life who made sacrifices during the Great War.

In order for students to get the most out of the discussion, their teachers were equipped with a set of education resources with which they could run a 30-minute warm-up session prior to the main event. Each education resource was tailored to a specific debate, and also provided background to the panellists. Running this session helped students to formulate questions to ask the panel directly throughout the event, and these questions shaped the direction of the discussion.

Thousands of young people took part in the series. To ensure that no one missed out, podcasts were created of all events, which are freely available from the First World War Centenary Battlefield Tours website.

431 Sixth form and GCSE students were invited to The Great War Debate, which was free to attend and gave students insight into the range of opinions and perspectives held by expert academics on the First World War.

First World War Centenary Battlefield Tours Programme

432 A student explores Railway Hollow Cemetery on the Somme battlefields in France.

433 Students locate the name of a local soldier from their own community and place remembrance crosses at the Tyne Cot Memorial in Belgium.

A national education programme led by UCL Institute of Education (University College London), the First World War Centenary Battlefield Tours Programme ran between May 2014 and March 2020, and was jointly funded by the MHCLG and the Department for Education. The programme allowed two students and a teacher from every state-funded secondary school in England to go to the battlefields of the Western Front. More than 6,500 students and teachers went on the four-day trip. Accompanied by a UCL National Education Co-ordinator and an experienced guide, they visited battlefield sites, museums, cemeteries and memorials, considering the significance of events 100 years ago as well as what we can learn from these sites today. Each tour was tailored to the relevant region of the school and included visits to individually researched graves and memorials.

434 A serving soldier from the British Army accompanied each tour.

435 All students took part in remembrance activities including the Last Post ceremony at the Menin Gate in Ypres, Belgium.

436 Students also participated in the Flemish project 'Coming World Remember Me', helping to create an art installation which went on public display in 2018.

All the students arranged a commemoration event in their community on their return, through Legacy 110 – an award-winning initiative where students participating in the battlefield tours created an enduring legacy by impacting upon at least 110 people within their local community. To date, student legacy projects have reached more than 15 million people across the globe. In addition the UCL Institute of Education provided an extensive range of teaching resources and professional development for teachers.

First World War Memorials Programme

437 Participants at a war memorial workshop at Stockport War Memorial Art Gallery. Listed at Grade II*, this is the only purpose-built war memorial art gallery in the UK.

438 University of Birmingham student Coralie Acheson assessing the condition of the Harborne War Memorial, Birmingham. The memorial is one of over 40 that Coralie applied to have listed during the centenary.

Throughout the centenary the First World War Memorials Programme went out into the community to help people engage with and protect their local war memorials. Civic Voice held almost 200 workshops with civic societies, universities and community groups to help people care for and safeguard their local war memorials by undertaking condition surveys and sharing their results with War Memorials Trust. For the first time in such a large-scale national project, volunteers were also invited to submit their local war memorials for inclusion on the National Heritage List for England.

In 2018, Civic Voice and War Memorials Trust worked together to run a series of workshops to help community groups to engage young people in their local war memorial heritage projects and ensure that they remain cared for many years to come. Historic England and War Memorials Trust also worked with schools to help pupils understand the significance of their local memorials. Pupils carried out research into the names of those listed on the memorial and worked with professionals to understand the importance of conserving memorials for future generations. They also made films based on the lives of local people

during the First World War and those listed on the memorials. Some schools even used their research to help their local memorial gain listed status. By contributing directly to the National Heritage List for England and having their memorials recognised as being nationally significant, pupils learnt how they can make a real difference to their local heritage.

Throughout the centenary, Historic England, IWM and War Memorials Trust worked with volunteers across the country to ensure that online information about war memorials was as accessible as possible. This information remains an important resource to enable communities to care for and protect their local memorials. There is now one central location, the IWM's War Memorials Register. Here you can access information not only on the history of memorials, but also link directly to War Memorials Online – where you can find information about the condition of the memorials and, if a memorial is listed, access the list entry on the appropriate national heritage website. The IWM War Memorials Register also holds the names of over one million men and women commemorated on memorials across the country. A new search tool, launched in March 2018, allows individuals to find the memorials on which their family members are commemorated.

439 Pupils from Moat Community College in Leicester shooting a film about the First World War at their local war memorial.

440 War Memorials Trust with a group in Edinburgh carrying out a condition survey of *The Call 1914* (also known as the Scottish-American War Memorial). This memorial was donated by Scottish-Americans to honour those from Scotland who served in the First World War.

Cathedrals Repair Fund

England's cathedrals contribute more than £220 million to the economy each year, drawing in more than 11 million visitors. They are often complex and historic buildings, facing the ongoing challenge of maintaining their fabric while ensuring comfort, safety and accessibility for all.

The First World War Centenary Cathedral Repairs Fund, launched by the government in 2014, invited applications from Catholic and Church of England cathedrals to address urgent repair works. The fund prioritised making buildings weatherproof, safe and open to the public – as well as ensuring that they would be able to host acts of remembrance for the

441 Comprising over 400 single pieces in the shape of a fleur-de-lys, the unique lead crestings along Exeter Cathedral roof needed extensive repair and resetting. Work was carried out to remove and examine each piece, and cost £70,000. The project was partly funded by the First World War Centenary Cathedral Repairs Fund.

442 At Peterborough Cathedral, the Victorian tesserae (mosaic) floor near the high altar had been roped off as it was dangerous to walk on. Thanks to the fund, over 30,000 small tiles were set or reset, and the beautiful Cosmati-style geometric patterns were restored to their former glory.

443 Restoration work was carried out on the tower of Durham Cathedral in 2016.

centenary of the First World War Armistice in 2018. Grants were awarded over two phases between 2014 and 2018, each totalling £20 million. A total of 146 awards were made to 57 cathedrals.

Projects supported by the fund were all deemed by architects to require urgent attention either immediately or within 12 months. Approximately one third of the projects were for roof repairs. Many also related to external masonry, with other works including guttering, heating, sound systems and window refurbishment.

Grants were awarded by an independent panel, and the fund was administered by the Church of England's Cathedrals and Church Buildings Division (CCB) on behalf of the Department for Digital, Culture, Media and Sport (DCMS).

NSI: Poetry and Art Competitions

Founded by Lady Lucy French, great-granddaughter of Field Marshal Sir John French, the charity Never Such Innocence (NSI) was set up to engage children in the First World War centenary through learning, poetry, art and music. The charity's name comes from Philip Larkin's poem 'MCMXIV'.

In 2014, NSI launched an annual Centenary Competition, inviting young people aged 9-16 to produce a piece of art, write a poem or create a song inspired by the events of the First World War. The charity produced a resource to provide a child-friendly journey through the First World War, which was sent to schools and was available online. Songwriting workshops were also used to inspire entries. All resources and events were provided at no cost for schools.

NSI toured the UK and Europe with an annual roadshow, inviting local schools to prestigious venues such as Edinburgh Castle, RAF Valley, HMS *Caroline* and the CWGC headquarters with Prime Minister Theresa May. NSI children participated in national centenary commemorations including the Battle of Jutland, Passchendaele and the Armistice service at Westminster Abbey.

The competition grew at an incredible rate, with international take-up increasing year on year. In total, the four Centenary Competitions received over 11,000 entries from 47 different countries, territories and dependencies, across five continents.

In Armistice year, the Centenary Competition culminated in a centenary finale at Buckingham Palace, bringing together winning children from every year of the competition.

444 Martha Potts, age five, reciting her poem 'Life in the Trenches' at the Never Such Innocence Centenary Finale at Buckingham Palace.

445 *Remember* by Jessica Rizova, first place winner of the 2015/16 Art Competition. Her painting was used as the front cover artwork of the hardback anthology *Never Such Innocence: The Centenary of the First World War: Children's Responses through Poetry, Art & Song*, published in November 2018.

Royal Mail

At the time of the First World War, Royal Mail was part of the General Post Office (GPO), operating postal, telegraphic, telephone and banking services. As well as dealing with thousands of letters to and from home, the GPO's global communication lines enabled officers to keep up-to-speed with the changing situation at the front. The GPO also released over 75,000 employees to fight in the war, including 12,000 men who fought with its own regiment, the Post Office Rifles. Four GPO employees became VC recipients. To keep the organisation running, the GPO recruited tens of thousands of women.

Commemorating the centenary, Royal Mail developed a searchable database of all known memorials in the company's care. Each record includes information about the location of the memorial and the names of the individuals featured. The Royal Mail works closely with the sites to ensure that the memorials are appropriately maintained.

Other centenary initiatives included, in both 2014 and 2018, the sending of information leaflets to Royal Mail's 140,000 employees, detailing Royal Mail's involvement in the war and in restoring the country after the war was over. They created postmarks to commemorate Amiens100 and Remembrance Day, and they also organised centenary services at locations appropriate to the Post Office Rifles.

446 A dedicated memorial and battle flag of the Post Office Rifles is at the church of St Botolph's-without-Aldersgate, London. This detail shows the regiment's badge.

447 Centenary service at St Botolph's-without-Aldersgate. The chuch is in Postman's Park, so-called because staff from the London Chief Post Office used to eat their lunch there.

Fields of Battle, Lands of Peace 14–18

448 The battered helmet of Corporal Edouard Ivaldi sits atop the last marked battlefield grave remaining on the Western Front. He was killed in April 1917. While his body was re-interred in a French cemetery, his equipment, together with a memorial plaque placed here in 1919 by his father, still marks his original burial place.

449 The remarkable 'Loos Football' is the proud possession of the London Irish Rifles. On 15 September 1915 it was kicked into no-man's-land as the battalion made an attack on the coalmining town of Loos.

450 Tyne Cot is the largest CWGC cemetery in the world. On his visit here in 1922, King George V said, 'I have many times asked myself whether there can be more potent advocates of peace upon earth through the years to come than this massed multitude of silent witnesses to the desolation of war'.

UK, BELGIUM, FRANCE

451 The marshes of the Ancre inspired the scene in the film of J.R.R. Tolkien's *The Lord of the Rings* where Frodo looks into a pool in the 'Marshes of the Dead' and sees the faces of men who 'died in battle long ago'.

452 View of the exhibition in St James's Park, London, November 2018.

Replacing the familiar black-and-white images of war-torn France and Belgium with stunning colour photography of how the sites look today, *Fields of Battle, Lands of Peace 14–18* revealed the history of the First World War and the Western Front in a powerful new way. This series of outdoor photographic exhibitions was mounted in prominent public places throughout the First World War centenary, and was viewed by over 11 million people. The exhibition was invited to many countries, including Germany and Turkey. The biggest exhibition programme proved to be in the US, while the longest single period of showing was in Dublin. Bookending the centenary commemorations in London, the exhibition was held in St James's Park in both 2014 and 2018.

Creator of the exhibition, photographer Michael St Maur Sheil, explains: 'This collection represents a legacy which I hope will create a visual gateway to the battlefields themselves, thus encouraging people to visit these historic landscapes and create awareness and understanding of the events and historical implications of the First World War.'

Often using the evocative light at dawn or dusk, and taken at the low eye-levels that would have been experienced by soldiers in battle, the photographs reveal how places which were the scenes of death and horror have become landscapes of great beauty and tranquility through the healing power of time and nature. Captured over a period of ten years, the photographs present a unique reflection on the transformation of the battlefields of the First World War into the landscape of modern Europe.

The National Archives: First World War 100

453 The launch of a virtual reality site about Great Wharton, a fictional online town, was a centenary initiative to tell real but little-known stories from the home front.

With historical records at its heart, The National Archives was well placed to organise an informative and engaging centenary programme. First World War 100 aimed to introduce new audiences to the collections, as well as to offer historians and regular archive users fresh insights into the conflict.

First World War records were opened up as never before, through a series of digitisation projects timed to coincide with the centenary commemorations. This included the digitisation of a variety of military records and government papers, including unit war diaries – one of the most popular collections held by the Archive. Operation War Diary was a crowdsourced collaboration between The National Archives, Zooniverse and the Imperial War Museum, which saw over 16,500 volunteers tag over 75,000 names and places in the unit war diaries. Providing unrivalled insights into life on the front line, the diaries are arranged by operational theatre, before being broken down into series reflecting operational arrangements, down to unit level within each division.

The National Archives collaborated with a variety of organisations during the Centenary. In 'Fighting Talk: First World War Telecommunications', records reveal how technology rapidly developed to meet the demands of a global, mechanised war.

Other centenary initiatives included *Somme Tales*, a creative film interpretation of the archive's First World

454 This painting of the Cenotaph, by Matthew Lee, was inspired by records at The National Archives, and was created at a 2018 workshop to create graphic novel collection 'Armistice and Legacy'.

War records which won the 2017 MEDEA Award for User Generated Media. The National Archives also created Great Wharton, a virtual town which allowed users to explore life on the home front during the First World War through records in the collections.

A useful tool for those wishing to learn more about the global reach of the First World War was the new interactive First World War map, highlighting key events and figures that are documented in the archive's records.

In addition to digitising the collections, another key aspect of the Archive's centenary work was to improve and develop ways in which users could search the records. This included better catalogue descriptions for searching and browsing in the online catalogue, Discovery. New resources and tools, aimed at helping both first-time and experienced users to get the most out of the collection, were made available, including the popular My Tommy's War blog series, taking a personal approach to providing practical advice to family historians researching their First World War ancestors. Publishing research, such as the Battle Babies, enabled staff to explore previously unknown aspects of the First World War.

The centenary events programme comprised a diverse and informative range of activities, exhibitions, talks and displays. A series of talks focusing on varied aspects of the war included some conducted online, for the benefit of users not able to visit in person. A number of conferences were held throughout the programme, including the Home Front conference 'Everyday Lives in the First World War' in September 2016.

Learning opportunities included partnering with Anglia Tours to provide teachers and students with an unrivalled opportunity to investigate every aspect of the conflict using original sources and trips to First World War battlefields. Education sessions included All Pals Together, a video-conference session which allowed schoolchildren to pose questions to Henry Fairhurst, a First World War soldier recreated by an actor using original sources held by The National Archives.

455 Graphic to show National Archive research on how words associated with the First World War became popular babies' names.

PICTURE CREDITS

We are grateful to all who provided images. Copyright resides with:

14-18 NOW: 31, 315, 333

Age-Exchange: 397
Amelia Allen: 346
John Archer: 223
Stuart Armitt/Edinburgh Arts Festival: 43
Johnny Armstead/Alamy: 96
Katielee Arrowsmith/SWNS: 314
Arterra Picture Library/Alamy: 20
Ross Attenburgh: 40
Stewart Attwood/HLF: 7
Avpics/Alamy: 388

Steven Baker/Historic England: 65, 255, 343
Balletboyz: 260
Jane Barlow/PA Images: 88, 324
Stephen Barnes/Alamy: 135, 386
Alison Baskerville/Impressions Gallery: 276
Mark Baynes/Alamy: 222
BBC Scotland: 327
Beaverbrook Collection of War Art, Canadian War Museum: 359
Belfast City Council: 381
Andrew Bell/Alamy: pp 210-11
Guy Bell/Alamy: 63, 76
Kevin Bennett/Alamy: 27
Subel Bhandari/dpa/Alamy: 62
Big Ideas: 419, 420, 422, 424, 427, 428
Big Ideas/Nick Hayes: 274
Stuart Black/Alamy: 213
Michael Bowles/Getty Images: 189
Kelvin Boyes/Press Eye: 136, 337
Gianmarco Bresadola: 261
Anna Bridson/Historic England: 64, 182
British Embassy, Copenhagen: 127
British High Commission, New Delhi: 200, 201, 202
Michael Brown: 383
James Brunker/Alamy: 61
Alun Bull/Historic England: 104, 181, 183, 256
Graham Burke: 393
Peter Byrne/PA Images: 90

Geoff Caddick/PA Images: 265
Colin Cameron: 342
Cardiff University/Trwy garedigrwydd Prifysgol Caerdydd: 369
Eoin Carey: 162
Niall Carson/PA Images: 70, 137, 138, 161, 212, 214, 215
Cavell Nurses' Trust: 93, 95
Russell Cheyne/WPA Rota/PA Images: 14
Hi Ching/Meridian Society: 365
Chronicle/Alamy: 66, 300
Civic Voice: 437
Ant Clausen: 30, 39
Collection Musikinstrumenten Museum Berlin: 91
Commonwealth War Graves Commission (CWGC): 11, 12, 13, 72, 97, 98, 99, 121, 154, 155, 156, 157, 224, 225, 226, 227, 238, 241
Ashley Coombes/PA Images: 131, 133
Guy Corbishley/Alamy: 278
CPG Photography: 429, 430, 431
Crown Copyright: 28, 29, 172, 173, 174
Crown Copyright (Welsh Government)/ Hawlfraint y Goron (Llywodraeth Cymru): 175, 176, 177, 248, 249, 250, 316, 317, 318, 320, 321, 322, 370, 374, 376

Simon Dack/Alamy: 84
Park Dale/Alamy: 83
James Davies/Historic England: 45
Philip Davies: 178
Colin Davison: 109
Dirk Debleu: 100
Kurt Desplenter/Belga /PA Images: 244, 245
Anthony Devlin/PA Images: 128, 263
DCMS: 293, 297, 298, 299, 301, 302
Benoit Doppagne/Belga/PA Images: 234
Mark Douet: 35, 164

Arthur Edwards/The Sun/PA Images: 231
Tim Etchells: 92
Laurence Blyth/Exeter Cathedral: 441

Theo Fernandes: 270
Joel Chester Fildes/Shady Lane Productions: 262
Tabatha Fireman/Getty Images: 185, 352
Fitzalan High School/Ysgol Uwchradd Fitzalan: 373, 378
Wayne Fox: 416
Johnny Fraser: 163, 259
Gareth Fuller/PA Images: front cover, 18, 19, 147, 280
Ian Gavan/Getty Images: 267
Getty Images: 106, 107, 334, 349
Joe Giddens/PA Images: 242
Jeff Gilbert: 396
Glasnevin Trust: 282
David Green: 425
Camilla Greenwell: 415
Paul Grover/Daily Telegraph/PA Images: pp 162-63; 311, 312

Dinendra Haria/Alamy: 281
Brian Harris: pp 124-25; back cover
Mike Hayward/Alamy: 355
Heritage Lottery Fund (HLF): 8, 391, 394, 395
Historic England: 46
Historic England Archive: 439
Jamie Howden: 191
Huckleberry Films: 166, 167
Humphries & Jones: 210, 258
Paul Hurst: 94

IWM: 3, 4, 5, 6, 67, 68, 171, 275, 338, 339, 340, 341, 353, 354, 398, 399, 400, 401, 402, 403, 404, 405, 406, 407, 408, 409, 410, 411
David Ivison, Royal Parks Guild: 271, 356

Chris Jackson/PA Images: 17, 21
Alun Jenkins/Alamy: 229
David Jensen/EMPICS Entertainment: pp 12-13
Benny J. Johnson: pp 2-3; 233, 239
Victoria Jones/PA Images: 288, 291

Matt Keeble/Getty Images for 14-18 NOW: 268
Murray Kerr: 86
Darren Kidd/Press Eye: 266, 330, 331, 332
Nicholas Knight/Public Art Fund: 41

Anna Kornatovska/Impressions Gallery: 277

Jack Ladenburg Photography: 113
Danny Lawson/PA Images: 124
Andrew Lee: 389
Matthew Lee: 454
David Levene: 296, 303
Dean Lewins/AAP/PA Images: 69, 73
Christian Liewig/ABACA/PA Images: 144
John Linton/PA Images: 132, 134
London Transport Museum: 53, 118, 203

Jon Macleod: 368
Nicolas Maeterlinck/Belga/PA Images: 232
Virginia Mayo: 101
Marshalls Mono Ltd/Marshalls PLC: 412
Jen Martin: 426
John Martin/Alamy: 50
Andrew Matthews/PA Images: 146, 149, 230
Kippa Matthews: 9, 10, 188
Mayflower Primary School: 221
Douglas McCalman AIIP: 329
Aaron McCracken Photography: 158, 159, 160
Topher McGrillis: 165
Mark McNulty: 37, 108
Gideon Mendel: 33
Andrew Milligan/PA Images: 126
Lucy Milson-Watkins/Historic England: 47, 105, 220, 438
MoD: 74, 75, 77, 78, 79, 80, 119, 122, 123, 125, 139, 140, 141, 142, 143, 148, 209, 228, 235, 236, 237, 243, 246, 247, 287, 289
Modern Designers: 55
Yui Mok/PA Images: 290, 292, 294, 295
Moonie's World Photography/Alamy: 49
Graham Morley/Alamy: pp 50-51
Keith Morris/Alamy: 319, 323
Brian Morrison: 44
Graham Mulrooney/Alamy: 71
Museum of Liverpool: 208

National Archives: 453, 455
National Library of Wales/Llyfrgell Genedlaethol Cymru: 372, 377
National Memorial Arboretum: 58, 60, 111, 204, 205, 272, 273
National Museum of the Royal Navy: 81, 82, 198, 199
National Railway Museum: 193, 194, 195
Nerve Centre: 279
National Museum of Northern Ireland: 380
Nubian Jak Community Trust: 423

Ayman Oghanna: 184
Stella Olivier: 348
Oosoom/Alamy: 51

Steve Parsons/PA Images: 282
Patricia Payne/Historic England: 48
People's History Museum: 54
Jonathan Perugia: 42
Paul Pickard: 392
Mike Prior: 89
Oskar Proctor: 313
Purcell UK: 371, 390

Chris Radburn/PA Images: 150, 151, 152, 153
Chris Redgrave/Historic England: 211, 344
RAF Museum: 56, 57
Jessica Rizova: 445
John Rainford/WENN.Com: 240
Matthew Roberts: 442
Royal Pavilion & Museums, Brighton & Hove: 117

Sabela Music Projects: 36
Science Museum: 196, 197
Science Museum Group Collection: 115, 116
Jeremy Shaw: 145
Mike Sheil: pp 80-81
Tim Skelton: 102
David Sneath: 103
Jeff Spicer/Getty Images: 351
Jeff Spicer/PA Images: 446, 447
Michael St Maur Sheil/Mary Evans Picture Library: 448, 449, 450, 451, 452
John Stiles/London Transport Museum: 52
Richard Stonehouse/Getty Images: 192, 264
Stow Maries Great War Aerodrome: 387
Sang Tan/PA Images: 22, 23, 24
Tank Museum: 110, 206, 207, 357
Steve Tanner/Wildworks: 34
Alan Taylor/Meridian Society: 364
The Other Richard: 363, 444
Geraint Thomas Panorama: 375
Jez Tozer: 187
Tributaries/Halsey Burgand/Tyne & Wear Archive & Museums: 112
Andy Tryner/Lincolnshire County Council: 190

UCL First World War Centenary Battlefield Tours Programme: p.11; 432, 433, 434, 435, 436
UK MoD Crown Copyright: 129, 130, 360, 361, 362

War Memorials Trust: 257, 440
War Memorials Trust/Grave Image: 257
Damian Walker/HLF: 2
Stuart Walker/English Heritage: 350
Washington Imaging/Alamy: 443
Tony Watson/Alamy: 26
Mark Waugh Photography: 120, 168, 169, 170
Jason Wells/Alamy: 32
Jack Welson: 335, 336
Westminster Abbey/Picture Partnership: 306, 307, 308, 309, 310
Stephen White: 38, 186
Kirsty Wigglesworth/PA Images: 421
WingNut Films with Peter Jackson (colourised footage); IWM (original b/w film): 347
WW100 Scotland 366
WW100 Scotland/Michael Boyd: 85
WW100 Scotland/Alan Richardson: 87
WW100 Scotland/Royal Edinburgh Military Tattoo (REMT): 15, 16
WW100 Scotland/Warren Media: 217, 218, 219, 251, 252, 253, 283, 284, 285, 286, 325, 326, 328, 367
Woven Films/Historic England: 345

James Young: 216

Peter Zabek/London Transport Museum: 358

First published in 2019 by
DCMS Centenary Publications
100 Parliament Street
London SW1A 2BQ

British Library Cataloguing in Publication Data
A catalogue record for this book is available from the British Library

ISBN: 978 1 5272 2861 0

Editor: Miranda Harrison
Designers: Caroline and Roger Hillier, The Old Chapel Graphic Design
Reprographics: Altaimage
Printed and bound by Gomer Press Limited

Front cover: Night view of war graves during the vigil to commemorate the Battle of the Somme at Thiepval, 2016
Back cover: Wooden cross and poppy at CWGC (Ypres) Menin Gate Memorial, Ieper
pp 2–3: The Cloth Hall, Ieper (Ypres), during the Centenary of Passchendaele – The Third Battle of Ypres commemorations on 30 July 2017
pp 12–13: Night view of *Blood Swept Lands and Seas of Red*, Tower of London, 2014
pp 50–51: First World War memorial at Freshwater West, Pembrokeshire, Wales, dedicated to sailors lost at sea including at the Battle of Jutland
pp 80–81: View of Thiepval Memorial at dusk, on the eve of the first day of the Battle of the Somme commemorations, 2016
pp 124–25: Close-up of CWGC (Ypres) Menin Gate Memorial, Ieper
pp 162–63: HM The Queen and the German President, Frank-Walter Steinmeier stand together at the Grave of the Unknown Warrior during the Service to Mark the Centenary of the Armistice, Westminster Abbey, 2018
pp 210–11: Silhouette of First World War soldier in the New Community Field, Pilling, Lancashire, surrounded by red poppies made by local children from recycled plastic bottles.

Acknowledgements
We would like to thank all our partners and contributors for their input to this publication and for their invaluable part in memorably marking the centenary of the First World War. Without their hard work and co-operation over the past four years, this book could never have been published.

We would also like to acknowledge and thank all those who took part in, attended and observed the vast array of activities that took place to mark the centenary. Each project and event that took place was integral to creating a lasting legacy for future generations.

A special thank you goes to the Imperial War Museums, to Miranda Harrison, the editor of this publication, and to the designer, Caroline Hillier, for their invaluable help, advice and expertise.